To Chris
with thanks
for all your
support of my work

Cynthia Enloe

DESIGN DETAILS FOR HEALTH

Wiley Series in Healthcare and Senior Living Design

Alfred H. Baucom
Hospitality Design for the Graying Generation: Meeting the Needs of a Growing Market

Sara O. Marberry
Healthcare Design

Elizabeth C. Brawley
Designing for Alzheimer's Disease: Strategies for Creating Better Care Environments

John E. Harrigan
Senior Residences: Designing Retirement Communities for the Future

Clare Cooper Marcus and Marni Barnes
Healing Gardens: Therapeutic Benefits and Design Recommendations

Joan M. Whaley
Wellness Centers: A Guide for the Design Professional

Cynthia A. Leibrock
Design Details for Health: Making the Most of Interior Design's Healing Potential

DESIGN DETAILS FOR HEALTH

Making the Most of Interior Design's Healing Potential

Cynthia A. Leibrock

JOHN WILEY & SONS, INC.

New York • Chichester • Weinheim • Brisbane • Singapore • Toronto

Copyright © 2000 by Cynthia A. Leibrock. All rights reserved.
Published by John Wiley & Sons, Inc.

Published simultaneously in Canada.

This publication is designed to provide accurate and authoritative information in regard to the subject matter covered. It is sold with the understanding that the publisher is not engaged in rendering professional services. If professional advice or other expert assistance is required, the services of a competent professional person should be sought.

Library of Congress Cataloging-in-Publication Data:

Leibrock, Cynthia
    Design details for health : making the most of interior design's
healing potential / Cynthia A. Leibrock.
        p. cm. — (Wiley series in healthcare and senior living design)
    ISBN 0-471-24194-6 (alk. paper)
    1. Health facilities — Decoration   2. Interior decoration — History
— 20th century. I. Title II. series.
NK2195.H43L45 2000
747'.8551 — dc21   99-29983

Printed in the United States of America.

10 9 8 7 6 5 4 3 2 1

To my family and our Christian faith,
which inspired this book

CONTENTS

LIST OF DETAILS AND RESEARCH ABSTRACTS

DETAILS *(continued)*

FOREWORD

Thirteen years ago, I initiated a rigorous inquiry into better understanding the ways that the physical environment could be more supportive of human health and well being. Thirteen years ago, this was like
whistling into the wind. Today, as you might attest from your own experience, the physical environment in which healthcare is delivered is very
different—and far more supportive. Clearly, we have only touched the
tip of the iceberg and there is much more work to be done—but we
have successfully managed to shift the paradigm. Today, the idea of supportive environments to promote health and well being is widely accepted and is approaching mainstream application.

The big question is *how do we make our physical environment more
supportive?* If the major event was the initiation of the inquiry, then we
must develop the appropriate technology to have the possibility be real-
ized.

I have known Cynthia Leibrock and her work for the past thirteen
years. During this period, I have watched Cynthia's pioneering work
encourage the implementation of specific technical solutions that have
served to further the application of supportive physical environments for
health. Cynthia's tenacity in discovering or developing, evaluating, and
documenting these many practical solutions for improved accessibility is
unrivaled.

Cynthia Leibrock's new book, *Design Details for Health,* is the pattern book that has been needed to bridge the gap between theory and
practical reality. Whether one is a student, educator, researcher, design
practitioner, builder, client, facility manager, accessibility consultant,
product manufacturer, or a lay person considering strategies to remove
physical barriers to accessibility—this book is a reference standard with
timeless value.

The physical environment surrounds us all and has the inherent ability to support our health and well being—or not. For those who have an interest in improving the life enhancing nature of our physical environment, this book will provide the examples, technical solutions, professional resources, and references.

Perhaps 35 years from today, as we will look back from a world that embraces us with a more supportive and accessible physical environment, we will genuinely appreciate the advanced technical capacity that this book has contributed to our improved state of health and well being.

WAYNE RUGA, AIA, FIDA
Loeb Fellow, Harvard University
Cambridge, Massachusetts
1999

PREFACE

God is in the details. The power of a healing environment comes from the little things, the design details that empower patients to take responsibility for their own health.

Imagine a hospital where patients wear street clothes, where physicians and nurses must have permission to enter patients' rooms, and where care partners stay in the hospital with patients as they are educated in healing choices. Imagine a housing complex guaranteeing that residents will never have to live in a health-care facility; none will be institutionalized or be moved along a continuum to independent, assisted, or skilled care. Imagine a center for healing with an emphasis on wellness rather than illness, prevention rather than treatment, self-care rather than service provision.

These models are no longer figments of the imagination. These hospitals of the future exist today in select demonstration projects filled with design details that empower patients to take responsibility for their own health, hygiene, medications, and nutrition.

U.S. health-care institutions are overbuilt. Patient care protocols are staff intensive. Patient outcomes are suffering. We offer the poorest-quality health care of the top ten Western industrialized nations (measured by longevity, patient satisfaction with care, and infant mortality). We also spend more dollars per capita on health care than any other industrialized country. Managed care has inherited these problems and is positioning for change. Managed care needs entirely different solutions, better health-care models that improve patient outcomes, lower liability, and reduce costs. The purpose of this book is to offer specific design details that improve patient outcomes by returning authority to patients. Case studies are offered that reduce liability by leaving the responsibility for health-care decisions with patients. Finally, research is presented that demonstrates how empowering design details can reduce costs as patients take responsibility for their health care and decrease their reliance on staff.

Without these details, health-care facilities are places where patients are overexposed to strangers and separated from family, where independence is lost to providers or to disabling design. Such facilities are threatening places filled with odors, noises, and invasive equipment. Without appropriate design detail, institutions are places where patients are kept in the dark, literally and figuratively. They cope with a stressful environment at the worst possible time, a time when they are already coping with illness or the threat of death and with problems of pain and medication.

Several years ago, I spent one night in a hospital recovering from minor knee surgery. My family had received good care in this hospital during the past 20 years, but things had changed. Under new management, staffing levels had been reduced and nurses replaced by aides. The night after my surgery, I only called for help three times—once because I needed pain medication, and twice for help to use the bathroom. No one answered any of my calls in less than an hour.

Forty-five minutes after the first bathroom call, I could wait no longer. I hopped on one leg across a slick floor, trying to make it to the toilet. I was wearing slippery surgical hose. The bed had no footboard for support and there were no handrails in the room. If I had slipped, I could have damaged my knee beyond repair.

The toilet had an elevated seat with a large, unprotected gap that allowed urine to spray on the floor. My surgical hose were soaked. I called for help again, and no one came. I tried to return to my bead, hopping on a wet, slick floor. I barely made it across the room. I will not soon forget crawling under those clean sheets wearing urine-soaked surgical hose.

Finally someone answered my call, an attendant who could not speak English. I could not make her understand that I needed medication. During my entire stay, a nurse never entered my room and I never received my prescribed pain medication. I spent a sleepless night in pain, waiting for a nurse and worrying about the care.

The next morning I called for the hospital ombudsman. When she arrived, I was stressed to the point of tears. I related my story, and she said that the problems arose because I was placed on a floor "for the elderly." She said I would have received much better care on another floor. It is hard to believe that older people still suffer from that degree of discrimination; it is harder yet to believe she would admit it.

I could have taken my own pain medication if I had been trusted to do so. I would not have required help to go to the bathroom if the bed had been planned for support, if the floor offered traction, if the trim above the wainscoting had been designed as a handrail, and if the bathroom had offered the dignity of self-care. I would never have called for help if a family member had been allowed to stay in the hospital with me and if my room had been detailed to accommodate rooming-in.

The ombudsman put a check in the mail the same day I complained, fearing litigation (even though I had never suggested it). If the room had been designed for self-care, the hospital would have had happier administrators (profits would be up), happier providers (no cleanup would have been required), and a happier patient (I'd rather do it myself).

I had to tolerate this abuse for only 24 hours, but many older people end up living in health-care facilities for the rest of their lives. Inferior care of older people is endemic, as I learned on the floor "for the elderly." We think nothing of segregating our elders. Whether we call it a nursing home, a manor, a retirement village, or residential care, it is not OK to live in a health-care facility. It doesn't make it OK if the health-care facility is decorated to look like home.

For three years, my offices were located in a beautiful assisted living facility where older people get great care. I worked with the residents to test some of the design solutions and products featured in this book and to offer feedback to the manufacturers. The facility has a caring staff, excellent food, a rehabilitation emphasis, and a nurse on duty at all times (which is not required by regulations). I thought I could adjust to having my office there, but I never did. I finally closed the office, realizing that I could not adjust to the concept of older people living in health-care facilities.

There are better solutions. I have conducted design research in Japan and most of the Northern European countries. The book focuses on contemporary emerging models rather than traditional places of service provision, such as university medical centers or nursing homes. One of my favorite models is in Holland in an apartment complex that virtually guarantees that residents age in place. The residents are offered 24-hour medical intervention in their own apartments. They never have to move to assisted living or skilled nursing units.

In addition to these field studies, this book offers findings from four other types of design research: experiments, surveys, evaluation studies, and historical research. A small amount of new experimental research is presented, but most of the new findings were produced by surveys I conducted of hundreds of health-care designers and architects. Their expertise is shared in each chapter. Also included are findings from my own postoccupational evaluation studies of health-care facilities from the patient's point of view. There is little information about improving facilities for the benefit of maintenance or other staff. Much has already been written about this subject. The majority of the research is historical; I present existing data on topics ranging from acoustics to lighting, complete with citations for additional study.

I provide lists of details from my first book, *Beautiful Barrier Free,* and its revision, *Beautiful Universal Design.* Using these lists, I have never surveyed an existing health-care facility that is truly accessible to older and disabled people (or even in compliance with the Americans with Disabilities Act). Where else is this technology more needed? Every day, I see people who are disempowered and even disabled by the design of health-care facilities. I truly hope this book will help.

ACKNOWLEDGMENTS

This book was conceived on a research trip to Scandinavia that was sponsored by the National Symposium on Health Design. In Motala, Sweden, I met Barbro Beck-Friis, a world-renowned gerontologist and innovator in the care of people with dementia. She introduced me to a self-care philosophy, keeping patients in charge and responsible for their own health. I saw innovative group homes offering patient-centered care in residential settings, replacing provider-centered care in institutions. I was inspired. I gratefully acknowledge the support of Wayne Ruga, who made this trip possible.

With this vision, I began my research on the power of design to return control to patients. This work was continually encouraged by my fellow members of the board of directors of The National Symposium of Health Design, especially Jain Malkin, Derek Parker, and Roger Leib. As my research progressed, seven people offered limitless support of my mission and countless opportunities to disseminate my research: Wayne Ruga, Deborah Carlson with DuPont, Barbara Henn with The American Society of Interior Designers, William Saunders with The Harvard Graduate School of Design, Amanda Miller with John Wiley and Sons, Jim Terry with Evan Terry Associates, and Elizabeth Brawley with Design Concepts. Without their ongoing support, this book would not have been possible.

I especially wish to thank my husband for the hours of editing and rewriting that he contributed to this project. I also wish to thank my parents for 50 years of empowerment and my brother, Eric Hildebrand, for all of his help with my work. He is winning a 30-year battle with mental illness and is a tremendous example of a person who takes responsibility for his own health.

I would also like to acknowledge the support of my colleagues at Colorado State University, especially the sustaining friendship of

Antigone Kostiopolis. For contributing professional expertise to the book, I wish to thank Barbara Heulat, Jain Malkin, Joan Baron, Karrie Frasca-Beautieu, Gregory Scott, John Robinson, Nancy Pattyn, Dian Love, Lisa Gerovac, Wanda Hailey, Cathy Bajo, and Judy Smith. In Japan, Hiroko Machida, Dr. Kose Satoshi, Mino Yokiyama, and Yoshiaki Goto shared their research, and in Holland, Filo Lanken offered innovative approaches to research on aging. In the United States, I wish to thank Gary Schexnaildre of Interface Flooring Systems, Jack Murph of DuPont Antron, Larry O'Neil of Genon, Tom Hakes of Construction Specialties, and Cindy Howley and Diana Schrage of The Kohler Company for their support of my research. Special thanks to Jane Langmuir of The Rhode Island School of Design and Bruce Arneill of The Slam Collaborative for sharing their research libraries and to Mary Beth Rampolla of Eva Maddox Associates for design and research collaboration.

It has been a joy and a privilege to work with my dear friend Debra Levin, who has spent countless hours providing wonderful illustrations for the book (and a great time for all in the process). Two other special friends are always there for me when I need expert advice on health design and a little encouragment: Patty Moore and Margaret Christenson. So many others have unselfishly contributed their ideas — Jane Rohde, Louise Jones, Elaine Ostroff, Marsha and Mark Mazz, John Salmen, Susan Dimotta, Charlie Pruitt, Vic Hanson, Sara Marberry, Steph Crosby, Chris Buscaj, Vija Berzins, Felicia Borkovi, Anne Carlyle, and Mary Jean Thompson, to name a few. I am grateful for their friendship and willingness to share their expertise. Finally, I wish to thank Jerry Younkin and Johnny Square, my Christian mentors, who initiate and sustain my mission.

P A R T

O N E

LONG-TERM CARE

This book is written on the premise that no one should have to live in a health-care facility. In the early 1970s, people with severe disabilities lived either in institutions or at home in the care of family members. Few lived independently. Today, many older people find themselves in the same position. Eighty-five percent of those needing help are forced to depend on care by their family and friends, receiving no community services.[1] Without these services, they cannot live independently. When friends and family are exhausted, older people are forced to move into health-care facilities.

Many are moved four times in their later years, primarily for the convenience of staff. It is not OK to move older people out of their home into an "independent living" facility and then on to assisted living, skilled nursing, and death in a hospital. Older consumers are demanding supportive and affordable residential long-term care in housing, not in facilities. We have the technology to meet this need. Health care is now portable. It can be brought to the consumer. With design support, older people can live independently in their communities for the rest of their lives.

Unfortunately, fully 15 percent of Americans over 85 have to live in nursing homes.[2] This is because more than half of older people have at least one disability[3] and try to live without design or staff support. The number of older people without a significant caregiver is growing because fewer older people have married, they have had fewer children, and there are more divorces. By the year 2030, about 70 million people will be over the age of 65[4] and 30 million will be living alone without a caregiver. They will need design intervention to age in place and avoid institutionalization.

Today, at least one out of every five U.S. citizens age 15 and over need help with activities of daily living (ADL): over 2 million people are in wheelchairs; 16 million have a visual impairment; 22 million have a hearing impairment; 37 million have arthritis.[5] Forty percent of all homeless men and 50 percent of homeless women have a chronic mental disability. All need supportive housing.

COST CONTAINMENT

The home is not only the hospital of the future; it is the hospital of today, and cost containment has been the result.[6] If the cost of caring for a child in a hospital is $250,000, the same care can be provided for $50,000 at home.[7] Research demonstrates that residential care for older people reduces the length of stay in acute care by an average of 15.6 days.[8]

A study called the Channeling Demonstration was conducted in ten communities to substitute case-managed care at home for care in nursing homes. This was a comprehensive three-year national test of residential care. At the time, only $440 per month was needed by each client for care at home (compared to over $2,000 per month for nursing-home care).

The United States has the largest percentage of people in nursing homes among all developed countries in the world[9] and there is little incentive to return patients to their homes. In 1998, less than 2 percent of Medicare-Certified health-care agencies were based in nursing homes.[10] At least 20 to 40 percent of the older population in nursing homes or long-term care facilities could be cared for at less intensive levels or in alternate settings, including the home.[11] In 1989, Oregon estimated that 93 percent of its Medicaid nursing home population are inappropriately placed.[12] Nursing homes have become a "solution" to what is basically a housing problem rather than a health problem. It is an inappropriate and expensive solution at best.

Nursing home care costs anywhere from $30,000 to $60,000 per year. Those patients inappropriately housed in nursing homes could receive equal or higher-quality care from an attendant at a cost savings of $15,000 to $40,000 per year.[13] Although many of these patients do not need 24-hour medical intervention, Medicaid pays only for full-time assistance in a nursing home. The money currently spent on nursing home care could pay for home care for three times as many people, who would achieve a better quality of life in the process.

To care for those who require 24-hour care at home, aides receive far less compensation than skilled nurses. In a 1989 study, Florida estimated that attendant services at home cost $4,000 to $6,000 per year, and Montana averaged about $4,300.[14] Again, care in a nursing home costs between $30,000 and $60,000 per year.

Residential health care also reduces the legal costs of practicing medicine. Litigation has been a negligible factor in residential health care to date. In institutional settings, fear of litigation forces physicians to practice "defensive medicine," ordering expensive tests and treatments that often prove unnecessary. When the provider is on the patient's turf, displays of power and authority are less common. Personal relationships develop between provider and patient in the home and patient satisfaction with services increases. Medical malpractice carriers do not recognize residential care as a high-liability practice.[15] The reduced risk of liability may keep insurance costs low and reduce the unnecessary costs of defensive medicine.

REIMBURSEMENT DRIVING DESIGN

An issue of concern to proponents of residential health care is the cost of supportive housing. Affordable housing is difficult to find, and affordable, accessible, available housing is nonexistent. There are waiting lists in most major cities.

The National Association of Home Builders estimates that compliance with American National Standards Institute (ANSI) accessibility standards adds between 6 percent and 14.5 percent to the overall size of most units, with resulting cost increases. Compliance with Americans with Disabilities Act (ADA) accessibility standards in large-scale commercial projects adds less than 1 percent to the cost of new construction.[16] Cost increases can be kept to a minimum if adaptable (rather than accessible) elements are planned; for example, bathroom walls can be reinforced to hold grab bars at a later date.

In some states, new housing is already required to be accessible, eliminating the need for modifications. Local Law 58 in New York City requires some new housing to be accessible and adaptable. The Fair Housing Amendment has taken the first national step in this process by addressing multifamily dwellings. But we are already too late for the baby boomers. We will not have enough adaptable housing stock to meet their needs.

Limited government funding is available for minor home modifications, meals on wheels, and accessible transportation. In addition, tax breaks are offered to those purchasing accessible vans or modifying their homes and offices. Home equity conversions and reverse annuity mortgages allow residents to age in place while offering a steady stream of funding from the equity of the house. This funding source can also be used for modifications.

The national need for coverage of in-home long-term care is growing. By the year 2020, over 14 million older people will depend on self-care for their long-term needs.[17] The home is the preferred long-term care setting, but most of this care is now offered by inexperienced volunteers. Nearly 90 percent of older people living in the community already receive help from an unpaid caregiver.[18] Over 50 percent of the caregivers are over 60 years old and

18 percent are over 70.[19] Seventy-five to 80 percent of caregivers are women with other obligations, including careers, child rearing, and household management.[20]

To contain costs, an interesting system has been established in a number of U.S. cities. Volunteers are compensated with "time dollars" exchanged for services at a later date. These volunteer service credits can be spent for rides to get groceries, cleaning services, or even just friendly visits. Medicaid will not pay for most of these services, and many who need the services are too proud to beg for them. With this system, even frail older people can accumulate credits by telephone—by keeping in touch with others or placing calls for them. This allows them to earn credits to pay for the help they need. Support groups have also formed to offer needed services to their members.

QUALITY OF RESIDENTIAL LONG-TERM CARE

Consumers are increasingly required to make quality-of-care decisions, and the uneducated consumer can easily make the wrong choices. Should innovative new technologies always be used? What level of care should be selected? Should a blood transfusion be given to a terminally ill patient? Who makes the determination? To what extent should such choices be driven by reimbursement?

In the past, physicians made many of these decisions. But most physicians were schooled in the disease-focused biomedical model, which minimizes the role of patients in managing their own health. This model does not address the psychological, social, and spiritual needs that become critical in long-term care. The model views aging as a disease that must be "treated" in a medical facility.

As a result, many well people are placed in nursing homes simply because they are old.

This problem is the direct result of uneducated consumers turning the responsibility for their own health care over to physicians who are biased toward the institutional settings in which they have been trained. Most physicians have had minimum exposure to residential care.

Institutional environments are stressful, and we know that stress is associated with changes in immunity that make people more susceptible to infection and viruses.[21] High-quality home care often prevents the need for institutionalization and resulting illnesses.

Long-term care is offered in the home by some physicians, registered nurses, home health aides, medical social workers, and therapists (most often physical, occupational, speech, and respiratory therapists). Geriatric evaluation and diabetic assessment services provide in-home assessment and referral to community services.

Home therapies are becoming commonplace, including provision of immunoglobulins, pain management, growth hormones, total parenteral nutrition, and enteral nutrition. Patients receive home treatment for infectious diseases such as hepatitis-B and AIDS. Dressing and wound care, ventilation therapy, and phototherapy for babies with jaundice are also frequently done at home. Physical therapy accounts for about 10 percent of the services in the home,[22] and occupation therapy at home is also popular.

The days of home care by Marcus Welby, M.D., are returning, but with a high-tech twist. Physicians are finding innovative ways to meet the demand for care at home. In the process, they are rewarded with the personal and professional satisfaction of home care and relief from the frustration of the impersonal medical office. One example could be found in Broward County, Florida, where two mobile clinics offered free care and medication in 22 neighborhoods. The clinics served patients whose average income is under $4,000 per year.[23] This was a volunteer effort, and most of the 15 physicians and staff were seniors.

In San Diego, physicians make house calls in vans, arriving within 60 minutes of each time-sensitive call. Each van contains necessary medications, a mobile lab, and X-ray, electrocardiograph (EKG), and other diagnostic equipment. Specialized vans offer cardiology and orthopedic care to chronically ill patients. Kidney stones can be crushed on an outpatient basis and gallbladders removed with a trocar the size of a straw. Gel diapers that turn urine to gel that never touches the skin eliminate the need for Foley catheters. Teleradiolo-gy uses a home video camera to digitize images that are sent through the telephone to the radiologist. Teleconnective cable allows physicians to diagnose from the office using a video camera. Arthroscopic procedures (which use a camera that fits through the eye of a needle) and laser surgeries will make many acute medical procedures possible at home.

Dr. Gresham Bayne, one of the leaders in the home care movement, predicts that as home health care progresses, two thirds of today's hospitals could be closed, with the remainder becoming intensive care units. He foresees that 90 percent of health care services will be performed by nonphysicians, but says qualified aides are the missing link in the system.[24]

Universal design will contribute to the solution. Through accessible design and supportive technology, individuals can function independently without assistance, and the demand for staff assistance can be reduced.

DESIGN INTERVENTION

Traditionally, the design solution to a variety of long-term care needs has been the continuing care retirement community (CCRC). Here patients are moved from level to level as their acuity changes. Most CCRCs offer three levels of care: independent living, assisted and skilled nursing. Residents are moved to more intensive levels of care as their health deteriorates. Each move becomes a defeat. This negative approach is exacerbated by the discrimination it fosters. Assisted living residents refuse to eat with skilled nursing patients, and independent seniors won't enter the assisted living wing. Residents are shuffled from level to level, destroying any networks established in the interim.

Most older people hate to move. If continuing care were truly offered in a retirement community, at least ten residential options would be considered without requiring frequent moving from one choice to another.

1. Community-based group homes
2. Foster homes
3. Supervised apartments
4. Shelters
5. Housing with live-in roommates
6. Host homes where the resident becomes part of the family
7. Boarding houses
8. Shared homes
9. Semisupervised apartments (without live-in managers)
10. Subsidized support programs where individuals receive payments to follow a plan for self-sufficiency (or discounts on insurance for healthy houses and healthy habits)

These choices support all ages and financial abilities. Designers trained in universal design can make each approach adaptable and flexible. The Stein Gerontological Institute offers innovative technological options for aging in place. This research center provides a model kitchen, bathroom, and a high-technology apartment that allows older people and caregivers hands-on access to education and information. The center also features portable "try before you buy" models that can be left in the home. A questionnaire measures residents' ability to self-treat medical problems, maintain personal hygiene, and take care of business affairs. A team of professionals, including an occupational therapist, social worker, architect, and interior designer, offers turnkey design that involves assessment, modification, and assisting devices.

Most people want to age in place, using the home as a orthopedic environment that functionally restores the independence of the individual. The design of a residence can significantly affect care. We know, for example, that many long-term care services can be eliminated by making changes in a person's dwelling.[25] In addition, studies show design elements influence the ease with which long-term services can be provided in the home.[26,27,28] For older people, design improves ability to adapt to and recover from stressful activity. It also maximizes the use of existing mobility as well as the auditory, visual, and tactile senses.

Forty percent of deaths from injuries to people 65 and over result from accidents at home. Tripping, fire safety, handrails, lighting, hot water temperature, heating ventilation and air conditioning (HVAC), kitchen safety, and security are issues that become critical for long-term care. Research confirms that the most important issues for older people involve health and security. In a congregate care survey of 500 Southern California seniors (over the age of 65), the most requested features were 24-hour security on the premises, an arrangement with the local hospital, an attendant on the premises trained in cardiopulmonary resuscitation (CPR), emergency call systems, and a television security system in the building.[29] Although an ergonomically designed kitchen was rated second out of 77 features, other amenities like shopping assistance, gardening space, and maid service were surprisingly low in priority.

TECHNOLOGY

Contrary to popular belief, older people are not always afraid of technology. Many use computers, initially enticed by e-mail for communicating with grandchildren. High-tech services are increasingly popular, especially to accommodate disabilities. At the Stein Gerontological Institute, residents receive computer training to encourage communication and discourage isolation. With this training, residents can maintain contact with others without leaving their homes. In addition to word processing, the computer provides access to community services, coursework (like language tutoring), and a senior newsletter. Checkbook balancing, banking, shopping, games, and travel services are also available.

Computers have become so accessible that they can be operated through simple eye movement, reflecting an infrared beam off the cornea of the eye. The Eyegaze System costs up to $25,000, but its user can perform a wide range of tasks. By focusing the reflected beam on the screen, the user can communicate with others, do word processing, control lights, operate appliances, and enjoy the television or VCR.[30]

Interactive cable uses a small television camera to film residents in their home. It can also be used to monitor patients, to more adequately control records, and to improve diagnosis and treatment. It can provide patients and their families with access to records together with the best medical expertise and information on specific illnesses. Video conferencing on interactive cable allows visiting without travel. In the future a system of pneumatic tubes may bring food, medicine, and supplies to the patient and family at home.

RESIDENTIAL LONG-TERM CARE
IN OTHER COUNTRIES

According to the 33 European nations that belong to the World Health Organization (WHO), "By the year 2000, all people of the region should have a better opportunity of living in houses and settlements which provide a healthy and safe environment." They are developing specifications for safe design and construction of buildings, furniture, fittings, and domestic equipment.

France has had more than a quarter-century of home-care experience and has developed an outstanding system to evaluate patient outcomes. In the French system, patients have direct access to national funding authorities and some control over service delivery.

In Ireland, boarding-out has been explored. Patients are placed with nonrelatives in private homes. The client and the state split the costs.

Demographics in Japan project an increase in the older population from today's 14.8 million to 31.9 million by 2020, creating a tremendous market for long-term care design services. Japanese people 65 years and older will represent 24 percent of the total population by then. In Japan today, 16 percent of the population is 65 or older, but more than 50 percent of all health care dollars are spent on these older Japanese.[31] For this reason, the government already provides preferential interest rates on universally designed homes that prevent institutionalization.[32]

Elders are traditionally treated with respect and honor in Japan, but they have had to rely on the women in their families for care. These women have now traveled more widely and are aware of other choices in long-term care. They work outside the home more frequently and are not available to offer day care. They do not always live close to their parents. The elders live longer lives with more disabilities and require more care. Older Japanese are demanding residential long-term choices offering independence, personal growth, support for activities, security, privacy, and dignity.

Sweden and Denmark have moved many health services to residential environments. Sweden has been reducing nursing home beds by about 900 beds per year.[33] Existing nursing homes are viewed as subacute facilities where only the most severely impaired patients belong.

Most older patients do not need skilled nursing care but do need assisted living at home because they cannot organize a network of services that would allow them to live independently. Twenty percent of the 65+ age group in Sweden receive residential long-term health care, almost all concentrated on the 80+ population.[34] The physically frail individual requires assistance with bathing, toileting, mobility, grooming, medication, and meal preparation. The mentally frail person may become confused or lost, even in familiar surroundings, and need assistance.

In Europe, much of this care is delivered in sheltered-care houses, which are typically smaller than U.S. assisted living facilities. They are not based on a medical model or integrated into a larger facility or CCRC. In Sweden, five to six people may each live in his or her own small apartment grouped around a large living area and kitchen. At a minimum, each apartment has a separate bedroom and small kitchen. Couples frequently have two bedrooms, which offers the flexibility to hire live-in help at a later date. Some units are equipped with passive energy systems that summon help if the toilet has not been flushed or if the refrigerator door has been left open. Motorized windows sense rain and close automatically. Toilets have built-in rinse and dry features. Sinks tip forward to ease hairwashing from a seated position. The Swedes have found that design intervention is less expensive than staff intervention and that care in the home is less expensive than institutionalization.

In Motala, Sweden, the hospital successfully provides 24-hour home care to both acute and long-term care patients. One study at Motala found that 89 percent of terminal cancer patients could be cared for at home until they died.[35] Employees are allowed to take off 30 days per year from work (at full salary) to care for an old or seriously ill relative.

Denmark is considered the most advanced country in Europe in terms of social policies for older people. Services are typically brought to people in their independent living units until that becomes impossible. Then, every attempt is made to find long-term care within the immediate neighborhood of the individual. Housing complexes often offer intergenerational care, integrating children and seniors while still offering privacy. Considerable effort is made to blend these facilities into the neighborhood. Commercial restaurants, rather than dining rooms, are located within the facility. Day care and therapies are offered to the public by the facility, encouraging community interaction.

There is a moratorium on new construction of nursing homes in Denmark. "In the future, independent dwellings not resembling institutions are to be built."[36] Very extensive modifications to existing houses are paid for by the government. It is considered good economic housekeeping to empower a disabled person to continue living at home. If fact, disabled people have a *legal right* to do so.

By 1984, over 3,000 universal kitchens had been installed in Denmark, complete with counters adjustable to six heights. Bathrooms were modified, and ramps and lifts were frequently added.[37] Doors and halls were widened and three levels of alarm systems were available. Legislation requires all ground-floor flats to be accessible.

As general housing in Denmark has become accessible, special housing for people with disabilities is no longer needed. Design demonstration centers are in place, allowing citizens to learn about their choices. These centers also help in the development of new equipment, providing consumer feedback to designers and manufacturers.

Denmark has also led the world in innovative elder care. Residential services include meals on wheels, housekeeping, and medical residential long-term care, including full-time aides if necessary. Denmark is developing housing that is oriented toward singles, not couples or nuclear families. The Danes keep elders involved in today's tasks and issues, considering them valuable consumers who need choices. Elders are aware of their choices, which include meaningful activities and tasks that are valuable alternatives to the working life. This is part of the Danish goal to offer continuity as a choice to seniors. The Danes maintain high expectations of their elders, making use of their experience and knowledge. They respect the decisions of their older population and make self-determination a high priority.

In the United Kingdom, most older people are cared for at home. Individuals pay rent for their housing, but long-term care is provided in three categories. In Category 1, services are generally supplied by neighbors. In Category 2, wardens offer services, and Category 3 is skilled nursing.

In Category 1, neighbors are paid to care for each other. This is an innovative attempt to provide caring caregivers. Neighbors help with ADLs, ensure that the home is properly heated and cooled, and even cook meals (if their charge has refused meals on wheels, thinking he or she could still cook). Because they are neighbors, caregivers frequently develop close relationships with the older people they serve. Supportive home design is also offered to facilitate self-care by those in Category 1.

In Category 2, wardens prepare at least one meal per day, sometimes in a congregate setting. Homes providing long-term care for four or more people must register and are subject to inspection. Most people with dementia are cared for at home under this category.

Category 3 (skilled nursing) is limited to older people with aggressive psychosis. Living with the extended family is seldom an option, but any form of institutionalization will not be accepted until it becomes absolutely necessary.

Residential long-term care is the care of the future in the United Kingdom. Reimbursement changes are forcing hospitals to compete for patients by introducing more ambulatory and residential care services. As in the United States and Scandinavia, the home is becoming the hospital of the future.

REFERENCES

1. Joanne G. Schwartzberg, "Reimbursement, Physician Case Management, and Home Health Care," *Group Practice Journal* (March/April 1991): 24–26.
2. Department of Health and Human Services, *A Profile of Older Americans: 1997* (Washington, D.C.: GPO, 1997), 5.
3. Ibid., 11.
4. Ibid., 3.
5. Bureau of the Census, *Statistical Abstract of the United States: 1997,* Vol. 117 (Washington, D.C.: GPO, 1997), 143.
6. Charles Honaker, "Home Healthcare Renaissance," *Group Practice Journal* (March/April 1991): 8–12.
7. Ibid.
8. P. J. Schwartz, S. Blumenfield, and E. P. Simon, "The Interim Home Care Program: An Innovative Discharge Planning Alternative," *Health and Social Work* (May 1990): 152–160.
9. House of Representatives Select Committee on Aging, *Housing for the Frail Elderly: Hearing, May 4 and July 26, 1989* (Washington, D.C.: GPO, 1990), SD cat. no. Y 4Ag 4/2:H 81/26.
10. National Association for Home Care (1999) *Basic Statistics about Home Care* Washington D.C.: NAHC, p. 2.
11. Janet Simons, "Assisted Living Demand Outstrips Supply," *Senior Edition USA/Colorado* (March 1989): 9–11.
12. House of Representatives Select Committee on Aging, *Housing for the Frail Elderly.*
13. Kerri S. Smith, "The Nursing Home Dilemma," *Rocky Mountain News,* 4 June 1991, *Lifestyles* section.
14. John Melcher, "Keeping our Elderly Out of Institutions by Putting Them Back in Their Homes," *American Psychologist* 8 (August 1988): 643–647.
15. Honaker, "Home Healthcare Renaissance," 8–12.
16. Kim Beasley, "Design Lines: The Cost of Accessibility," *Paraplegia News* (June 1990): 42.
17. J.M. Keenan and K.W. Hepburn, "Home Care Needs Physician Leadership," *Group Practice Journal* (March/April 1991): 14–23.
18. Honaker, "Home Healthcare Renaissance," 8–12.
19. John Melcher, "Keeping Our Elderly Out of Institutions," 643–647.
20. Keenan and Hepburn, "Home Care Needs Physician Leadership," 14–23.
21. Mike Snider, "Stress May Be Something to Sneeze About," *USA Today,* 29 August 1991, sec. 1A.
22. Honaker, "Home Healthcare Renaissance," 8–12.
23. Maxi Dewolf, "Health Care on Wheels: Retired Doctors Come to Aid of Elderly," *USA Today.,* 1 March 1990, sec. 4D.
24. Gresham Bayne, "A Mobile Emergency Room: A New Option in Comprehensive Home Care," *Caring* (July 1988): 25–27.
25. R. Stuyk, "Current and Emerging Issues in Housing Environments for the Elderly," in *America's Aging: the social and Built Environment in an Older Society,* Committee on an Aging Society (Washington, D.C.: National Academy Press, 1988).
26. S. J. Newman, "Housing and Long-Term Care: The Suitability of the Elderly's Housing to the Provision of In-Home Services," *The Gerontologist* 25, no. 1 (1985): 35–40.
27. L. Noelker, "The Impact of Environmental Problems on Caring for Impaired Elders in a Home Setting" (paper presented at the 35th Annual Scientific Meeting of the Gerontological Society of America, Boston, Mass., 1982).

28. B. Soldo and C. Longino, "Social and Physical Environments for the Vulnerable Aged," in *American's Aging: The Social and Built Environment in an Older Society,* Committee on an Aging Society (Washington, D.C.: National Academy Press, 1988).

29. V. Regnier and J. Pynoos, *Housing the Aged: Design Directives and Policy Considerations* (New York: Elsevier, 1987).

30. Bernie Ward, "Overcoming Barriers," *Sky* (September 1991): 52–61.

31. Hiroko Machida, "Why Housing Coordinator(s) for the Elderly" (paper presented at International Conference of Living Environment Health and Well Being for the Elderly, Izu, Japan, March 1997).

32. Satoshi Kose, "Aging in Place: From Barrier-Free to Universal Design Dwellings" (paper presented at the International Longevity Center Conference, "Living Environment, Health, and Well-being for the Elderly—Cross National Perspective," Izu, Japan, 10 March 1997).

33. Gilbert Dooghe and Lut Vanden Boer, *Sheltered Accommodation for Elderly People in an International Perspective* (Amsterdam: Swets and Zeitlinger, 1993), 64.

34. Linda Boise, "Family Care of the Aged in Sweden," *Viewpoint Sweden* (February 1991): 2.

35. Barbro Beck-Friis, "Physical Dependence of Cancer Patients at Home," *Palliative Medicine,* 3 (1989): 281–286.

36. Royal Danish Ministry of Social Affairs, *The Pensioner in Denmark.* (Copenhagen, Denmark: [Author], 1990).

37. Ibid.

1 ASSISTED LIVING APARTMENTS

The future of assisted living is lifetime care in one location. It is not the continuing care concept where residents (who are often treated like patients) are moved from independent living to assisted living to skilled care units. The best of assisted living provides the independence and dignity of a home, individual assistance with daily activities, and physical medical care for life in the same apartment.

Traditionally, assisted living has been defined as a housing model offering support for unscheduled needs,[1] including assistance with ADLs, personal care, and some health care. Skilled nursing has been defined as 24-hour medical intervention in a health care facility. But the line has blurred between the two; skilled nursing is trying to become a housing model and assisted living is providing more medical service.

Health care is now portable; many interventions can easily be brought to patients and their families with advancements in home health care. In addition, most assisted living complexes offer transportation to ambulatory care. Others have nurses on call, if not on the premises, 24 hours a day. Some complexes have two-tier call systems that let residents choose between minor assistance and emergency help. Prevention is a priority; nutrition, exercise, security, and safety are addressed (see Details on page 49).

The worst of assisted living is a skilled nursing facility decorated to look like home to ease the guilt of family members institutionalizing a loved one. These models are easy to identify; the exterior clearly reads *facility*, not *housing complex*. They are basically medical models inappropriately used as housing models.

In the United States, many older people are forced to live in health-care facilities. This is not true in much of Europe, where a distinct separation is maintained between housing and health-care facilities. Rehabilitation, emergency assistance, and 24-hour skilled nursing are available at home, but fewer Europeans actually live in health-care facilities. The United States has the largest percentage of people living in nursing homes of all developed countries in the world.[2]

ASSISTED LIVING IN EUROPE

In Rotterdam, Holland, 60 nursing home patients were moved into apartments at The Bergweg Project (see Figure 1-1). They will not be moved along the continuum of care from independent living to assisted living to skilled nursing. Bergweg residents can now live with their spouse of any age, have their children stay overnight in the apartment, and develop friendships with their neighbors without fear of being moved out of the neighborhood into a healt-care facility. This project has literally returned life to residents who were previously subsisting in semiprivate (which means almost public) rooms in nursing homes.

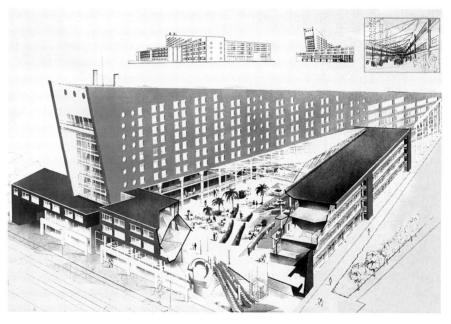

Figure 1-1 Lifetime care without moving. *Courtesy of Stichting Humanitas Rotterdam.*

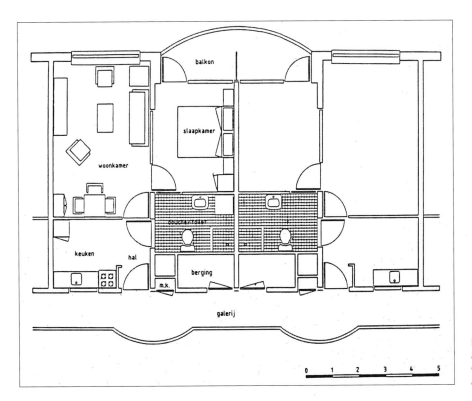

balkon

slaapkamer

woonkamer

keuken

hal

berging

m.k.

galerij

0   1   2   3   4   5

Figure 1-2 Gurney-accessible apartment. *Courtesy of Stichting Humanitas Rotterdam.*

The complex consists of 180 lifetime apartments, each with two or three rooms totalling 660–740 sq. ft. The apartments are not only accessible to people in wheelchairs; they are accessible to people in hospital beds as well (see Figure 1-2). Even bedridden residents can be bathed on a gurney in the privacy of their own bathroom (see the Research Abstract on page 101). A special shield can be used to keep the attendant dry (see Figure 1-3).

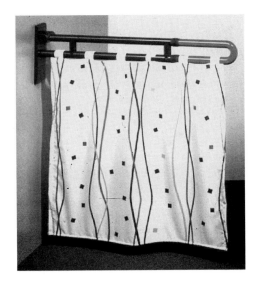

Figure 1-3 Shield for attendant care. *Courtesy of HEWI, Inc.*

The apartments are built over an ambulatory health-care facility (see Figure 1-4) offering skilled nursing to 60 patients and assistance to an additional 60 in the apartments. No one lives in the health-care facility. Many apartment residents, however, spend a portion of each day there receiving therapy and rehabilitation.

Each apartment overlooks an atrium whose glass roof provides year-round protection from the elements. Atriums are appreciated by older people with concerns about safety and security (see Figure 1-5). Even though the Bergweg atrium is located on the second floor, a stream runs through it. Sculpture, trees, and plants are all bathed in daylight, a major contribution to a healing environment. Surrounding the atrium is a 20,000 sq. ft. shopping mall that is not just for the elderly—the entire community uses the shops, restaurants, hairdressers, kiosks, etc. Next to the elevator, an escalator from the street invites walk-in traffic and community interaction with the residents (see Figure 1-6).

In addition to serving 180 apartments, the ambulatory health-care facility provides daycare for 20 community residents and is staffed with occupational therapists, physical therapists, a full-time general practitioner, a dentist, and a massage therapist. Its offices open to the street, encouraging community use. The entrance to the facility is also on the street level, well away from the apartment entrance. The Dutch want clear separation between housing and health-care facilities.

Bergweg is a truly integrated complex offering shopping, dining, and health care to the entire community in a mode sensitive to the security and dignity of the older residents. This housing model is emerging in many countries in Northern Europe. Increasingly, Europeans are not required to move out of their homes into a health-care facility. If a resident does not function well in an apartment, other housing choices are available (e.g., group homes for people with advanced stages of Alzheimer's; see Chapter 2). But most older people can receive services in their own apartments for life, even if they lose ambulatory ability and are confined to bed.

Apartments are frequently constructed over a geriatric rehabilitation clinic (see Chapter 5), but again, the separation between the place in which one lives and the place in which one receives health care is well defined. If necessary, one can receive treatment all day in the clinic and still have the dignity of returning to one's own apartment at night.

In many Scandinavian complexes, therapy equipment is displayed in visible public areas to encourage residents to exercise. Residents are actually expected to exercise to maintain ability and elevate self-esteem. They are expected to perform at their highest level to save staff time and maximize independence. These expectations are not in place in many U.S. complexes.

Figure 1-4 Geriatric rehabilitation in an apartment building. *Courtesy of Stichting Humanitas Rotterdam.*

Figure 1-5 Atrium for year-round protection. *Courtesy of Filo Laken, Stichting Humanitas Rotterdam.*

Figure 1-6 An escalator to attract visitors. *Courtesy of Stichting Humanitas Rotterdam.*

ASSISTED LIVING IN THE UNITED STATES

Much of U.S. assisted living design was built by former nursing home administrators and is still based on a nursing home model. This model is the result of the social programs of the 1960s and 1970s, when the federal government became the principal payer for care of elderly residents in nursing homes. Government reimbursement drives nursing home design and staffing, dictating such details as square footage per patient. Reimbursement is dependent on government approval through the certificate of need (CON) process and state inspections. There is little change in revenue when these inspections determine that quality of care exceeds the level required by regulations, and every incentive exists to maintain minimal care. Design improvements are discouraged by lengthy waiver, conditional-use permit, and variance processes.

On the other hand, the best designers are willing to jump through hoops to build innovative models, and theirs is the work that raises overall quality levels. Theirs is also the work that gets published and becomes the latest standards of good design. For example, when assisted living is combined with historic preservation, requirements can be modified to preserve the historic significance of the project (see Figure 1-7). One restoration was able to hide sprinkler heads in cornices and visual alarms under chair rails, retaining their function but eliminating the institutional appearance they convey.

Many licensure codes, however, would need to be changed to construct affordable Scandinavian lifetime models in the United States.[3] Scandinavian fire codes for long-term care are less stringent than those in the United States, allowing fireplaces in skilled nursing homes, reduced separation requirements, and natural (flammable) materials. Scandinavians are willing to take some risks to improve quality of life.

On the other hand, some U.S. health-care construction requirements are not stringent enough. For example, the minimum space required for dining rooms may be as little as 9 sq. ft. per person; for people using wheelchairs, walkers, or medical equipment, the minimum should be 25–30 sq. ft. per person.[4]

In the lifetime model, the separation between health care and housing may actually reduce code compliance requirements. For example, if the apartment is not considered part of a nursing home, there is no requirement to keep all rooms within 120 ft. of a nursing station. Apartments may not be required to be sprinkled (although it is a good idea to do so). But even lifetime apartments are overregulated in some areas. For example, the quantity of apartment parking required by code is not needed. Many older residents in a lifetime model no longer drive.

What are the program requirements of a lifetime model? In addition to transportation, the model must include optional assistance with the

Figure 1-7 Assisted living and historic preservation. *Courtesy of John Bertram House, Assisted Living Residence.*

ADLs. These activities include housecleaning, daily bed making, linen service, personal assistance (e.g., bathing, dressing, and medication), meals, and health monitoring (e.g., pulse rate, blood pressure, and weight).

Some of these services can be provided by family members, reducing costs as much as 40 percent and encouraging family participation with the resident.[5] Residents should also be encouraged to help one another to bolster self-esteem, reduce dependence on staff, and reduce costs. A case manager must track volunteer involvement and ensure that all needs are being met.

Cost is the issue that reduces demand for the lifetime model in the United States. Existing models are expensive, and assisted living has never been a high-end market. Wealthy people generally receive their care at home, seldom moving into assisted living complexes that do not offer life care. The wealthy also avoid the CCRC model which moves residents from level to level. They do consider a condominium model that provides health-care security for life with most medical care at home. The Stratford is one such project.

This ten-story condominium complex is located in San Mateo, California. It offers 65 condominiums that can all be converted to assisted living. This is one of the few complexes in the United States licensed for both independent living and assisted living in each residence. Amenities include hotel services; a concierge keeps treats on hand for the many pets. Design details include an electronically controlled entrance, a maple-paneled library (see Figure 1-8), and an enclosed swimming pool. The first-class restaurant is nothing like the congregate dining halls frequently found in assisted living. It offers several choices in dining: an elegant restaurant, two private dining rooms, and a chef's bar for a quick meal (see Figure 1-9).

Figure 1-8 Homelike public space. *Courtesy of Seccombe Design Associates, Inc.* © *Chas McGrath.*

Figure 1-9 A restaurant, not a congregate dining hall. *Courtesy of Seccombe Design Associates, Inc.* © *Chas McGrath.*

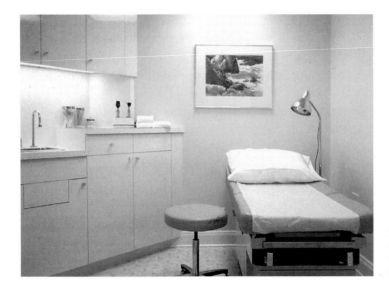

Figure 1-10 Exam room in a condominium complex. *Courtesy of Seccombe Design Associates, Inc. © Chas McGrath.*

The Stratford plan includes a lifetime medical program, including an on-site physician for consistency of care (see Figure 1-10) and a full-time registered nurse. Transportation is provided to all medical and dental appointments, and medical insurance forms are processed by the staff. The wellness program includes health education (in the penthouse lecture room overlooking the bay), fitness classes, and nutritional consultation.

An alternate model for lifetime care is been offered on many college campuses — Cornell, Iowa State, Indiana University, University of Connecticut, Dartmouth, Duke, University of Washington, Stanford, Princeton, and Lehigh, to name a few. Assisted living apartments are provided on campus, offering all of the perks of college life with none of the course requirements. Residents can attend classes, parties, free concerts, and collegiate games. Sophisticated medical care is often available on these campuses and there is a strong emphasis on rehabilitation. Although skilled nursing is not generally offered in the apartments, most schools have a fine record of getting residents out of nursing homes and back on their own.

PLANNING PUBLIC SPACES

The best of assisted living apartments provide environmental layers to allow residents to gradually enter social situations. A deck overlooking the entry permits residents to screen visitors without making a social commitment. The deck can also be used as a place for residents to smoke away from the entry. The first impression at many complexes is an entry littered with cigarette butts and a group of smokers as the official greeters.

Entry landscaping must be carefully planned with no place for an intruder to hide. Even in safe locations, older people may perceive danger lurking in a highly landscaped entry. Night lighting contributes to the perception of safety and empowers the many older people who have trouble with night vision.

Landscaping should offer distinctive layouts for each entry. Courtyards assist residents with orientation by spacially differentiating exterior landscaping. Parking lots should also be small and clearly differentiated (see Details on page 49). To maintain a residential environment, delivery vehicles should not use the main entrance. They should deliver close to the staff kitchen, perhaps through a residential garage.

As in any apartment building, the public spaces of assisted living complexes should be homelike and inviting (see Figure 1-11), but not at the expense of clear spacial definition. Forty percent of assisted living residents have some degree of dementia, and they may become confused in unfamiliar spaces like large congregate dining halls.

Interior spaces should be small, intimate, and clearly defined (see Research Abstract on page 21). Interior social layers can be created by half walls, balconies, window seats, greenhouse enclosures, and atriums. Glassed-in porches can provide the dual benefit of a social layer as well as access to nature in a safe environment for socialization. Exterior views of nature keep residents alert to the weather and to seasonal changes.

An exterior swimming pool offers an opportunity to exercise, spend time outdoors, and socialize. Tables with umbrellas can define personal space in the pool area and create another social layer (see Details on page 54). A swimming pool also offers an excellent opportunity to invite the community into the complex for exercise classes or an afternoon of family fun.

Figure 1-11 An apartment building, not a facility. *Courtesy of Alterra Healthcare Corporation*

RESEARCH ABSTRACT
Experiential Research in Detailing Assisted Living

Lisa Gerovac is director of interior design at one of the world's largest assisted living providers, Alterra Healthcare Corporation in Brookfield, Wisconsin. She offers the following design priorities for empowering residents:

1. Provide a large variety of social and private spaces in residential scale (rather than one or two large adaptable spaces). When space planning, subdivide spaces into areas for social functions, hobbies, and everyday life activities as well as for supportive services. Plan comfortable, intimate seating arrangements that will encourage conversation and offer privacy (see Details on pages 117 and 119).

2. For older people, safety and security are perhaps the issues of greatest concern. Appropriate lighting levels offer a sense of security and safety while maximizing visual acuity. These higher lighting levels empower residents with increased confidence, mobility, and function. Don't forget matte finishes to reduce glare with higher lighting levels. Residents also stay in control when color and pattern is planned for wayfinding and texture is selected to reduce ambient noise levels (see Details on pages 266 and 267).

3. A homelike ambience can be created with color, pattern, and texture (see Details on pages 82 and 214). A residential palette should consider context reflecting the location and cultural preferences. Homelike environments also encourage pleasant daily rituals. Whether they involve enjoying the morning paper with a cup of coffee or watering the flowers, daily rituals establish a sense of identity and inner peace. Identify specific scenarios and heighten the experience through design.

Design in context. *Courtesy of Alterra Healthcare Corporation.*

Water aerobics (followed by a sauna or spa) can provide significant pain relief. Swimming pools must be planned for users in wheelchairs as well as those with reduced hearing and vision (see Chapter 8). An interior pool may be a good place to increase sensory stimulation by adding live butterflies and the relaxing sound of falling water. If the pool is located in the basement, provide access to daylight and extra attention to acoustics. The concrete surfaces may reflect sound, making therapy and instruction difficult. Consider an instruction pit, a sunken area next to the pool that keeps the instructor dry and at the same level as the swimmers. Instruction and treatment areas should be acoustically isolated from the rest of the complex to prevent sound transition.

Access to natural elements may also be provided by large windows that open onto protected interior gardens and invite exploration. Double-loaded corridors (with rooms off both sides) offer few opportunities for window placement. A corridor that circles an atrium or patio tends to have shorter horizontal stretches and offer more articulation. When this design is not possible, the corridor can be deconstructed with jogs or curves. Corridors can be planned to encourage chance encounters and excuses to meet people. Resting places should be provided and supportive handrails visually integrated (see Details on page 254).

Details define a residential environment. Seating breaks up long walks; kiosks offer snacks and drinks. Conversely, the design formula for an institutional environment is uniformity and lack of detail. Shiny beige composition floor tile and unfamiliar spaces like dayrooms are institutional clichés (see Details on page 181).

Rooms should be planned with clarity of purpose. Keep spaces understandable, with public spaces very public and private spaces very private. Residents do not understand a living room with 50 chairs in it. Spaces and finishes should anticipate behavior, particularly dementia and incontinence (see Research Abstract on page 23).

Most assisted living residents experience some degree of memory loss. Familiar details like a fireplace, a case filled with books, and a china cabinet can trigger long-term memory and serve as important wayfinding cues (see Details on pages 251 and 252). Fragrances like baking bread and morning coffee are also important cues. Music can be used to bring back long-term memories and cue the start of daily events, maintaining a sense of order.

Public space in assisted living can and should retain familiar, home-like qualities. Residents can be offered supervised options, like participating in laundry and cooking. A vegetable garden, aviary, greenhouse, aquarium, and liberal pet policy also allows the residents to express personal interests. Secure displays of personal collections offer important wayfinding and orientation cues. Abstract art can be problematic for some; choose realistic themes, perhaps including relationships with chil-

RESEARCH ABSTRACT
Bathroom Carpeting[6]

In research sponsored by DuPont Antron and Interface Flooring Systems and conducted by Cynthia A. Leibrock, two public bathrooms were carpeted at an assisted living complex. Carpet was used around all fixtures, including the toilets, even though approximately 40 percent of the residents using these bathrooms were incontinent. The purpose of the research was to measure microbial growth in carpeting in challenging health-care environments.

The carpet was specified to limit microbial growth. The fiber was solution dyed and inherently stain-resistant, with an integrated powerful antimicrobial system. The carpet construction included a moisture barrier, even though it was installed without a pad over an existing ceramic tile floor where odor retention in the subfloor was not a problem.

One bathroom was installed with carpet tile without sealed seams (for easy replacement); the other featured a wall-to-wall installation with sealed seams protecting the subfloor. After one year *with no maintenance*, the carpeting was to be evaluated for efficacy of antimicrobial characteristics. Tests measuring increases in bacterial and fungal growth were conducted. There were no significant increases in microbial growth in either the carpet tile or the wall-to-wall carpet with sealed seams. From this research, it can be extrapolated that this carpeting is suitable in other health-care environments–even in patient bathrooms, where slipping and falling frequently occurs and where injuries result from falls on hard-surfaced floors.

dren and pets. Residents feel more in control when designers humanize interiors with such elements as bay windows, mullions, balconies, and carpeting (see Details on page 24). Human scale should be maintained, especially in areas frequented by residents. Entries, porches, and transition spaces may include windows with small panes and doors with details on a traditional residential scale.

Public space should also encourage social activity. Lobbies become hospitality centers, with the receptionist sitting close to the guests to provide information. Reception may include serving beverages. Sometimes a bar may be provided to serve cocktails. Small, intimate dining areas may be planned to encourage socialization. Soft table cloths, fitted to prevent sliding, and fresh flowers maintain the ambience. Plan one of the smaller dining areas for those who have difficulty with eating and may be embarrassed to dine with others.

To improve visual acuity in dining rooms, it is important to provide contrast between the chairs and the floor covering and between the plates and the table. Specify 80 percent light reflectance from the wall and uniform levels of glare-free light at approximately 50 footcandles (fc)[7] (see Details on page 80).

DETAILS
Carpeting

- Light-colored carpeting increases light quantity throughout the space without increasing glare.
- Hard-surfaced floors are not safer than carpet for controlling fungal or bacterial growth in health care environments.[8]
- Hard-surfaced floors may hinder walking efficiency and confidence. In a study of 58 elderly hospital patients, carpeting significantly improved mean gait speed, step length, and walking confidence.[9]
- Carpet used with wheelchairs, carts, and gurneys cannot exceed ½-in. pile height, and a ¼-in. height offers less resistance to rolling traffic.
- High-cut pile may pull a wheelchair, gurney, cart, or stroller in the direction of the nap. Use an uncut or tip sheer in a high-density pile for an easy traverse.
- Carpeting with an antimicrobial system prevents microbial growth and resulting odors.
- For people with dust allergies, hard-surfaced flooring is a better choice than carpeting, which can harbor dust and dust mites.
- People with incontinence may associate cold, hard floors with going to the bathroom and thus appreciate carpet.
- Carpet reduces the incidence of falls and cushions falls that do occur. The carpet should have a pile height of ¼–½ in.; the pile should be of a high density. A carpet surface that is too soft is easy to sink into and may cause loss of balance. Large loops can catch on braces, canes, and walkers.
- For people with hearing differences, reduce electrical interference with hearing aids by installing static-resistant carpeting.
- For people with incontinence, seal concrete slabs with an acrylic polymer before installing carpeting. If the concrete flooring is hydrophilic, it absorbs liquids and their odors as it expands and contracts.[10]
- Area rugs should be permanently installed to prevent tripping. The small wheels of wheelchairs, gurneys, carts, and strollers may cause loose area rugs to gather in front of the user. People in power wheelchairs may also be immobilized, and rugs may become tangled with the mechanism.
- Borders can be used to blend carpet colors from room to room, but keep the contrast to a minimum so that a border is not mistaken for a step.
- It is often difficult to spot a slight elevation in floor level. Single steps, thresholds, carpet tack strips (especially across corridors), and the edges of area rugs all cause tripping. Use a bevel when changing from one floor surface to another if the change is between ¼ and ½ in. Use a small ramp if the change exceeds ½ in. (see Details on page 254).
- Metal carpet strips between rooms may pose a tripping hazard. Sew carpets together at doorways or use graduated transition strip.
- For the easiest wheelchair ride over carpet and for a stable surface offering sure footing, eliminate padding in the carpet installation. A glue-down installation also prevents rippling caused by wheelchair or gurney use.

Graduated strip. *Courtesy of Johnsonite*

Areas of decision like entries, reception lobbies, and elevators require increased lighting levels, up to 100 fc for close work like reading instructions or signs[11] (see Details on page 83). Redundant cuing should also be provided in the elevator, and an emergency elevator phone should be connected directly to the building manager and receptionist (see Details on page 130). This phone cannot replace the elevator alarm system required by the Americans with Disabilities Act (ADA).

Lighting can also be used to reinforce the change from public to private space. Increased lighting levels at apartment entrances offer control, security, and clarity. Differences in detail, materials, and size can accentuate the transition, providing a unique apartment entrance as part of the wayfinding plan. The entrance can also serve as an important place to people-watch from a wheelchair or to charge a power wheelchair. For this purpose, plan a special outlet and ventilation from the odors caused by recharging. For ambulatory residents, provide a place to sit down to remove boots and overshoes before entering the apartment.

A NOTE ON APARTMENTS

Apartments are private; facilities are not. When people are shuffled from level to level, possessions must be eliminated and physical territory is reduced. The value of privacy and independence increases dramatically.

The apartment represents a place to maintain independence when, through aging, all forces seem to lead to less control. An individual's home allows that person to stay in touch with "the person they were in the past." It provides a place to accumulate memories.

As we age, each change can represent a loss of territory and possessions. Symbols of life like a flower box, a mailbox, a doorbell, a clothesline, and holiday displays become increasingly important. Residents need to remain connected with others, but through windows, doorways, and porches that permit the choice of privacy.

Chapter 3 is filled with universal design detail that should be integrated into apartments. As a closing thought to this chapter, please consider that social spaces and bedroom spaces are culturally incompatible. At a minimum, apartments should offer separation between sleeping areas and living areas.

REFERENCES

1. M. Kalymun, "Toward a definition of assisted living," in *Optimizing Housing for the Elderly: Homes, not Housing* (New York: Hayworth Press, 1990), 97–132.
2. House of Representatives Select Committee on Aging, *Housing for the Frail Elderly: Hearing, May 4 and July 26, 1989* (Washington, D.C.: GPO, 1989): SD cat. no. Y 4Ag 4/2:H 81/26.

3. Regnier, Victor, and Hoglund, David, "Expanded Housing Choices for Older People: Building Codes Impact on the Environment of Older People" (paper delivered at the American Association of Retired Persons White House Conference on Aging, Mini-Conference, August 1995), Tab 700, 69.

4. S. DiMotta, B. Dubey, D. Hoglund, and C. Kershner, "Long-Term Care Design: Blazing New Territory—Code Reform and Beyond," *Journal of Healthcare Design* 5 (1993): 198.

5. Victor Regnier, *Assisted Living Housing for the Elderly* (New York: John Wiley & Sons, 1994): 179.

6. Daniel Price, "Collinwood Nursing Home Case Study Samples," *IRC Microbiology Laboratory Report* (March 15, 1999), (Atlanta: Interface Research Corporation): Lab Log #3175, 98–293.

7. Pat Hennings, "Long-Term Care Design: 16 Solutions to Implement on Monday Morning," *Journal of Healthcare Design* V (1993): 206.

8. Julia S. Garner and Martin S. Favero, "CDC Guidelines for Handwashing and Hospital Environmental Control, 1986," *Infection Control* 7(4): 231–243.

9. M. Wilmott, "The Effect of a Vinyl Floor Surface and Carpeted Floor Surface upon Walking in Elderly Hospital In-Patients," *Age and Aging* 15 (1986): 119–120.

10. Lorraine G. Hiatt, "Long-Term-Care Facilities," *Journal of Health Care Interior Design* 2 (1990): 203.

11. Hiatt, "Long-Term-Care Facilities," 199.

2 CARING FOR PEOPLE WITH DEMENTIA

A locked nursing home is not appropriate housing for people with dementia. It is also inappropriate for such people to be isolated in their own homes. A group home with trained staff in a residential neighborhood is often the better solution. Hundreds of these homes have been constructed in northern European countries.

This movement started in 1985, when six older people with geriatric dementia were moved to the Baltzargarden group home in Motala, Sweden. This lovely ten-room home was used as a demonstration project for the care of people with Alzheimer's disease. Most were moved from institutions; all of the residents were incontinent and heavily medicated. Within three months, none of the residents required diapers, sleeping medication, or psychopharmaceuticals. Aggressive behavior, wandering, anxiety at night, and periods of screaming ceased. The residents became happier and more outgoing and started to take notice of their surroundings and their fellow human beings.

These remarkable results were achieved by Barbro Beck-Friis, the world-renowned Swedish physician and gerontologist who founded this movement. According to Dr. Beck-Friis, people in advanced stages of geriatric dementia "should be cared for in a group home of no more than six to eight people and in an environment that is as homelike and secure as possible."[1] In the United States, the National Institute on Aging confirms that housing for a small number of individuals is less confusing and less stimulating than larger groups.[2] Small scale encourages activity and mobility.

Dr. Beck-Friis's successful demonstration of this concept opened the doors of group homes to over 7000 Swedish residents.[3] Attendants in these homes help residents to care for themselves using "active participation" in such tasks as grocery shopping, cooking, and folding laundry. Care is individually tailored to the needs of each resident. When compared to those in an institutional environment, residents in group homes experience marked improvement.

Medical experts from many countries have traveled to Sweden to receive training in this model of care provision. The method of care at Baltzargarden is designed to strengthen residents' self-esteem and reinforce their remaining healthy resources and brain functions. Resident care is highly individualized and is based on positive contact; the staff is encouraged to express praise, warmth, appreciation, happiness, and laughter, reinforcing positive behavior. Therapy includes the use of music, and some residents who were unable to speak can now sing songs fluently. All of the senses (sight, hearing, taste, smell, and touch) are activated to trigger long-term memory. Residents even grow their own food, which they eventually harvest and consume.

Design intervention at the group home incorporates wayfinding cues, like hearts on the floor leading to the bathroom. Lighting is also used in wayfinding, including a night light so residents can find their way to the toilets (see Details on page 83). Furniture and carpets from the 1930s, 1940s, and 1950s are used to trigger memories. Familiar objects like chamber pots are used by residents who were used to them. Program repetition, familiar surroundings, and set routines with the same staff contribute to memory reinforcement.

In Sweden, care in group homes for people with dementia costs 30 percent to 40 percent less than nursing home care for the same population.[4] Nursing homes are viewed as subacute facilities where only the most severely impaired residents belong. The quality of care in group homes is viewed as superior. Even though this discussion is limited to family-centered ideas, it should be noted that a higher degree of staff work satisfaction was found in group homes than in nursing homes, even though the work is exhausting.[5] Group homes unite the best parts of institutional care with the quality of life at home. They are often located close to senior centers offering a wide variety of programs and services.

As the movement has grown, the housing models have been fine-tuned to truly serve the needs of older people with dementia. A typical plan includes six apartments, each with a living room, safe kitchenette, and bedroom alcove. The L-shaped building reduces the perceived length of the corridors. Residents can view both corridors from the central space, a boon to wayfinding (see Details on pages 251 and 252). The common space includes a small living room, a family dining room, and a large kitchen designed for resident participation The central kitchen table and window seat are used by residents during meal preparation. Staff members dine with the residents, which encourages a sense of family. Dining with others stimulates the appetite and prompts the use of appropriate table manners, a fact confirmed by research. In one interesting U.S. study, residents with psychogeriatric disease, including dementia, improved their eating behavior when dining in groups around tables (compared to those eating from trays in chairs along corridor walls).[6]

In the United States, the average cost of caring for one person with Alzheimer's disease is $47,000 per year.[7] The number of Americans with Alzheimer's disease and related dementia is well over four million. Many others suffer from dementia caused by stroke, AIDS, Parkinson's disease, or vascular disease, sometimes in combination with high blood pressure and diabetes.[8]

Unfortunately, funding for the long-term care of people with dementia is seldom based on the medical diagnosis of the resident; it is most often based on the location of their care. Although people with dementia seldom require 24-hour medical intervention, many are forced to move into nursing homes by Medicaid reimbursement policies. An appropriate setting, like a group home specializing in their care, is generally funded by private pay sources. As a consequence, people without private pay sources end up living in health-care facilities.

Eighty-five percent of older people plan to age in place, never even considering other living choices like group homes (see Chapter 3). But too much privacy can be dangerous to one's health; elderly people who live alone consistently have longer stays in the hospital and fewer discharges than people living together.[9] When dementia forces a move, most Americans can choose only between nursing homes or assisted living facilities specializing in this care. Minnesota offers other options.

Reimbursement drives design. Minnesota has experimented with reimbursement based on the health of the residents rather than the place where they receive the care. Individuals can receive the same amount of reimbursement whether receiving care in a skilled nursing facility or in a group home. Minnesota has used a Medicaid waiver process based on 12 levels of care assessment, not on the facility offering the care.

This unique process has encouraged design innovation. One of the first U.S. group homes for people with dementia was built in Buffalo, Minnesota. Four cottages, each housing six residents with dementia, are located in a wooded residential neighborhood (see Figure 2-1). The homes were designed to be converted to individual apartments if the

Figure 2-1 Cottage.
Project name: Karrington Cottages of Rochester, MN. Designer: Cini & Associates.

reimbursement pattern changes. Each cottage offers a common area with a living room, dining area, and family kitchen. Daily chores are shared by the staff and residents. They dine together around a kitchen table, and staff is required to eat the food they prepare.

When a demonstration project pushes the envelope, codes become problematic. Even though these cottages are sprinkled, fire code requires some exits to remain unlocked, a real danger to residents unless the perimeter of the property is secure. Fortunately, it is easier to monitor these exits with only six residents per cottage. Outside each open exit, a gate is installed with a difficult latch as well as a soft bell to warn staff. Locked doors are visually integrated so residents are not tempted to try them. Residents who are cognitively capable of using them have keys to the locked doors.

Innovative details include felt on the feet of chairs to reduce noise on the hard-surfaced flooring and a phone equipped with a soft chime rather than a disturbing ring. The kitchens have diffuse tungsten track lighting that conveys a more residential ambience than does fluorescent lighting. Handrails are installed in the halls.

Another innovative U.S. project addresses the isolation from loved ones frequently caused by dementia. Ten people with dementia live with their families in a complex that offers case management, home health care, and adult day care in rent-controlled apartments (see Figure 2-2). The apartments are connected with a covered walkway (see Figure 2-3) and a secure walking path is also provided. The project is accessible, affordable, and available to families facing the institutionalization of a loved one.

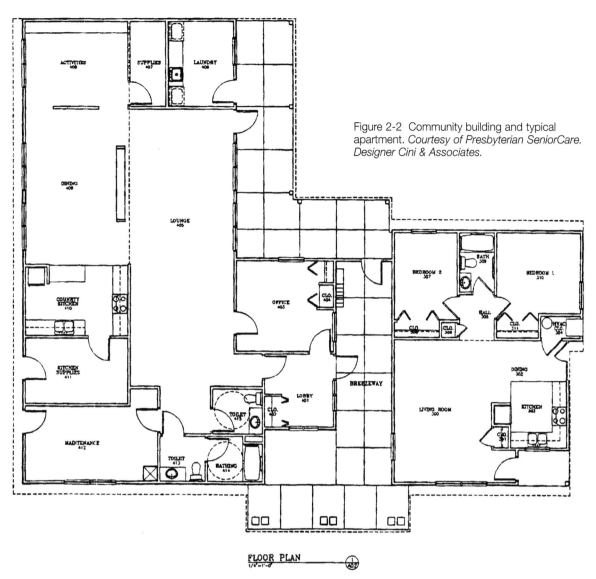

FLOOR PLAN
1/4"=1'-0"

Figure 2-3 Covered walkway and gazebo. *Courtesy of Presbyterian SeniorCare*

31

PROGRAMMING FOR DEMENTIA

Elizabeth Brawley provides comprehensive coverage of programming for dementia in *Designing for Alzheimer's Disease*.[10] She emphasizes that the design program must be a team effort involving staff, residents, and families. She stresses the need for personal experience with the disease; every architect and designer should experience a day in the life of a person with dementia before beginning the design process.

For people with Alzheimer's, the design program should offer a better quality of life, not just more therapies. It should focus on competency, not simply medical intervention for incompetency. It should support health maintenance and stabilize declining mental health rather than focusing on improvement.

People with Alzheimer's disease experience the following symptoms:

- Recent memory loss, including the memory of tasks as familiar as eating and drinking. (This may lead to dehydration, dizziness, and confusion.)
- Problems with language caused by memory loss of simple words and sentence combinations
- Disorientation of time and space characterized by a disrupted wake-sleep cycle and problems with orientation and wayfinding. (For orientation, write the date and day of the week on a whiteboard using nontoxic markers. Don't mark off days on the calendar, which reinforces the loss of time.)
- Problems with abstract thinking, resulting in bizarre behaviors such as putting the iron in the refrigerator
- Changes in mood or behavior resulting in confusion, fear, and overreaction to stimuli.[11]

These changes may lead to difficulty with the expression of appropriate emotion, problematic social skills (especially in large groups), and impaired judgment characterized by reduced ability to plan and anticipate. Dangerous situations are particularly problematic and are complicated by an inability to change behavior to override the situation.[12]

The balance of this chapter offers a discrepancy analysis of cognitive impairment only, looking at the alignment or otherwise of individual need and environment. Many older people with cognitive impairment must deal with a reduction in sensory and motor skills as well, particularly in balance and coordination. Design intervention for these changes is addressed in Chapter 5.

REDUCING DISTRACTIONS

Individuals with dementia generally respond more positively to small spaces with few distractions. See-through dividers and planters allow

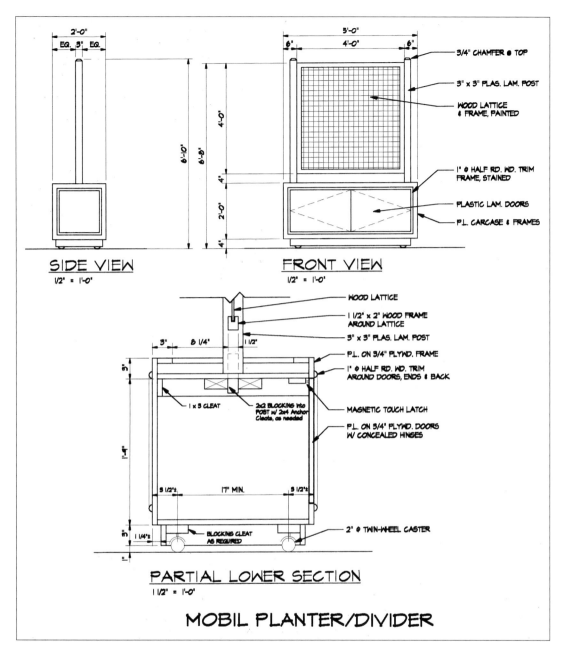

Figure 2-4 Divider detail. *Courtesy of John M. Robinson, PE, RA; Robinson Design. Photography: Frank Guiliani.*

residents to gradually enter social situations while separating large spaces into smaller, private areas. The design shown in Figure 2-4, with its open lattice filled with plants, allows staff to supervise while still offering privacy to residents. Cluttered spaces may be too distracting; people with dementia need variety but not overstimulation.

Incorporate a range of color values, but use pattern with care (see Details on page 82). Some patterns are distracting and visually confusing; even light patterns from blinds may be disturbing visually.

33

A heavily patterned tablecloth may even prevent a resident from concentrating on eating.[13] High-contrast squares on the floor may look like things that need to be picked up or like holes.

Noise is a major distraction for all of us, and ambient noise levels should be reduced (see Details on page 265 and 266). Eliminate the public address system; use vibrating beepers instead. Constant music may also be distracting and certainly adds to the ambient noise level. Periodic use of nostalgic tunes may serve as an important memory cue, however, and music may be used to announce events like dining or special activates. Keep in mind that older people with hearing loss have a hard time accurately identifying most sounds, including announcements, and responding appropriately.

Startling sounds, like sudden vacuum cleaner noise, may contribute to falls. Prevent doors from slamming (using a closer that requires less than 5 pounds of force to open). Use a chime on the telephone. Eliminate the doorbell or buzzer; in a group home, a knock on the door will suffice.

ESTABLISHING LINKS WITH THE FAMILIAR, HEALTHY PAST

People with dementia need design that stimulates interest and curiosity, especially in mastered skills. Many spent the majority of their lives in the workplace, and an office environment may be filled with memory cues like an antique typewriter, a bentwood coat rack, a clock with hands (digital clocks may be unfamiliar), and a rotary dial phone (not touch-tone, even though it requires less manual dexterity). There is often a trade-off between familiar products and accessible products.

Residents should be empowered to perform familiar tasks; they should be encouraged to dress themselves, even if it takes an hour for them to do so. Provide a place to arrange clothing each day in order of use: underwear first and socks and shoes last. Everyday tasks should be performed in familiar spaces, not a dayroom or congregate dining hall. How many of us regularly dine in a congregate setting? Everyday events should take place in rooms with clarity of purpose. Without meaningful activity in familiar space, residents may focus on inappropriate activities, like raiding a neighbor's room.

The resident's personal space may present the best opportunity for establishing links with the past. It's not easy for any of us to adjust to communal living, and personal possessions help with the transition. A personal photo (redundantly cued with a name plate) can personalize the entrance, distinguishing it from similar doorways in the corridor. A collection can be displayed at the room entrance, secured under glare-free glass and recessed in the wall. A protruding Plexiglas box with sharp corners is a hazard and an institutional cliché.

The resident's room should feature a place to display prized possessions including crafts, photo albums, and furniture from home. Institutional built-in furniture is certainly not as recognizable as free-standing personal display pieces. Valuables can also be displayed on a plate shelf out of reach of other residents. Each object must be permanently attached in earthquake zones.

Personal treasures can also be securely displayed in public spaces. Serving as landmarks, displays should be planned for every 20 feet; personal cues are 50 percent more effective than traditional signage. For example, a model ship made by a resident is more effective in wayfinding than a banner, plant, or other impersonal cue. Antique pocketknives, bows, combs, handkerchiefs, woodworking tools, and kitchen utensils can be displayed to stimulate conversation and trigger memories. Hat racks with a variety of caps, helmets, and scarves can stimulate the imagination. Resident art should be displayed in a variety of frames to improve differentiation. Picture books and magazines are so popular with the residents that shelving often must be added. Perhaps a library would be useful for residents as well as for family members who are seeking information about dementia.

PROVIDING SENSORY CUES TO PROMPT MEMORY

A crackling fire in the fireplace, the fragrance of bread in the oven, a hot cup of coffee in the morning, a warm room filled with daylight, the touch of a loved one—these are the memories of home. A home that appeals to the five senses can improve orientation and reduce loss of memory.

Family life often revolves around the kitchen. Provide aprons to encourage participation. Textural activities, like supervised cooking and dining, stimulate the sense of touch. Finger foods, touchable objects within reach, pleasant fragrances, and the warmth of the oven are all available in the kitchen. The kitchen should be planned to encourage resident participation, although this can get out of hand; sometimes one resident will take over the kitchen and not let others in.

Perhaps residents can grow some of their own food in an adjacent garden. Pulling weeds, raking, and digging in fragrant earth can be practical therapy to a gardener. Sunlight is also healing; insufficient exposure to daylight disrupts circadian rhythms and often results in sleep disorders and seasonal depression. Other outdoor activities can include hanging clothes on a clothesline, feeding and exercising a pet, and sweeping the sidewalk. These familiar routines bring back memories.

Plan a healing garden accessible to residents (see Details on page 234), who will truly value the freedom to go outdoors at will. Even a view of the garden can help with day-night orientation and awareness of seasonal changes. A bird feeder in the garden can provide lively entertainment. Plants can be selected to attract butterflies. For comfort, plan partial shade or filtered light, a feature often requested by families and residents.[14]

Staff is often encouraged to use eye contact, tenderness, closeness, and loving physical touch, but too often a high-touch environment is overlooked. Big, cuddly bath towels in bright colors, textural wall hangings, and soft bedspreads just ask to be touched.

Encourage participation in arts and crafts; the process of painting allows memories to surface. Color preference can often be deduced from the colors residents select for paintings or projects. Residents may be encouraged to help with the color selection in their rooms. Often the colors of the 1940s are popular. Clear color, devoid of gray and black, is most easily seen. Maintain midrange values. Some older people have more difficulty discriminating between cool colors, like blue and green or blue and violet, than between warmer tones, like orange and yellow.[15]

ELIMINATING DANGEROUS OPTIONS

Ensure that interior design delivers the right message. Windows can tempt residents to escape from the home. Plan windows opening into secure interior gardens to invite exploration, not escape. Reduce visual access to people getting in and out of cars, a scenario that may encourage residents to leave. Residents are drawn to light; a poorly designed window can be used as an unsupervised exit. Exit strategy can be reduced to "out of sight, out of mind." Visually offset exits. Locked doors to janitorial closets, stairway landings, and other hazardous areas may be disguised by a mural or painted to match the surrounding wall. Residents are frequently frustrated by attempts to open locked doors.

To keep door controls out of sight, some residences have received permission to place an automatic door control around the corner and paint it to match the wall. Wristbands containing microchips are also available to automatically lock the doors for some residents and open it for others (see Figure 2-5). Unless the doors are visually concealed, however, this process may be frustrating to many.

Dangerous items should be stored out of sight in visually integrated locked cabinets. Kitchen appliances can be equipped with a control lockout feature, timer switch, or remote control for staff use. Magnetic induction cooktops cannot heat when the pan is removed and stay relatively cool during the process. Only the pan is heated, eliminating red-

Figure 2-5 Microchip for exit control. *Courtesy of Senior Technologies.*

hot elements. The flat cooking elements offer more stability for pots and pans than do raised burners.

AVOIDING CONFRONTATIONS

Many symptoms of Alzheimer's trigger confrontations. People with the disease may easily become suspicious, blaming other for stealing things that have only been misplaced. Fighting and hitting may occur, often because residents are defending themselves from something they don't understand. Inappropriate sexual behavior can be a real test of compassion, patience, and understanding. Some people with Alzheimer's disease deal with the same changes experienced by many older people: reduced mobility, visual impairment, auditory changes, and incontinence.

People with Alzheimer's disease may hallucinate; shadows and glare can further distort perception[16] (see Details on page 80). A wall of mirror produces startling and confusing images each time a resident walks by. A shadow turns into a demon and glare becomes the headlight of an approaching train. Appropriate design intervention calls for even illumination using high lighting levels without glare.

Confrontation and resulting frustration can often be avoided with minor environmental modifications. A medication cart can trigger a showdown; hand out medications from a basket instead. Specify twin size or double beds; dormitory beds are too narrow for people with Alzheimer's (who may have difficulty adjusting to an unfamiliar size). Don't expect people with dementia to learn to use high-tech devices like movable counters and adjustable cabinets. High expectations may lead to disappointments for residents, families, and staff.

Bathing is often a source of much frustration for both residents and staff. A private bathroom can help to alleviate many problems. When residents' privacy is not respected or when they are overstimulated by having too many people in the bathroom, they may act out. Residents may behave badly because they are cold or are surprised by a sudden spray of water. Install a pressure-balancing feature on the faucet control to prevent surges of hot water. A carefully controlled hand-held shower can cause less agitation than a standard shower. Noisy whirlpools are overstimulating and even threatening if the water rises close to the head of the resident. Bathing can be less difficult, if not enjoyable, with the addition of fragrances and bubble bath, but oils may make the tub too slippery.[17]

Environmental cues can reduce incontinence and make toileting easier. In each resident's room, plan the space so the toilet is clearly visible from the bed when the private bathroom door is open. In public

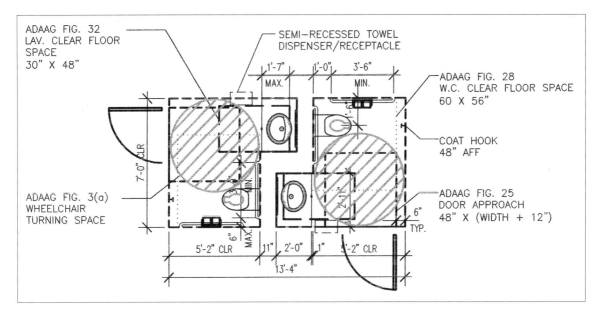

Figure 2-6 Recessed sink providing clear floor space for the toilet. *Courtesy of Evan Terry Associates, P.C.*

bathrooms, leave stall doors open so toilets are in view when the outer door is first opened. Increase the number of public bathrooms, shortening the trip required by the resident. Plan sufficient space on both sides of the toilet for a two-person transfer. To reduce the size of the bathroom, recess the sink or shower in these spaces (see Figure 2-6). Provide soft paper towels for cleanup, hidden under the countertop or over the toilet. A chamber pot or container may need to be installed under the toilet seat to catch objects residents drop in the toilet.

Thoughtful prevention and creative staff intervention can resolve many confrontations. Sometimes inappropriate resident behavior can be redirected by a favorite food or another enjoyable activity. At other times, an individual away space may be necessary. A private room or a quiet place in the garden may suffice. Staff must constantly supervise residents without hovering. Low dividers, interior windows (if not confusing), and vision panels or side lights in doors can be used for this purpose. A vision panel can also be used to create a social layer, a transition between spaces that allows the resident to become oriented before entering a room. The panel must not generate glare and must be usable by shorter residents and those in wheelchairs.

In summary, people with Alzheimer's disease need a supportive, calm, consistent environment, not a climate of constant change. Moving is particularly difficult. Every attempt should be made to keep the resident in one location (and one room or apartment) for life, not requiring a move to a nursing home or to other space within the residence.

ENCOURAGING SUCCESSFUL SOCIAL INTERACTION AND FAMILY PARTICIPATION

When a new residence opens, it is helpful to have everyone move in at the same time. Residents in the early stages of dementia will be more tolerant of familiar neighbors as they work together to cope with the changes of aging.

Tolerance is difficult in a residence for people with dementia. From the point of view of the resident, much of the social interaction is negative. Precious possessions are stolen by the other residents. Sleep is disturbed by a noisy neighbor. Much of the behavior of other residents is distracting at best and threatening at worst. Some residents may cry for long periods. Others perpetually wander. Some may engage in public sexual behaviors.

It is no wonder that the reactions of residents are sometimes catastrophic, especially late in the day. But sundowning (increased agitation at sunset) is not the fault of residents. Most can't control the reaction or fake agitation for attention. It may be possible, however, to reduce this behavior by design. Research has shown that bright light exposure can reduce agitated behaviors in people with advanced Alzheimer's disease. Increased exposure to light may also help to regulate variable wake and sleep cycles.[18]

Every effort should be made to reset residents' internal clock. If these efforts fail for some, the residence must support dining, sleeping, bathing, and wandering at will. For safety, consider wiring the night-light to be activated by a motion sensor in the resident's room. Maintain an even lighting level in the corridors. Keep juice, fruit, and rolls out at all hours. As an added benefit, a breakfast bar becomes a destination where people can stop and socialize at any hour, as well as an invitation for friends and family to drop in for a visit.

Moving a loved one to a long-term care setting is often viewed by family members as a failure, and each visit is a painful reminder. An institutional environment filled with noise and odor may tip the scales against the decision to visit. The residence must be warm and welcoming, encouraging family and friends as well as the residents. Visitors should be allowed to room in occasionally. The resident's room or apartment may include a daybed or window seat that makes into a bed. Bedding can be stored underneath the window seat as long as a clear kick space is planned (8¾ in. a.f.f. by 6 in. deep).[19] To rise from the seat, older people may put their feet back into the kick space and lean forward to redistribute body weight (see Details on page 117).

The residence must also be planned to accommodate children and pets. Perhaps a play area could be included for children. Art, music, exercise, and dance classes offer opportunities for child involvement. Pet therapy can be a wonderful activity to share. Pets offer unconditional love, and permanent pets can be included in many settings.

RELEASING EXCESS ENERGY

People with dementia need meaningful activity and plenty of exercise. A well-designed walking path in a secure setting offers an opportunity to release excess energy, stay in shape, get some sunshine, and explore.

An exterior walking path should incorporate two basic design criteria: the path should circle back to the beginning, and this point should be clearly cued and visible from most points on the path. The cue can be a canopy over the door to the residence, a change in the landscaping, or a tall sculpture. The path should be designed to create a safe surround without the feeling of confinement. A fence can be hidden within the foliage; a black chain-link fence is nearly invisible when covered with foliage. Fencing must be high and secure, located well away from architectural elements and trees that could be climbed. Plant trees that will not drop fruit on the walking path and foliage that is safe to eat and sturdy enough to take some abuse. Shallow water features may be used as barriers to reduce access to more fragile plants.

The garden can feature raised beds so that residents can grow their own vegetables and flowers or just release energy by digging. The path through the garden must be stable, firm, and slip-resistant; a covered pathway is necessary in many climates. A boardwalk or pressure-treated lumber is a good choice; asphalt, dark concrete, and fine decomposed granite may also be used. Gravel is unstable, and people with Alzheimer's disease have been known to eat it. Light-colored concrete reflects light, causing glare.

An interior courtyard is an ideal location for a walking path and can also serve as an extension of the indoor path around its. This path should accommodate industrious activity (the need to stay busy) and searching behaviors (e.g., looking for home). Searching behaviors can be accommodated by providing displays along the way, perhaps recognizable objects from home. "Window shopping" is a popular and familiar activity. Collections can be exhibited on rotating shelves or in recessed shadow boxes. Consider an aquarium or an aviary filled with interesting birds.

Offer a wide variety of activities. A place to snack provides a popular destination and encourages socializing. Cabinets along the way can be planned for exploration, perhaps with interesting hardware and drawers for rummaging. The laundry can include a place for residents to fold towels; the living room may offer pillows to fluff and furniture that rocks, bounces, or swivels safely. A rocker stimulates the vestibular canal, which provides a calming effect.[20] Platform models provide better stability.

Encourage a safe adventure along the interior walking path. Resting areas and bathrooms should be provided along the way. As with the outside path, interior walking paths must be circular, bringing residents home again.

Wayfinding to accommodate dementia differs from standard practice. Color-coding corridors, for example, doesn't help most residents. Alzheimer's disease combined with visual impairment limits the ability to recognize color and to attach significance to it.[21] Residents rely on tactile cues, like actual objects or air currents, for orientation. Fragrances and visual shapes are also important orientation cues.[22] Spaces can be differentiated using the scents of childhood: pine trees, flowers, burning leaves, the smell of hay, and even the fragrance of suntan lotion.[23]

The interior path must be a slip-resistant level surface. Even though standards permit a ¼ in. change in elevation,[24] ⅛ in. would be less of a tripping hazard for older residents, who shuffle and drag their feet. The interior path can be defined by furniture arrangements and other movable items, but once defined, these items should remain in place. Change is disorienting.

ENCOURAGING INDEPENDENCE

The Swedish philosophy of care for people with dementia literally translates into "sitting on the palms of your hands." Staff members are required to take a hands-off approach, encouraging residents to do for themselves and to maintain their skills. Most residents prefer private rooms, although shared rooms are available for those who want the companionship and security of a roommate. Resident rooms should include simple storage systems that are clearly defined—socks stored in one drawer, underwear in another, and so on. The smallest detail can make the difference between staff dependence and independence.

Residents can more easily maintain control in small spaces that are clearly differentiated. Large spaces are disorienting and sometimes noisy. Each small space should have a clarity of purpose; flexible space planned for multiple uses is confusing to people with dementia. Keep public zones very public and private zones very private. Dining, for example, should take place in a small, private dining room, not in a noisy dining hall.

Select furniture and accessories that are familiar and easy to use. Well-meaning designers often specify accessible products that cannot be

DETAILS
The Seven Basics of Housing for Home Health Care

1. *An accessible entrance on an accessible route.* Include access to the street (and public transportation), a covered transfer space adjacent to the vehicle, and an accessible route into the dwelling, preferably not exceeding a 1:20 grade or an abrupt change in elevation in excess of ¼ in. Ramps should only be used as a last resort.

2. *In public housing, usable common areas.* Public bathrooms, for example, should be in compliance with ADA Accessibility Standards (see Details on pages 166, 167, and 168).

3. *A clear width of 32 in at all doors.* A clearance of 36 in. is preferable, to allow clearance for the open door and elbow room to the wheelchair user. Each door to the master bath and master bedroom should have a side panel that can be opened to provide a clearance of 44 in. This extra width is necessary to move the bed into the living room or to transfer a patient on a gurney from the bed to the bath .

4. *A 36 in wide accessible route throughout the dwelling.* Hallways should be at least 42 in. wide, with doors swinging out of the hallway. To accomodate wheelchairs, greater widths are necessary if doors swing into the hallway.

5. *All controls in accessible locations.* Install controls at a minimum height of 15-in and a maximum height of 48 in. and provide a clear floor space of 30 in. by 48 in. Pay special attention to the location of switches, outlets, thermostats, and breaker panels (see Details on page 99).

6. *Reinforcement in bathroom walls.* (Use ¾ in. plywood from floor to ceiling around the bathroom perimeter. This will secure towel bars grabbed in an emergency and support the addition of grab bars or a shower seat as needed.

7. *Usable kitchen and baths.* A 60-in. turnaround space can be used for a T- turn or U-turn in most wheelchairs and provides space for those using walkers, canes, or assistants. This clearance can include space under the counter and sink. Removable cabinets can be used to clear the space for access by a wheelchair user.

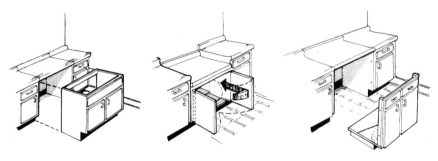

Removable cabinets. *Source: USDHUD.*

of home health care services, covering a wide variety of therapies that are offered at home. Accessible housing can be considered design intervention, replacing staff intervention as consumers care for themselves. In this housing, patients can increasingly make their own health care decisions, retaining responsibility for their own health. This trend will further reduce the responsibility (and liability) of practioners.

For these reasons, housing choices must return control to the consumer, with features to improve independence, safety, and security (see Details on page 49). Universal housing must adapt to specific diseases and disabilities. It must be integrated with the community rather than isolated in centers for older people or those with disabilities. Design demonstration centers in neighborhoods support this integration, offering an opportunity to try products and design ideas before purchase.

DESIGN DEMONSTRATION CENTERS

One such model is Sophie's Home in Horsholm, Denmark, a prototype for independent living. The demonstration center is part of a complex for all ages that features 650 sq. ft. apartments and a day care center serving 100 residents. The center provides training in the use of products like adjustable nightstands, remote controls used to operate doors, adjustable counters, lights, draperies, television, call systems, and lifts from the bedroom to the bathroom (see Figure 3-1).

The service house model of northern Europe has succeeded in maintaining older frail people in adjacent individual units as well as in the surrounding neighborhood. The model is similar to that of senior centers in the United States, with the addition of health and rehabilitation services. Most such houses offer physical and occupational therapy as well as home health care services and personal assistance. As in U.S. senior centers, these models also offer meals, day care, and social activities to prevent isolation.

COHOUSING

In the United States, cohousing communities are often clustered around a common house, similar to the Scandinavian service house, but without staffing. This space is shared by the entire community, not just the older residents. The common area often includes a kitchen, dining room, workshop, children's day care area, or laundry room. The community often dines together, sharing cooking and maintenance responsibilities.

Cohousing works well for older people who want an intergenerational setting. One older resident commented, "We aren't Sun City types. It's nice to be with a group of people who don't spend all of their time talking about

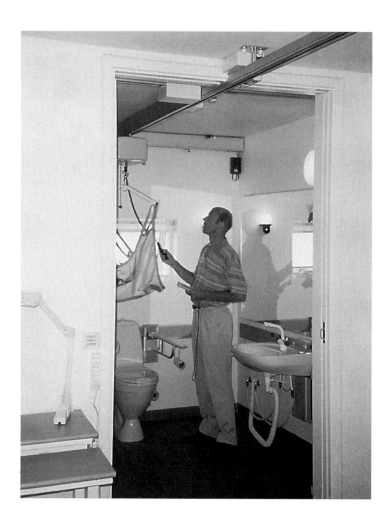

Figure 3-1 Sophie's House lift.
Courtesy of Aktivitetscentret Sophielund.

health and money." Another resident noted, "Children need to appreciate that people get older and may not be as physically able, but that doesn't mean they have to be isolated or waited on."[2]

In cohousing, residents often try to live simply, cutting down on space and sharing responsibilities. Residents may pick up the mail for their neighbors, tend a community greenhouse, or house guests at the common house. The community may share some possessions, including tools, snowblowers, and camping gear. Cohousing is not a commune, however. Homes are individually owned and income is not shared.

This style of living offers the advantages of community support without the problems of a commune. Neighbors watch the house while you are away. Some may put out a colored flag before they leave for the grocery store, inviting people to drop off their shopping lists. Many communities focus on conservation of energy and resources, and the residents contribute to the cost of landscaping and maintenance.

DETAILS
Security

- At least four types of security systems are available: ultrasonic motion detectors, pressure mats, passive infrared photoelectric sensors, and switch sensors. Each type can be powered by batteries or direct wiring.
- Ultrasonic sound motion detectors in the security system can interfere with hearing aids. Use pressure mats, passive infrared photoelectric sensors, and switch sensors instead.
- For a private residence, consider an electric locking system for the entry door coupled with an intercom system. When a noise is heard, the lock can be checked by remote control from anywhere in the interior. The doorbell can be answered and the door unlocked without having to move to the entry.
- A video monitor can also be added to the system, giving a clear picture of visitors at the front door.
- Outdoor lighting is an essential part of this system. An entry light that comes on automatically at night is another good choice.
- With any electrical security system, plan for backup if power is lost.
- Proximity to the call system becomes a critical issue in the event of a medical emergency or security breach. Many portable alarm devices enable the use to call for help with the push of a button.
- It may be important to include an emergency call system in the bathroom. A touch system could be installed on the baseboard, for example, so that a person could call for help after a fall to the floor. A redundant system should be available higher on the wall.
- In less critical situations, a telephone or intercom in the bathroom may be sufficient. Most intercoms can be monitored in other rooms when the channel is left open, so a call for help can be heard throughout the house.

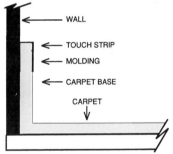

Baseboard call system. *Courtesy of Cynthia Liebrock with illustration by Susan Behar.*

- A commercial call system may be as simple as a buzzer or as involved as a video teleconferencing device.
- An automatic garage door opener makes an essential contribution to security. The garage door system should include an automatic light with at least a 15-second delay to allow time to drive into the garage. Some systems are equipped with touch pads, smoke detectors, carbon monoxide detectors, and burglar alarms for added security.
- For security purposes, bay or bow windows provide a more complete view of the surroundings. Glass windows can be more easily broken than plastic and do not provide intruder protection. Wired glass can also be used, but it has an institutional appearance.

Continued

- Look for windows with pins that extend into the frame to prevent the window from opening even if the lock is breached. Locate the lock as far away as possible from the glass on windows and doors.
- Use a quick-release combination lock on doors to potentially dangerous areas, such as the head of a stairway or the entrance to a furnace room.
- A metal door and frame provides the best security. Wooden entry door frames (even with a dead bolt) can be forced with a well-placed kick.
- Add screws to the top of existing sliding glass doors to prevent them from being lifted out of the frame.
- Add a peephole with a scope that can be viewed by a child, shorter person, or wheelchair user.
- To increase response time to a fire, specify flame-retardant fabrics, furnishings, and carpet. For window treatments, modacrylic or fire-resistant polyester fabrics drape well.

Door scope. *Photo courtesy of Evan Terry Associates.*

Although fiberglass is flameproof, it does not drape well and can cause skin irritations. Furniture should comply with California Technical Bulletin 133, which tests the entire piece rather than the individual components; the most flame-retardant carpet should also be selected.

Evaluation Guide: Performance Characteristics of Carpet Fibers

| Property | FIBER | | | | | |
	Nylon 5,6	Nylon 6	Acryl	Olefin	Poly	Wool
HEALTH AND SAFETY						
Flame Resistance	4	3	1	3	2	3
Static Resistance	3	3	3	3	3	2
Mildew Resistence	3	3	3	3	3	1
WEAR LIFE						
Durability						
Abrasion Resistance	4	4	2	3	2	2
Appearance Retention						
Resiliency	4	3	3	1	2	3
Soil Resistance	4	4	2	4	2	3
Stain Resistance	3	3	2	4	3	2
Fade Resistance	3	1	3	4	3	3
Maintenance						
Cleanability	4	4	2	4	2	3
ENVIRONMENTAL						
Dying Flexibility	4	4	3	2	2	3
Styling Versatility	4	4	2	2	2	3

- Every kitchen should be equipped with a fire extinguisher. Specify a multi-purpose ABC model to combat electrical and grease fires as well as ordinary combustibles.
- In a residence, smoke detectors should be installed adjacent to each bedroom and at the top of the stairway. Another smoke detector should be installed in the living room if it is more than 15 ft. away from a bedroom unit. A third should be installed in the basement. Other possible locations include the kitchen and furnace room. Be sure to consider location in relation to air supply and air return registers.
- A gas leak detector may also be required. Select a model with photoelectric and ion chamber detection to warn of both smoke and heat.
- The detector should sound a warning when the battery needs to be replaced.
- Some localities allow use of a smoke detector that activates a recorder that in turn dials the nearest police or fire department.

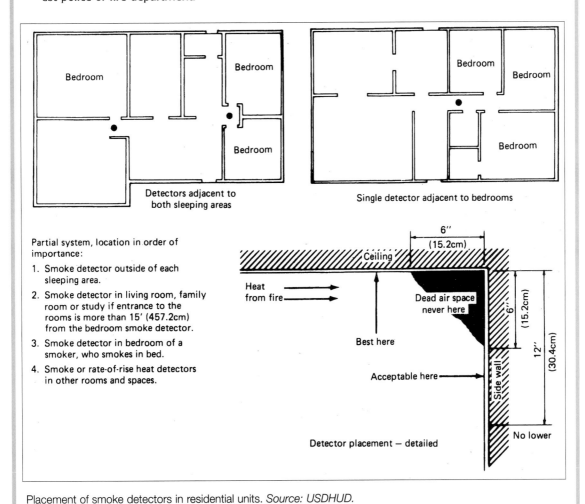

Placement of smoke detectors in residential units. *Source: USDHUD.*

One cohousing community offers disabled people of all ages the opportunity to assist one another. It began with a critical need: affordable housing and assistance for people faced with institutionalization because older family members could no longer provide care. It culminated in a demonstration project offering a common house for shared activities and 32 accessible and adaptable units. Each resident received 60 hours of training in maintenance and project management to ensure user autonomy.

GROUP HOMES

Group homes offer independence to people who require assistance with bathing, toileting, mobility, grooming, medication, or meal preparation. Group homes have also been used successfully to accommodate mentally frail people who become confused and lost, even in familiar surroundings (see Chapter 2). Most group homes in the United States serve people with developmental disabilities.

Innovative models that serve other populations are found in northern Europe. In one such model in Sweden, four to eight people may live in their own small apartments grouped around a larger living area and kitchen. This model offers more dignity and autonomy than the typical group home, where residents live in a bedroom. The European group homes may even offer two-bedroom apartments so that couples may stay together, sleeping in different rooms if necessary. The second bedroom may also accommodate live-in help.

As mentioned on page 7, Scandinavian governments have found that design intervention is less expensive than staff intervention. The Swedish government pays for passive energy systems that summon help if the toilet has not been flushed or if the refrigerator door has been left open over a programmed period. Motorized windows sense rain and close automatically and manual controls are designed for independent use (see Details on page 54). Toilets have built-in rinse and dry features. Sinks tip forward to ease hair washing from a seated position. This technology has been added to reduce staff-intensive programs and the need for institutionalization.

In a Swedish group home, individual apartments are typically grouped around two public spaces (see Figure 3-2). One of these spaces is shared as a great room and the other is used for staff, including a work space and two small bedrooms for the night shift. The great room has a large kitchen, dining table, and living area. The apartments also features a kitchen, dining, and living space separate from the bedroom and private bath. All spaces have a private patio, including the staff area. For a comprehensive discussion of northern European group homes, see Victor Regnier's book, *Assisted Living Housing for the Elderly.*[3]

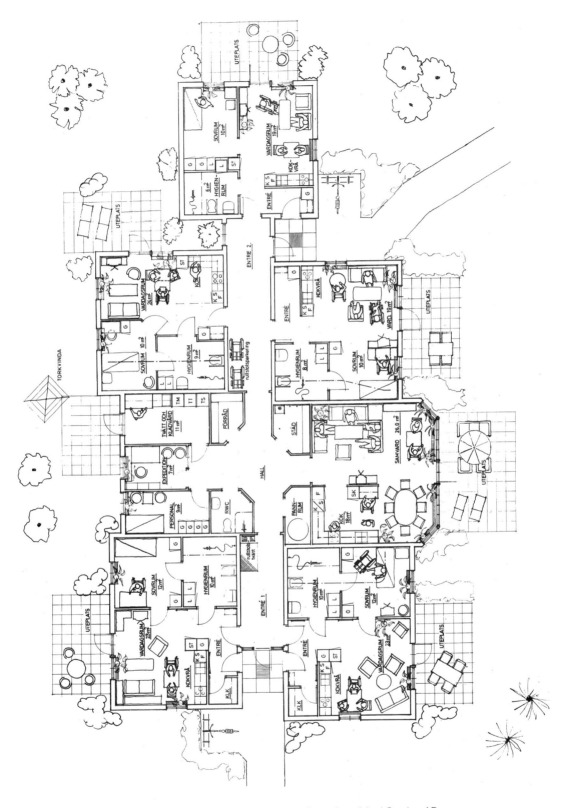

Figure 3-2 Five-bedroom Swedish prototype. *Courtesy of Gruppbostäder i Sverige AB.*

DETAILS
Windows

- Both the design of the window and the location of the controls should be accessible by children, shorter people, and wheelchair users. Casement, sliding, hopper, and awning windows with controls on the bottom are easier to reach.
- Latches should be operable with a closed fist.
- Corners of sills must be rounded to prevent injury.
- Double-hung windows can drop unintentionally, are difficult for everyone to open, and are often too high to be reached from a wheelchair. Add a crank control to an existing double-hung window.

Crank control. *Courtesy of A-Solutions.*

- An awning window is easier to reach and open than a double-hung installation. An awning window can also be installed inside an open double-hung window.
- Many crank-type casement windows are easier to use than sliders, although a slider with ball bearings may also be easy to operate.
- A longer crank or lever arm multiplies the force. Place levers so that they can be operated with the strongest hand for greater power.

Push rod on a casement window. *Courtesy of Lifease, Inc.*

- Casement windows with levers do not require as large a range of motion as do horizontal sliders and pivoting sashes.
- Casement windows and horizontal pivot sashes are easier to clean than are other types. The window lock should be installed within reach of wheelchair users and shorter persons.
- A sliding window panel or shutter on a track may be easier than a hinged panel to operate from a wheelchair. The top panel of a double-hung shutter is often higher than 48 in. and not reachable from a wheelchair.
- For safety, choose windows and shutters that won't drop unintentionally or swing in the wind.
- People with limited circulation often need higher ambient temperatures, yet people in wheelchairs or on gurneys must operate in the lower, often colder, part of a room. For these clients, heat loss and solar gain become critical issues. Reduce the header or window height and create an overhang to reduce solar gain.
- Double-glazed sliding windows conserve energy but may be too heavy for many people to operate. For people with strength limits, specify a double-glazed power window with a breakout feature for emergency exit in a power failure.
- Window treatments mounted within the window frame block some of the light and view but free extra wall space for storage within reach of children, shorter people, and wheelchair users.
- Keep wands on blinds a maximum of 48 in. a.f.f. and ensure that cords on roller shades are no higher with the shade rolled up.
- Wall-mount cords on blinds and draperies to keep them handy and within reach. Do not mount cords over counters, where they are difficult to reach.
- Consider electric drapery rod controls. Wands on blinds and shades can also be operated electrically by switch or remote control. Remember that all electrical devices require additional maintenance.

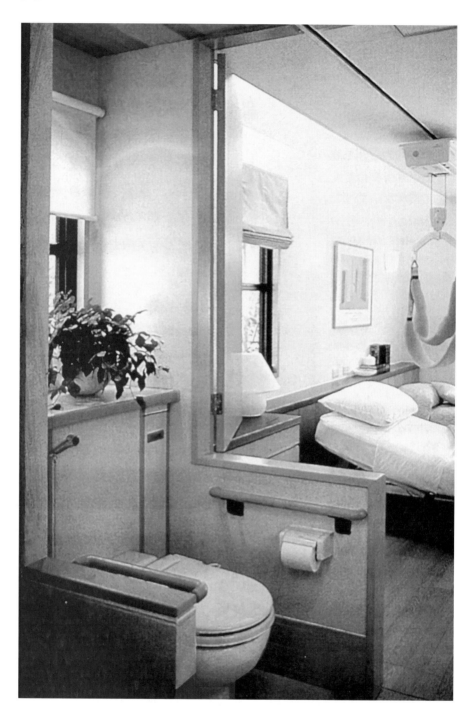

Figure 3-3 Remote-controlled lift. *Courtesy of Sekisui House, Ltd.*

INDEPENDENT LIVING

Without financial limits, most people with disabilities would choose to live independently, caring for themselves with the support of a universally designed home. Much of the design intervention takes place in the kitchen and bath. The balance of this chapter discusses innovative kitchen and bath design. (Comprehensive coverage of universal design is available in *Beautiful Universal Design*[4]; additional tips on kitchen and bathroom design can be found in Chapter 5.)

In Japan, the Sekisui Corporation has constructed hundreds of accessible homes and demonstration projects, including the Mitaka Model Home for independent living. This unique installation showcases a ceiling-hung lift offering direct access between the bedroom and the toilet area (see Figure 3-3). This product alone could delay, if not prevent, institutionalization, supporting home health care with minimal assistance.

In the bathroom, the toilet features a heated seat, automatic flush, a wash-dry feature, and an internal odor exhaust system. The track extends into the bathing area to a transfer seat and wooden tub (see Figure 3-4). No comfort was spared; even the quarry tile floor is warmed by heating coils.

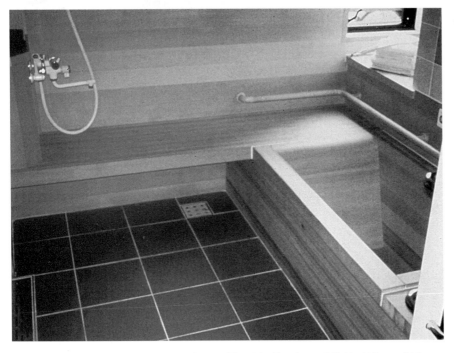

Figure 3-4 Smooth transfer to a wooden soaking tub. *Courtesy of Sekisui House, Ltd.*

Figure 3-5 Universal kitchen. *Courtesy of RISD—Universal Kitchen, Mini and Maxi. Photography: Mark Johnston.*

Sekisui studies lifespan housing in a huge research and development facility near Nara, Japan. Consumers are encouraged to tour this facility as well as the adjacent model homes and to participate in sensitivity training on the mobility and sensory changes of aging. In the United States, the Rhode Island School of Design has conducted extensive universal design research, resulting in production of model kitchens displayed at the Smithsonian (see Figure 3-5 and Research Abstract on page 59).

While these innovations offer a glimpse of the future of universal design, many universal design ideas are already in common use to support health care at home. Lever controls, side-by-side refrigerators, and C-grips are invisibly integrated into most of our homes, accommodating people of all sizes and abilities. Many larger cities offer mobile hospitals, interactive cable, and sophisticated computer systems to support home health care (see Details on page 139). Increasingly, home health care services and technologies are prescribed by teams of therapists, designers, and social workers dedicated to helping residents cope with changes in ability as they remain at home.

RESEARCH ABSTRACT
Universal Kitchen Project[5]

The Rhode Island School of Design has restructured kitchen standards and developed prototype kitchens that adjust to meet the needs of a full range of users. Time-motion studies revealed that over 400 steps are needed to prepare a simple dinner in a standard kitchen; this number has been greatly reduced by these unique designs. Instead of an interrelated work triangle in one work area, three separate major work areas were identified: the food preparation area, the cleaning area, and the snack area, each with their own sink. The research also identified a comfort zone on the countertop that is 16 in. to 18 in. deep. Two small refrigerators are placed in this zone, one in the food preparation area and one in the snack area. Redundancy throughout the kitchen reduces the reach, mobility, and time required for each task.

The research also identified a need for seating in the food preparation area. Communication problems and environmental concerns were also addressed. One kitchen recycles gray water through a waste channel. A continuous wet surface drains into this channel, encouraging a clean-as-you-go work style.

Three kitchens were developed, including a standalone mini-kitchen that is perfect for dormitories, hotels, assisted living, and independent living models. The mini kitchen cabinets unfold to reveal a standard kitchen that contains everything needed to make a moderately complex meal for two. Appliance components are interchangeable with storage components, and the disappearing doors on both do not sweep over the countertop.

Mini-kitchen. *Courtesy of RISD—Universal Kitchen, Mini and Maxi. Photography: Mark Johnston.*

REFERENCES

1. Department of Housing and Urban Development, "Final Fair Housing Accessibility Guidelines," *Federal Register* 56, no. 44 (6 March 1991).
2. Colleen Kelly, "Older Residents Find Way Back to Community," *Spectrum* (October 1993): 6.
3. Victory A. Regnier, *Assisted Living Housing for the Elderly: Design Innovations from the United States and Europe* (New York: John Wiley and Sons, 1994).
4. Cynthia Leibrock and James Evan Terry, *Beautiful Universal Design* (New York: John Wiley and Sons, 1999).
5. Rhode Island School of Design, "The Universal Kitchen: Research, Analysis and Design" (paper presented at the Universal Kitchen Project Advisory Board Meeting, Providence, Rhode Island, 1997).

4 HOSPICE

Historically, death has been viewed as a failure, something to be hidden from public view.[1] In today's hospitals, many terminal patients and their families are still brought in through the back door, as if there is shame in dying. The deceased leave by the service entrance near the trash containers.

How should we view the process of dying? The philosophy of hospice maintains that we should enhance the life that remains. Hospice emphasizes palliative care, controlling pain and other symptoms but not necessarily prolonging life. At the end of life, time must be measured by quality instead of quantity.[2] Each moment takes on greater importance, each sensory experience a special meaning. A window is not just an opening for light an air; it frames a vista of the last sunrise. A door is more than a functional entrance; it brings in friends and family members.

Design details in hospice are selected to improve life quality, not necessarily for their healing attributes. Design goes beyond problem solving to plan the setting for a wide choice of comforting scenarios. The key is choice, providing the hospice guest (not patient) access to positive experiences. Spaces must be flexible and easily adapted to the desire of the guest. Hospices are not designed for the average user; they must be planned to adapt to individual needs of guests and their families. The hospice must be easily personalized and controlled, even by users with reduced strength, coordination, and mobility. Short travel distances should be planned between spaces, especially to bathrooms (see Details on pages 166, 167, and 168 and Research Abstract on page 101). In general, spaces should be small and clearly differentiated to aid in wayfinding and orientation (see Details on pages 251 and 252). They must also be visually pleasing and appealing to all the senses through choices in music, dining, fragrance, and tactile experiences.

The entrance to a hospice should welcome the guest and offer a welcoming first impression (see Figure 4-1). Guests should not be required to use the institutional entrance for staff and consultants; they should have their own dignified entrance. The approach should be designed to accommodate a person on a gurney or anyone using a wheelchair or walker (see Details on pages 63 and 148).

The building should offer a residential ambience. This can be established by reducing larger elements to a human scale. Dormers and window boxes can be added to the exterior. Seen from the inside, window boxes serve as a garden at bed height. Interior scale can be reduced through the use of multiple windowpanes, trim in the hallways, and handrails on stairs (see Research Abstract on page 230). Institutional scale can also be reduced by space planning. Four to six private rooms can be clustered around an intimate shared living area (see Figure 4-2)

Figure 4-1 Entrance with a welcoming first impression. *Courtesy of Engelbrecht and Griffin Architects, P.C.*

DETAILS
Building Approach

- Plan smooth, firm, and stable sidewalks with good traction. Brick, sand, and cobblestone surfaces are examples of textures that are difficult for many people.
- Abrupt edges and drops in the sidewalk pose a tripping hazard and a barrier for people in wheelchairs. Specify adequate drainage and sidewalk sub-base construction to prevent settling and the resulting changes in level.
- Ramp existing changes of level exceeding ½ in. Bevel changes of level between ¼ in. and ½ in.[3] (see Details on page 254).
- Where an accessible route crosses a curb, provide a curb ramp built to ADA Accessibility Standards in slope, location, width, and surface[4] (see Details on page 248).
- Curb ramps should not reduce the width of the level accessible route. When a curb ramp is cut into the level accessible route, the resulting slope can pull people in wheelchairs into the street.
- Specify flared sides on curb ramps, as steep sides can pose a tripping hazard to pedestrians.
- Plan a covered exterior route for emergency escapes. Such a route usually consists of a covered sidewalk around the perimeter of the building. For security and safety, the sidewalk should be well lighted. It should be adequately drained yet free of gratings, which could catch on wheels and crutches.
- Gratings used in other areas should have spaces no greater than ½ in. wide.[5]

At the end of life, basic human needs do not necessarily change, yet people with terminal illness are often isolated from friends and family, enduring painful treatment and an unending procession of providers. More than ever before, they are in need of privacy, comfort, and the support of friends and family.

DESIGN CRITERIA

Privacy

As death approaches, privacy seems to become more elusive. Interruptions by staff become more frequent. Family and friends may visit more frequently. A private room offers the guest more control, especially if visitors and staff enter by guest permission only. Some guests prefer a room-

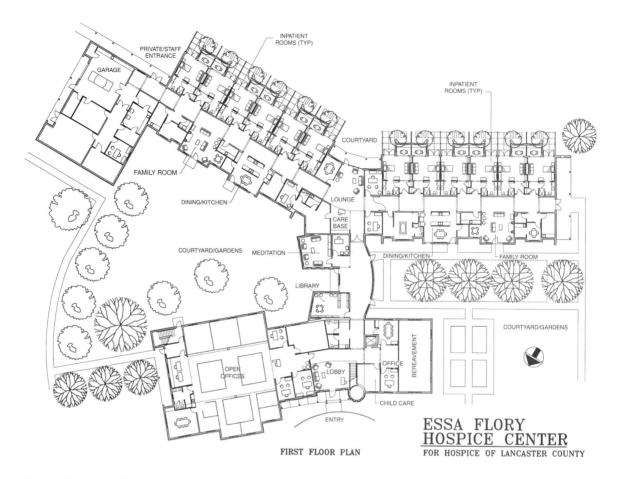

Figure 4-2 Clustered bedrooms. *Courtesy of Hospice of Lancaster Co. Designer: Reese, Lower, Patrick & Scott, Ltd.*

mate, so double rooms should be available, but, generally, a private bedroom and bathroom offer guests much greater control. The private bedroom can also be used as a viewing room after death.

In hospice, the bedroom is often larger and more private than a hospital patient room. Privacy is ensured with acoustical design planned to absorb ambient noise and prevent transmitted noise. Acceptable noise levels are generally lower than those in other health-care facilities; levels as low as 80 decibels can produce auditory trauma and stress[6] (see Details on pages 265 and 266).

Comfort

Comfort is the major provision of hospice. It involves more than relief from pain; comfort comes from pleasant memories, hours spent in the garden, the sound of a crackling fire, soothing music, appealing fragrance, and a loving touch. Hospice provides these final pleasures; hospice design strives to evoke pleasant emotional responses.

Norman Cousins states that memory is where the proof of life is stored. Guests in hospice often spend time reviewing their life, looking for meaning as they become reconciled to death. Personal possessions and family photographs can trigger comforting memories. Windowsills should have plenty of room for personal treasures. A bathroom shelf can house personal photographs as well as grooming items. A trunk could be placed at the end of the bed, offering a surface on which to display cards and photographs as well as a secure place for storage. Familiar furniture brings back memories, and guests should be encouraged to bring their own furnishings. Storage for existing hospice furniture should be planned to make room for the guests' own furniture. In public spaces, elements of home like a piano, a grandfather clock, a game table, and French doors can evoke pleasant memories (see Details on pages 68 and 70).

Nature is comforting to many, and access to the outdoors is important (see Figure 4-3). A garden provides a comfortable place to visit and produces flowers to adorn the guests' rooms (see Figure 4-4). Bring the natural elements of light, water, and fire indoors through the use of skylights, fireplaces, and fountains (see Figure 4-5). Special care should be taken with the hearth of the fireplace, which may be viewed as the heart of the hospice. This is an appropriate place to display personal photographs of the staff and their families.

Bring nature in by provide sufficient space in guest rooms to place the bed close to a window with a comforting view. The bed must be adjustable (see Details on page 225), and the window must be easily operated to offer the guest access to fresh air. Orient the window to provide good sunlight without glare, even in the late afternoon. Soft sheers on the window produce lovely shadows. Designer bed linens are a relatively inexpensive extravagance that adds a comfortable residential touch. Choose linens with a high thread count for softness and comfort.

Leave enough space around the bed for a guest to receive care and comfort; extending the bed diagonally from the corner of the room does not provide sufficient space for family and caregivers at the head of the bed. Comfort and reassurance come from human touch. Plan space for a portable massage table. Integrate touchable textures in upholstery and floor covering (see Details on page 181). With proper specification, fabric and carpet can be used in guest bedrooms, bathrooms, and other high-maintenance areas (see Details on page 24).

The warmth of a soaking tub or a soothing whirlpool bath can also be a great source of comfort. Some tubs have doors that swing up or open out for easy access. These doors are tightly sealed and can be used with a whirlpool bath. A tub with a swing-up door can be ordered for a left or right approach, allowing full use by a person with hemiplegia. The strong side of the body can be used while transferring and accessing tub controls. Make sure that drain controls are within reach. A high-volume drain allows the tub to be quickly emptied before the bather exits.

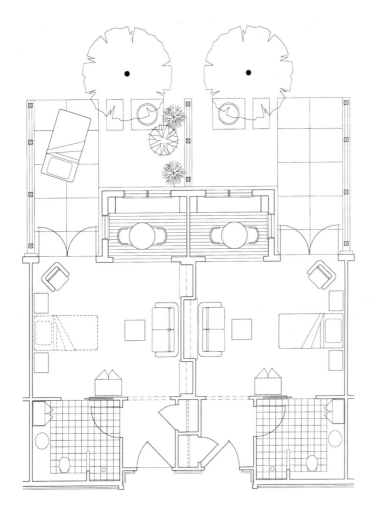

Figure 4-3 Bedrooms with private gardens. *Courtesy of Hospice of Lancaster Co. Designer: Reese, Lower, Patrick, and Scott, Ltd.*

Figure 4-4
Flowering gardens.
*Design: Delawie
Wildes Rodrigues
Barker & Bretton,
616/299-6690.
Photography:
David Hewitt/
Anne Garrison.*

Figure 4-5 Skylight
and fountain.
*Design: Delawie Wildes
Rodrigues Barker &
Bretton, 616/299-
6690. Photography:
Kim Brun Studios, Inc.*

Family comfort must also be considered. Provide a private place for the family to grieve and a private telephone to call home. This room could also be used for counseling and meetings with providers. It could even double as a guest room with the addition of a fold-down bed or sofa sleeper. Other comforting family options include a place to nap and a children's day care area. A coffee shop is a great place for a quick break, and it could be open to the community to encourage integration and acceptance of the hospice.

DETAILS
Doors

- French doors are often specified for wheelchair access, but it is difficult to open both doors at the same time from a wheelchair. One leaf must offer at least 32 in. of clearance.
- Eliminate the vertical strip between French doors, as it is often not detected by blind people who use canes. Doors that open at an angle into high-traffic areas may also be hazardous to people using canes. Plan sliding interior doors to eliminate this problem.
- For people who must spend part of the day in bed, use wide French or atrium patio doors that allow the bed to be moved outside. Wide doors also facilitate moving large pieces of furniture into the room.
- Sliding glass exterior doors can be difficult to operate because of the width and weight of each door. Also, the accumulation of dirt in the door track can render the doors inoperable. Consider a hinged glass door as a replacement.
- For people who are autistic or prone to seizures and falls, use tempered glass in doors. Glass doors should be protected from wheelchair abrasion by a kick plate.
- Pocket doors often solve space-planning problems, but the recessed hardware is often difficult for many to use. An outside-mounted sliding door can eliminate the need for recessed hardware.
- Dutch doors are problematic, as the top half of double-hung doors often is not detected by a blind person using a cane.
- To operate swinging doors, people in wheelchairs must often reach, grasp, pull, back up, turn, and go around. Sliding interior doors that stack out of the way are the best choices for wheelchair and gurney access.
- Folding doors also work well, but it is easy for children and others to pinch their fingers in them. If these doors are on a track, make sure the track is recessed and not an obstacle for entry. Accordion-folding doors and draperies also work.
- Sliding top-hung doors with bottom guides may be easier to move than those that slide on a bottom track. Choose nylon wheels or roller bearings with self-lubricating metal tracks.
- Solid-core doors require more strength to open and close than hollow-core doors. Maintain a minimum width to keep doors light and easy to open.
- To measure the force necessary to open a door, attach a spring scale to it, then open the door slowly and evenly. Many people cannot open exterior doors that require more than 8.5 pounds of force (lbf). Interior doors and all sliding doors should require less than 5 lbf.[7]
- Doors that stick or drag require needless effort. The problem can often be corrected by oiling the hinges or removing the old paint on the edges of the doors. If this does not work, remove the door, plane and sand the edges, shim the hinges, or rehang the door on new hardware.

- Sand leading edges of doors to eliminate a sharp edge and minimize possible injury.
- Specify an oil finish on doors for easy touch-up.
- In commercial spaces, specify alternative doors or gates adjacent to revolving doors and turnstiles. Some doors feature an extra panel that can be opened when wider access is necessary.
- People with reduced vision are often injured by swinging power doors or sliding doors with malfunctioning motion detectors. Air curtains and manually operated doors are better choices.
- Whenever possible, specify 34 in. (instead of the required 32 in.) of clearance in the door frame. This allows wheelchair users 2 extra inches for elbow clearance.

The aroma of fresh coffee signals break time for many, a time to relax with friends and family. The sense of smell may trigger more memories than sight or sound because of its strong link to the limbic system, the brain's emotional center. Color produces strong physiological responses (see Details on page 82) and auditory cues, like music, can reduce stress, change mood, and distract from discomfort, but fragrance evokes the strongest response. Pleasant aromas have been shown to reduce blood pressure, respiration, and pain perception levels.[8] Unpleasant odors, like urine and ammonia, trigger feelings of fear and anxiety. Appealing fragrances, like spiced apple and strawberry, have been shown to reduce stress.[9]

Support of Friends and Family

At the end of life, social rituals and celebrations of life have great value. The rituals of dining are small pleasures that add immeasurable quality to hospice life. Guests may prefer to dine in bed or at a table with family and friends. A small table set with beautiful linen and tableware in the bedroom is a nice touch. A choice of dining areas and cuisine is preferable. The meal could be served in individual courses with hot food storage available to give the guest time with each course.

Although most guests do not prepare their own food, a family kitchen offers them this option as well as a place to find a quick snack (see the Research Abstract on page 59 and Details on pages 96, 97, 98, and 99). It can also be used by families to prepare a favorite meal. A dining table in the family kitchen provides the guest one more place to spend time with family and friends.

DETAILS
Door Hardware

- Door accessories for wheelchair use include levers, door closers, thresholds, protective plates, vision panels, and hinges.

- A door can be equipped with double-action hinges so it can swing in both directions. Be sure the action of the door does not interfere with foot traffic.

- If an existing door is too narrow for wheelchair use, try removing the doorstop for added clearance. Offset pivot hinges can increase the width of an open doorway by 2 in.

- In case a person loses consciousness behind a locked door, specify rising pin-butt hinges for easy door removal. Be sure interior locks can be opened with a screwdriver. This is especially important on the bathroom door.

- A rising pin-butt hinge can also be used to elevate weather stripping from floor surfaces. Maneuvering over interior thresholds may be difficult for people in wheelchairs.

- Interior thresholds often serve no purpose and should be removed. Exterior thresholds should be no higher than ½ in. Bevel thresholds to a vertical slope no greater than 1:2.5.

- Exterior thresholds should be of a contrasting color to the floor.

- To totally eliminate the threshold on swinging doors, use movable mortise-type weather stripping that lowers to the floor when the door is closed.

- Limit the height of doormats to ¼ in. and secure them to the floor with beveled metal trim or tape. A recessed carpet mat should not exceed ½ in. in pile height.

- A pneumatic door closer can offer convenience for people in wheelchairs who have the strength to operate it. It is also useful for people with vision limits because doors left open at an angle into traffic areas may present unexpected problems.

- A power door opener can be activated by a remote control, a floor mat sensor, a wall switch, or a photo cell. If mounted on the pull side of the door, the sensor or photocell must open the door before the user reaches the sweep area. This is not an issue with folding or sliding power doors.

- A wall button or switch may be used if mounted within reach, close to the door or on the push side (but not in the frame). The button must be a minimum of ¾ in. in diameter, be flush mounted (not recessed), and require 5 lbf or less to operate. Make sure automatic doors have a break-out feature in case of power failure. Force required must be no more than 15 lbf.[10]

- A delayed-action door closer helps to keep the exterior door from blowing closed during use. Automatic doors must remain open to a full 90° for 20 seconds to allow wheelchair passage. Rising pin-butts are not sufficiently reliable as door closers.

- To close the door without a door closer, add a C-grip handle mounted on the hinge side of the door. Again, this requires strength to use, but it does offer convenience.

Hinge-side C-grip. *Courtesy of Barrier Free Environments.*

- To protect doors from abrasion, consider a high kickplate (16 in.) on manually operated doors. Extend the plate the full width of the door on the push side. The corners of metal plates should be filed or bent toward the door to avoid possible injury. A plate is preferable to projecting rails, which could catch on a wheelchair or gurney.

- A metal bar or decal over a sliding glass door makes the door more visible and can prevent accidents.

- Vision panels in doors (with the bottom of the panels no higher than 3 ft.) allow a child, shorter person, or a wheelchair user to see and be seen. On an exterior door, a vision panel helps to monitor visitors. On an interior door, the panel lets the person become oriented to ongoing activities before entering a room. Be aware that people with reduced vision can mistake panels that extend to the floor for door openings.

- Levers (mounted at a height of 36 in)[11] on both interior and exterior doors are convenient for people in wheelchairs, children, and anyone with reduced strength. They are much easier to use from a seated position than doorknobs are. Horizontal levers require less operating force than vertical levers do.

- Levers should turn toward door hinges for easy access. They should have a slight return to keep them from catching on clothing.

- Use extra-long doorstops to protect walls from door levers. Choose one that doubles as a hook for clothes. It is easy to trip over a floor-mounted doorstop.

- Paddles on doors can be specified if they can be easily maneuvered with one hand. Avoid doorknobs; never specify a knob on one side of the set and a lever on the other, because the spring of the lever is too strong for the knob.

- Avoid door hardware requiring simultaneous two-handed operation. One example is a lock that requires the user to turn the key with one hand and pull with the other. Specify a push-button system that can be operated with one hand.

- If a dead bolt is used, specify a set that disengages both the dead bolt and the door latch with one motion. For people who don't have the strength to operate the dead bolt, a slide bolt provides nearly the same amount of security and is easier to handle.

Extra-length doorstop. *Courtesy of HEWI, Inc.*

- Doors without latches should have a C-grip on the pull side and a push bar on the push side. Doors with C-grips on both sides give the misleading message that both sides should be pulled.

Design elements supporting socialization may be as simple as a reachable telephone on a usable nightstand (see Details on page 267) and as complex as programming and space planning to support excellent communication. Design details help families to communicate, to come to terms with death. Family members may feel afraid of death or confused about the situation. They may feel guilty, perhaps wishing they had done more. They may experience unresolved hurt, a feeling that the loved one is deserting them. For family members as well as guests, a place for private contemplation, prayer, and worship is a necessity. Both indoor and outdoor meditation and prayer areas should be planned.

Many hospice activities are quiet and contemplative. A reference library could offer recreational reading material, spiritual support, and research on coping with life's transitions. Spaces should be planned throughout the hospice for reading, listening to music, playing games, gardening, and watching television. A classroom or auditorium could be used for in-house education as well as community events that encourage community support. A beauty salon could also be open to the public while providing guests and visitors a needed boost in self-esteem.

Guests should be able to spend time with visitors in all locations; the entire hospice should be accessible to guests with mobility aids as well as those on gurneys. Since many guests are on gurneys or in bed, plan an interesting ceiling pattern (see Details on page 214). Light control on skylights is especially important to reclining guests.

Medical equipment should be out of sight to encourage repeat visits. Medical gases can be concealed in the headboard of the bed; and suitable storage should be planned for potentially frightening medical equipment like gastric tube pump feeders, intravenous (IV) stands, and portable oxygen supply.

HOSPICE FOR PEOPLE WITH AIDS

A specialized form of hospice provides physical, psychological, and spiritual support to people with AIDS and their families, enabling them to live out their lives with dignity. With advances in medical technology, life expectancy has been extended for people with AIDS. Hospice is sometimes used as temporary housing, offering respite for the caretaker, a chance to regroup. Hospice also becomes a permanent home for individuals living alone or for those living with families unable to care for them in the latter stages of the disease.

A hospice for people with AIDS is planned differently than other hospices. AIDS can be contracted by anyone, so the design program must reflect the needs of children, singles, couples, and people from a wide variety of cultures. The guests are generally younger than those in other hospices, which may increase interest in the positive distractions of younger people including computer games, video, television, and music. AIDS hospices generally see more social interaction and daily involvement of family members and friends, and more social interaction can mean more social problems. The population may reflect a diverse mix of potentially conflicting cultures, a wide range of ages, and clients with various conditions.

AIDS is frequently contracted from shared hypodermic needles, and substance abuse in AIDS hospices continues to be problematic. Medical needs may range from detoxification programs to treatment for dementia, which often occurs in the latter stages of AIDS. Care is less palliative and more therapeutic than in traditional hospice programs. Physical, occupational, and recreational therapy are usually offered. The program may also include massage, acupuncture, horticulture, art, pet, and IV therapy. Most AIDS hospices also offer transportation, meals, and temporary housing. The prevalence of homelessness among AIDS hospice guests is increasing, and poverty may be a more widespread condition than in other types of hospice.

With such a diverse program, AIDS hospice presents a significant design challenge. Like all hospice environments, the design priorities include comfort and privacy. Spaces should be planned to encourage socialization and the support of family and friends. As in any hospice, the spiritual and emotional needs of families and clients must be addressed by the design; a prayer and meditation area should be included. The space must be flexible and accessible, with choices for people of all ages, sizes, and abilities. In addition, the need for security and infection control is especially high for this vulnerable population.

Individual Choice

To meet the needs of a wide variety of consumers, design detail must accommodate a wide range of choices. For example, younger guests may need more electrical outlets for computers, CD players, and other electrical devices, but guests in the latter stages of the disease are very sensitive to noise. A slamming door or even the ring of a telephone can be physically painful. Sophisticated acoustical design (see Chapter 10) should be combined with simple solutions like soft phone chimes on the phones and door closers that prevent slamming.

Individual control of heating and ventilation is critical. Smoking and nonsmoking rooms should be planned. Flexible lighting is important for adaptation to a variety of needs (see Details on page 83). Public spaces require night lighting to accommodate variable wake-sleep cycles. During the day, numerous sources of natural light should be provided. Clients' rooms should offer visual access to the outdoors, a positive distraction

Figure 4-6 Greenhouse in an AIDS hospice. *Design: Bumgardner. Courtesy of Michael Jensen.*

from health problems. Bedrooms need large windows with good window controls to accommodate increased light sensitivity as well as ventilation. For people who spend some daylight hours in bed, use a reflective black-out lining to darken the room for sleeping.

Many rooms should provide secure access to the outdoors. A private balcony with sun and shade is especially appreciated by guests who need fresh air but are not well enough to go out in public. Access to nature can also be provided by a greenhouse (see Figure 4-6). This warm retreat is particularly welcome to guests with reduced circulation, who may prefer ambient temperatures as high as 78 degrees.

AIDS hospice must also accommodate a large number of visitors. Because the symptoms AIDS are so diverse, numerous health care providers arrive and depart daily. Demand for parking is higher than at other long-term care facilities. Friends and relatives also visit frequently. Rooming-in is common; family members may also request access to exercise areas, the kitchen, and laundry. The kitchen may need a larger freezer than is standard; some guests find relief from nausea by chewing ice and are soothed by a bowl of sherbet or ice cream. A sterilizing dishwasher should also be available for infection control.

Infection Control

People with AIDS are extremely susceptible to infection. Their immune system is suppressed by the AIDS virus, and even minimal exposure to an infectious disease can be life-threatening. Isolation areas must be considered for patients with a transferable disease. The heating, ventilation, and air-conditioning (HVAC) system should not recirculate airborne contagions. Small facilities with a limited client population create less opportunity to encounter infection. Antimicrobial materials should be specified, and finishes should stand up to bleach and other harsh cleaning fluids. Many people with AIDS have diarrhea and bowel incontinence; specify sofas and chairs that cannot collect fluids or dirt in seam welts or cushions. Medical waste disposal is also a critical issue.

Security

People with AIDS are a population at extreme risk, and entry to an AIDS hospice must be tightly controlled. Drug dealers seek access to guests with substance abuse problems, often with their help. Those suffering from dementia are at risk for wandering into the street. Egress must be limited in some situations but not restricted in case of fire. Twenty-four-hour supervision is required.

The accessible route must include doors that expand to 42 in. of clearance for the evacuation of guests on gurneys. This extra clearance also prevents these guests from being confined full time to their rooms, allowing them to be moved on gurneys to social functions and hospice activities. In addition to wide doors, client bedrooms and bathrooms should be equipped with an emergency call system (see Details on page 49).

One final detail: When a loved one dies, families frequently cannot find the strength to immediately claim the possessions, so long-term storage is needed in hospice.

> *The Bustle of a House*
> *The Morning after Death*
> *Is solemnest of industries*
> *Enacted upon Earth —*
>
> *The Sweeping up the Heart*
> *and putting Love Away*
> *We shall not want to use again*
> *Until Eternity*

EMILY DICKINSON

REFERENCES

1. Z. Bauman, *Mortality and Immortality and Other Life Stories* (Stanford: Stanford University Press, 1992).
2. Alan Lightman, *Einstein's Dreams* (London: Bloomsbury Press, 1993).
3. *Americans with Disabilities Act Accessibility Standards,* 1991, 4.5.2.
4. Ibid., 4.7.
5. Ibid., 4.5.4.
6. Millicent Gappell, "Hospice Facilities," *Journal of Health Care Interior Design* 2 (1990): 79.
7. *ADA Standards*, 4.13.11.
8. Beth Frankowski Jones. "Environments that Support Healing," *Interiors and Sources* (January 1996): 71.
9. Gappell, "Hospice Facilities," 79.
10. Ibid., 4.13.12.
11. Evan Terry Associates, *ADA Facilities Compliance Notebook Supplement* (New York: John Wiley and Sons, 1995).

5 SUBACUTE CARE AND REHABILITATION

In most Scandinavian countries, it is illegal to build a nursing home. Skilled nursing is rapidly being replaced by subacute care and rehabilitation. Even in the United States, these are among the fastest-growing market segments on the continuum of care.

Subacute units offer long-term acute care oriented toward medical-based outcomes. Although many patients in subacute care receive rehabilitation services, they are generally not as medically stable as those in rehabilitation hospitals.

Subacute care and rehabilitation are not housing models, but the length of stay in either may be as long as six months (or as short as two weeks). Subacute costs are typically 25 to 50 percent lower than costs in a similar setting in an acute-care hospital.[1] Patients in both subacute and rehabilitation facilities often have multiple afflictions requiring a wide variety of treatments. Progress is measured in tiny steps that are almost unrecognizable day to day.

DESIGN OF SUBACUTE CARE FACILITIES

Unfortunately, design for subacute care is driven largely by codes and reimbursement rather than patient and family need. The Americans with Disabilities Act (ADA), the Omnibus Budget Reconciliation Act (OBRA), and certificate of need (CON) regulations require compliance.

ADA prevents disability by design, OBRA addresses restraint-free environments (locked doors, etc.), and CON deals with a range of building issues, including minimum square footage per person. In addition, licensure requirements stipulate hours between meals and staffing issues with design implications (like training requirements and staffing levels). Health department standards regulate call systems and distances to the nursing stations. Building codes regulate everything from fire-rated corridors to door closers, some of which conflict with independent testing standards like those of the National Fire Protection Association (NFPA).

These requirements are minimum standards; only 50 percent of skilled nursing patient rooms and baths are required to be accessible under the ADA standards, yet 70–75 percent of the patients are in wheelchairs (see Details on page 238). In New York, only 540 sq. ft. per bed are required, but it is best to offer 700–800 sq. ft. The Department of Health requires a call system that only 12 percent of the nursing home population can use.[2]

In Scandinavia, traditional residential materials like wood, brick, and stone, are commonly used. These materials are restricted in U.S. subacute facilities. Scandinavia's liberal attitude about the fire separation between public corridors and rooms allows designers to explore overlapping spaces, often creating niches in larger spaces. The Scandinavians do not take away life by trying to eliminate risk.

In subacute care, older people constitute the majority of the patient population, and the design must reflect the cognitive and sensory changes that often take place in aging (see Research Abstract on opposite page).

Design for Visual Acuity

Much can be accomplished with lighting to compensate for the visual changes we experience in aging. As we age, our eyes may adjust to light more slowly due to a reduction of elasticity of muscles. We develop an inability to adapt to changing light levels. The result is a dazzle effect called *contrast glare* that makes it more difficult to focus when moving between light levels. Sensitivity to glare may also be caused by macular degeneration, a deterioration of the central area of the retina. One third of people 70 years old or older have this disease, which produces a spot in the center of the visual field that gradually enlarges until it fills the field. Glare actually increases the deterioration rate of the retina.[3]

Contrast glare often occurs in subacute-care facilities with low levels of lighting. Patients are dazzled as they leave dark interiors and step into the daylight. Contrast glare is also produced by wall-mounted fluorescent fixtures on the head wall, a medical cliché that produces glare and contributes little to ambient light levels. Table lamps and sconces

RESEARCH ABSTRACT
Experiential Research in Detailing for Long-Term Care

Dian Love, healthcare interior architect with SHG ARCHITECTS in Detroit, Michigan, has personally designed over 6 million sq. ft. of interior space totaling over $500 million. She offers the following design priorities for empowering patients in long-term care:

- It is important for older people to maintain mobility. When color and graphics are well designed, they can help to move patients through the space.
- Older people may experience reduced awareness of time and location. To increase awareness of time, for example, select see-through window treatments, like blinds, that make the sunrise and sunset obvious.
- With a slower response time, hierarchies in design are critical. Arrival, circulation, and destination spaces must be clearly identified. Environmental information should be retrieved from a color system using contrast and brightness. Figure-ground relationships are most important.
- Older people have difficulty recognizing detail in a cluttered background. Keep the environment ordered and reduce clutter.
- Efficacy and control increase in importance. Many older people cannot use electric beds; high-low beds are essential and latch springs are important.
- As reflex and reaction times are reduced, safety issues become more important. Floor lamps and table lamps, for example, should be very heavy for stability. Floor lamps require a base weight of at least 80 lbs. Cloth shades help to increase and softly distribute ambient lighting levels. Point source lighting creates distorted, disturbing, and glaring lighting patterns (see Details on page 223).
- Many older people take their cues from the floor. Textural gradients are important for locomotion as well as depth perception. Differences in spaces should be cued by color and texture changes in floor finishes.
- Older people need bright and warm spaces. Warm northern and eastern exposures with light and warm colors. Balance southern and western exposures with cool, deep colors. Remember that warm colors are intensified in incandescent lighting and cool colors become cooler in fluorescent lighting.
- The sense of touch is sometimes substituted when other senses decline. Carpet feels warmer. Textural cues, like carpet and fabric, are stimulating and may be used to signal spacial changes from one area to another.
- As hearing diminishes, visual cues like strong color become doubly important. Other redundant cuing may also be helpful.
- With a reduction in the olfactory sense, textures that absorb odor become difficult to identify for maintenance. Hard-surfaced flooring, for example, may be preferable in some areas.

can also dazzle when their shades are above or below eye level (see Details on page 223).

As we age, the lenses of our eyes thicken, making us more susceptible to another type of glare called a *veiling reflection*, which we experience when trying to read a shiny printed page. In subacute care, veiling reflections may be more subtle. Reflections on a shiny floor look like water when perceived through a thickened lens. Older people are immobilized by a fear of falling. A window or door at the end of a shiny corridor can produce enough glare to cause an older person to trip over a threshold or fall down a stairway. These accidents can be easily prevented by design (see Details below).

DETAILS
Eliminating Glare

- Keep lighting levels adjustable and consistent from room to room. Keep corridor lighting levels low at night. Many people have trouble adjusting to sudden changes from a dark bedroom to a bright corridor. Night-lights in the bedroom can also help. Many falls occur when people try to get out of bed. Install a light under the lip of the nightstand or around the perimeter of the bed.

- Gradual changes in light levels are also needed in transition spaces between indoors and outdoors. Create a transition zone, such as a well-lighted entryway or porch, between the outdoors and the interior. Put side lights at the entrance to a bright room. Side lights and other accent lighting (instead of flat fluorescent light) can help people to maintain orientation within the room.

- Shield all lighting sources to prevent contrast glare. Chandeliers do not significantly increase light levels and can cause glare, unless frosted globes are used. Even then, unprotected bulbs have high-temperature surfaces capable of carbonizing dust, a source of irritation to many people with allergies.[4]

- Avoid directed sources like spotlights. Provide several low intensity light sources rather than one bright source. Keep all lights high and well diffused over the task area. Wall lighting strips can be mounted 12–18 in. from the ceiling, washing the wall as well as the ceiling with light.[5] Other successful choices include indirect pendant and cove lighting. Undercabinet lighting can illuminate matte-finished counters without glare.

- Control contrast glare at windows and doors through proper placement and treatment. Window glare can be controlled by draperies, blinds, and shades. Dark color schemes adjacent to bright windows can dazzle and make it difficult for people to distinguish objects located near the window. Doors should be placed in alcoves to reduce dazzle when open.

- Place doors to the sides of corridors, not at the ends. An open door causes both contrast glare and veiling reflections down the length of a shiny floor.

- Eliminate veiling reflections by specifying low-glare surfaces on counters, floors, furnishings, and walls.

Eighty-five percent of older people experience yellow tinting of the human lens.[6] The yellowed lens filters out short wavelengths. Cool colors, like blue-green and blue-violet become grayed. It becomes nearly impossible to see the edge of a blue chair or ottoman situated on a blue carpet, a contributing factor to falls.

Yellowing of the lens also reduces the amount of light perceived. In addition, pupil size generally decreases with age, so the pupil lets less light in. Many older people require 4 to 5½ times more light to distinguish a figure from the background (at least 100 fc for reading and close work).[7] The light level in a typical nursing home is about 20–30 fc[8] (see Details on page 82).

Low lighting levels affect more than the ability to read. Older people experience reduced ability to discern all detail. Sometimes patients don't eat because they can't see the food. Others suffer the indignities of incontinence because they can't see well enough to find or use the toilet. The Illuminating Engineering Society recommends at least 30 fc in the bathroom.

As the pupil becomes smaller and the lens denser, depth perception may become restricted, which can cause problems with spacial orientation and mobility. For example, a stripe across a hallway could be perceived as a stair or a change in elevation. Shadows from high-contrast lighting may have the same effect. To prevent the problem, keep lighting levels even (see Details on page 83).

In some areas, high contrast is needed. Reduced perception of contrast may make it impossible to distinguish between the floor and the wall, for example, or between foreground and background. High contrast also helpful to the many older people with reduced peripheral vision. Retinitis pigmentosa and glaucoma both cause this problem.

Design to Enhance Hearing

Many older people have difficulty hearing high frequencies, and increased volume may not help. Some amplified phones boost high frequencies and improve clarity. Ambient noise reduction is also important. Background noise is often amplified and distorted by hearing aids (see Details on pages 265 and 266).

Older people have difficulty understanding a conversation when ambient noise levels exceed 30 decibels. It is not unusual to find dining rooms with noise levels at 60–70 decibels.[9] Specify products with a high noise reduction coefficient rating (NRC). Low reflective ceilings amplify sound, increasing ambient noise. Long, rectangular rooms increase sound reflection and resulting noise levels. Ceiling light fixtures that reflect sound should be replaced with suspended or wall-mounted fixtures.

DETAILS
Color

- Appetite can be improved with warmer color choices for dining—for example, coral, peach, and soft yellow. Violet, yellow-green, gray, olive, and mustard are poor choices.[10]

- Yellow to green tones should be avoided because they are associated with body fluids. Yellow, green, and purple colors are not flattering to the skin and reflect jaundiced skin tones.[11]

- Use intense colors only for accents and for contrast to improve visual organization. Brightly colored grab bars, door frames, levers, and switches, for instance, are easier to find than those that blend into the background.

- Yellow color schemes may cause difficulties for people who have yellowing lenses. Bright yellow colors can intensify to the point of annoying. Pastel yellows are difficult to distinguish from white (which appears yellow).

- With yellowed lenses, blue, blue-green or violet color schemes may appear gray, especially in daylight or fluorescent light (in a blue color spectrum). Blue tones can be distinguished from other colors more easily at night when lighted by tungsten light (standard lightbulbs).

- Yellow tinting of the human lens has little effect on red tones. However, people with color-blindness have difficulty distinguishing between green and red.

- Texture makes tones appear darker,[12] absorbing important ambient light.

- Color values that contrast by more than two digits on the gray scale are adequate to increase the imagery of objects.[13] (The gray scale consists of ten increments from black to white; it is often illustrated on the back of many printer's rules).

- A monochromatic color scheme throughout the building may be perceived as institutional. It can become monotonous and boring when viewed for an extended period. It can contribute to sensory deprivation, which leads to disorganization of brain function, deterioration of intelligence, and an inability to concentrate. For those who suffer from a deficiency of perception, plan variety in color, pattern, and texture.

- Warm color hues are often associated with extroverted responses and social contact. A quiet, relaxing, or contemplative atmosphere is created by cool hues.

- Primary colors (red, yellow, and blue) and strong patterns are pleasing at first but may eventually become tiring. Highly saturated colors may also be too controversial, triggering unpleasant associations in the mind of the guest.[14]

- The boundary between two intense colors eventually becomes visually unstable.[15]

- Researchers in the field of anthroposophic medicine maintain that color can help patients regain health. Patient rooms in warm colors are used to build up from a "cold" illness like arthritis, and cool blue or violet tones are used to dissolve or break down inflammation.[16]

- Color can affect perceptions of time, size, weight, and volume. In a space where pleasant activities occur, such as a dining or recreation room, a warm color scheme makes the activities seem to last longer. In rooms where monotonous tasks are performed, a cool color scheme can make time pass more quickly.

DETAILS
Universal Lighting

- Sufficient lighting is particularly important in areas where concentration is required, decisions are made, or danger is present. Decision areas, like a reception room and entryway, may require increased lighting. A light ceiling color increases the quantity of reflected light.

- Many accidents occur in bathrooms; increase lighting levels without glare to prevent accidents.

- Stairways and landings, especially the head and foot of the stairs, are potentially dangerous areas (see Details on pages 253 and 254). Place lighting (and windows) to throw light toward, not down, staircases. Recessed lighting under stair treads prevents accidents without creating glare.

- As lighting quantity increases, be careful to avoid excessive heat by using luminaries with low heat output.

- Extra lighting is helpful when using a shower chair or seat. A steam-filled room makes vision more difficult, and high ceiling lights may not penetrate to the level of a shower seat. At a minimum, recess a vapor-proof light fixture in the ceiling of every shower stall. The light can be combined with an exhaust fan to reduce the steam.

- Flickering fluorescent lights have been found to trigger epileptic seizures.

- Studies have shown that people with Alzheimer's disease become agitated under fluorescent lighting.[17]

- Cool fluorescent light emphasizes the blue-green tones that are most difficult for people with cataracts to perceive.[18]

- When planning fluorescent lighting, keep in mind that a lighting spectrum as close as possible to daylight may reduce depression, fatigue, hyperactivity, and some incidences of disease. The daylight spectrum also may increase calcium absorption and reaction time to light and sound.[19] This, in turn, may increase staff productivity and patient progress. The ultraviolet light in the spectrum is also helpful in sanitizing the space for people with allergies.[20] Circadian rhythm can be disrupted by inadequate exposure to natural light.

- A less institutional appearance is achieved when only the light is seen, not the source of the light. Exposed lighting systems are often harsh and glaring and can visually take over a space. With concealed lighting systems, the emphasis is placed on the beauty of the room and its occupants rather than on the light fixtures. Concealed fixtures are often less expensive than decorative fixtures.

- When using wall fixtures, keep controls within the reach of patients. Fixtures must protrude less than 4 in. when placed 27–80 in. a.f.f.[21]

Products with a high sound transmission class (STC) rating prevent transmitted noise that adds to ambient noise levels. Wall construction, double or triple glazing on windows, and placement of doors and windows can also reduce transmitted noise. Place exterior windows and doors away from streets, playgrounds, and other sources of noise. Stagger interior doors so they do not face each other in corridors. Back-to-back outlets and medicine chests in bathrooms are also sources of transmitted noise that can be avoided.

Many people with reduced hearing unconsciously depend on body language and lip reading. For people with hearing differences, plan adequate lighting to allow facial expressions, body movements, and gestures to be distinguished. Lighting is especially important in areas of frequent communication, like nursing stations and reception areas. Avoid backlighting and shadows on speakers and interpreters.

Consider integrating flashing lights in a warning system for hearing-impaired people. Install light switches both inside and outside of patient bathrooms (see Details on page 98), dressing rooms, and other areas requiring privacy. The provider can flash the light before entering.

Fluorescent lighting, on the other hand, may interfere with hearing aids, and flickering ballasts should be replaced. Static in carpet can trigger a screeching noise in hearing aids. Most contract carpeting is inherently static free.

Design for Improved Cognitive Ability

Cognitive difficulties in subacute care may range from poor judgment about touching hot surfaces to reduced attention span, depression, disorientation, and even dementia (see Chapter 2). Many older people have some degree of forgetfulness, but most do not have dementia. Considering the extended length of stay in subacute care, orientation is particularly important. A bulletin board in each patient room can feature family photos. It can also be used for seasonal displays or to post the day of the week. A calendar and clock also help with orientation (see Figure 5-1). Patients also experience disorientation between day and night in subacute facilities, especially in spaces without windows. (For a more comprehensive discussion on orientation, see Chapter 13.)

Disorientation may also be caused by repetitive elements in the design. For example, doors repeated the full length of double-loaded corridors (corridors with rooms off both sides) are confusing. Long corridors themselves can be disorienting. Lighting and ceiling treatments can help to visually reduce the length of corridors (see Figure 5-2). Walking distances in corridors can be shortened with seating niches every 20 feet. This seating also supports mobility; without seating in corridors, older people may be reluctant to leave their rooms.

Figure 5-1 Clock and bulletin board for orientation. *Courtesy of Watkins Hamilton Ross Architects, Inc. Photography: Jud Haggard.*

Figure 5-2 Ceiling vines visually shorten a long corridor. *Courtesy of Judith-Myers Thomas/ Summer Hill Co., Inc.*

Figure 5-3 Visual connection between spaces. *Courtesy of TRO/The Ritchie Organization. Photography: Edward Jacoby, Jacoby Photography*

Orientation can be improved or reduced by pattern. Eliminate bold patterns, stripes, and undulating patterns in subacute care. Older people may feel more comfortable with patterns from the 1940s and 1950s, when they were financially and physically comfortable.[22]

Orientation can be significantly improved by planning small spaces that are clearly differentiated by finish and size. Visual connection of spaces also improves orientation and offers patients a chance to observe activities prior to entering (see Figure 5-3). Orientation (where you are) differs from wayfinding (how you get there). Chapter 13 offers a comprehensive discussion on signage and wayfinding.

Lighting can also be used to improve cognitive skills. Some people with concentration differences may experience a shortened attention span triggered by fluorescent lighting.[23] Access to sunlight may help. Research has also shown that access to daylight and nature can make a

significant difference in depression (see Chapter 11). Most older people have some degree of depression, and 15 to 50 percent of patients in nursing homes are clinically depressed.[24]

Design for Mobility

Beautiful Universal Design[25] is filled with ideas for people with reduced mobility. Most of these accessibility features meet the needs of older people, but a few do not. High toilets for wheelchair users, for example, don't work for many ambulatory older users. It may be easier to sit and rise, but older people (and shorter people) have bowel trouble with high toilets. Some have to use a stool to elevate their legs into a squatting position in order to have a bowel movement. Specify standard-height toilets; an elevated seat can always be added if necessary.

Many older people have a fear of falling, and with good reason. Osteoporosis and arthritis may have reduced their bone density and weakened their joints. The weakness may not be bilateral; older people typically are stronger on one side than the other. Unilateral weakness must be accommodated by grab bars on both sides of the toilet and handrails on both sides of the corridors. Handrails should be flat, not round, so the user can slide along using the forearm. A flat oval shape also increases grip strength (see Details on page 254).

The grab bars required by the ADA seldom meet the needs of older people. Although people with reduced strength often prefer grab bars on both sides of the toilet (see Figure 5-4), people using wheelchairs, walk-

Figure 5-4 Fold-down grab bars. *Photo courtesy of Otto Bock Rehab.*

DETAILS
Grab Bars

- Grab bars, sinks, and towel bars must withstand tremendous force (250 lb./ft.), including bending, shear, and tensile forces.[26] To help meet this standard, install grab bars with wood screws into studs, blocking, or plywood reinforcement. Molly bolts, nails, or screws into gypsum board are not adequate.
- With prefabricated showers, the blocking or plywood support for grab bars must contact the plastic over the entire reinforced area.
- Grab bars should not break or chip. They should have no sharp or abrasive edges, and they must not rotate within their fittings.
- An oval design requires less strength to grasp than a circular bar and the flat of the oval can be used to brace the forearm as well.
- A grab bar is often used by bracing the forearm between the bar and the wall for support. Install the grab bar no more than 1½ in. from the wall to prevent the entire arm from slipping through the gap.
- The color of the grab bars should contrast with the wall to ensure quick and accurate eye-hand coordination in an emergency. Chrome and metallic bars may produce reflected glare or blend in with the wall. Even better, visually integrate the grab bar into a contrasting wainscotting.
- Add fold-down grab bars on both sides of the toilet to support ambulatory users. Raise the grab bars for access from a wheelchair.
- Textured finishes are available for a sure grip.
- A transfer bar may be helpful over the bathtub; it should be installed on a ceiling trolley track or a ceiling eyebolt above the tub (with a minimum capacity of 300 lbf). The ceiling may need to be reinforced to install this bolt or track.
- Grab bars may also be necessary for transferring to a shower wheelchair. Clients whose doorway to the bathroom cannot be widened for wheelchair use may have the strength to transfer to the shower wheelchair through the doorway. In this case, grab bars should be installed on both sides of the doorway for support in transferring.
- In most showers, grab bars should be installed at a height of 33 to 36 in. on all sides, or just below elbow height. When a shower seat is wall mounted, no grab bar is needed along that wall. Shower grab bars for children should be no higher than 27 in.

ers, or assistants need one side clear for the approach. To accommodate everyone, install the grab bars required by the ADA and add swing-up assistance bars. These are wall mounted on both sides of the toilet (see Details above).

Edward Seinfeld has conducted interesting research on the needs of older people with disabilities.[27] He makes a case for a larger turning

- A vertical grab bar at the entrance to the shower may be desirable for a standing user. Vertical grab bars must not conflict with horizontal grab bars for wheelchair use.

- For the easiest approach to the toilet, grab bars should be located behind the toilet and on one side. Install them at a height of 33 to 36 in., depending on the user. The bars should be long enough to allow unobstructed movement.

- People with strength differences prefer grab bars on both sides of the toilet, and people in wheelchairs need one side clear for the approach. A swing-up assistance bar can meet both of these needs.

Integrated vertical grab bar. *Courtesy of HEWI, Inc.*

radius for older people in wheelchairs, up to 60 in. wide by 72 in. deep. He recommends resting places every 100 ft. on the accessible route and an optimal slope of 1:20, even on ramps (see Details on page 254). In addition, he recommends increasing corridor widths to 48 in. with doors swinging out of the corridor and 60 in. with doors swinging in. Doors to bathrooms should swing out and, in a typical 60 in. by 90 in. bathroom, the door should be on the long wall. In-swinging doors should have 24 in. of clearance on the latch side, not the minimum of 18 in. required by most codes and standards. Grab bar placement significantly varies by user; reinforce all walls to allow grab bars to be located for individual needs.

Older people frequently lean on furniture for support. Heavy furniture can be planned, and each bed should have a footboard at 33–36 in. a.f.f. for support (see Details on page 225). Although many older people can use a shorter bed, dormitory beds should not be specified. Patients may fall out of them, as they are about 3 in. narrower than twin beds.

Other Sensory Issues

Incontinence may be induced by long travel distances to the bathroom or by an inability to see the bathroom door. Subacute care facilities should generally increase the number of public bathrooms required, raise bathroom lighting levels, and maintain a clear path to each toilet (see Details on pages 166, 167, and 168). Carpeting may also reduce incontinence. Experiential research indicates that cold, hard-surfaced flooring may actually trigger the urge to go to the bathroom. Preliminary research substantiates that carpet may be maintained successfully in patient bedrooms and bathrooms of incontinent patients (see Research Abstract on page 23).

As we age, we may experience reduced senses of taste and smell as well as a loss of sensitivity to pain and temperature. Again, *Beautiful Universal Design*[28] is filled with ideas to accommodate these changes. For example, a pressure balancing mix valve in the shower can prevent surges of hot water that can easily burn a person with reduced sensitivity to temperature, reduced circulation, and reduced reaction time. Many older people experience all of these changes. In the bath, a temperature control can also prevent burns.

DESIGN OF REHABILITATION FACILITIES

Rehabilitation focuses on physical impairments as well psychological dysfunctions like stroke, head injury, cognition, and perception. But it goes beyond mere restoration of physical and mental function to the application of this function to the activities of daily living (ADLs).

The key to design for rehabilitation is patient motivation; the facility must provide the incentive for a patient to get out of bed every day, sometimes for months at a stretch, and endure painful and possibly embarrassing therapy. Although most inpatient rehabilitation is completed within three to six weeks, it may involve tedious and repetitious activity for months on end, perhaps playing the same games with the same therapist at the same time every day.

One unique model, Independence Square, features a large variety of training modules while providing rehabilitation therapists with an assessment tool, a real-life environment in which efficacy can be determined before discharge (see Figure 5-5). Patients gain confidence in their skills and lose their fear of returning to work and home. They also learn to accept their limitations. Patients relearn everything from climbing stairs and ramps to banking.

This rehabilitative environment offers modules including a grocery store in which the therapist can assess the patient's ability to read and

Figure 5-5 Rehabilitation modules. *Courtesy of Guynes Design Inc.*

recognize prices, count change, and stay within a budget. Patients also relearn to ring doorbells, retrieve mail, and use door hardware (see Details on page 70). In addition, patients learn to traverse a variety of floor surfaces, including brick, turf, stone, and broken concrete. They practice getting in and out of a car, operating a parking meter and gas pump, and walking through a crossing with a timed traffic signal.

The many disciplines in the field of rehabilitation medicine include physical therapy, occupational therapy, speech therapy, therapeutic recreation, physiatry, neuropsychiatry, and social work. Most of today's facilities are premised on a multidisciplinary rehabilitation philosophy. The physical plant features shared space in which turf battles must be minimized and patient care can be maximized.

Psychiatric Rehabilitation

Chapter 11 offers a comprehensive discussion of designing for mental health, but a more universal approach may be necessary in rehabilitation centers treating patients with multiple impairments. Patients in need of psychiatric rehabilitation may use wheelchairs, canes, and crutches. The patients may express their anger by abusing the facility, banging these

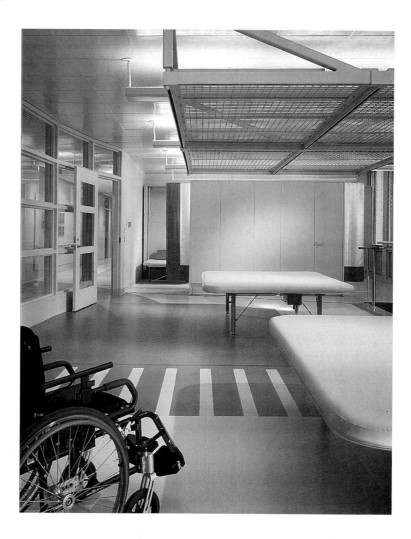

Figure 5-6 Indirect lighting above treatment space. *Courtesy of Rehabilitation Institute of Chicago. Interior Architecture and Design: Eva Maddox Associates, Inc., 300 W. Hubbard, Suite 300, Chicago, IL 60610; 312/670-0092. Photography: Steve Hall, Hedrich Blessing.*

devices against the walls. Flame-retardant wall fabric provides some protection from assistive devices. Use a Velcro-compatible finish to allow patients and their families to personalize their space without damaging the walls. Wall fabrics also offer some acoustical control of low-frequency noise. The texture is helpful to people who occasionally lean on a wall for support.

Physical Therapy

Much of physical therapy is performed on mats with patients staring at the ceiling. Indirect lighting is important (see Figure 5-6). Interesting ceiling detail should also be considered. Unfortunately, physical therapy areas are often the most institutionally designed spaces in the facility.

These areas could easily be planned to resemble an executive health club or spa (see Chapter 8). The spa atmosphere can boost morale for

both patients and staff. Physical therapy may include a hydrotherapy room, which can be treated as a Roman bath. Hydrotherapy is used for exercise as well as stimulation of circulation.

A fitness center or gym may be employed by physical therapists to restore function to patients' major muscle groups. Physical therapy involves a wide variety of equipment, some rather frightening in appearance. Some pieces are very large—apparatus for gait and motion analysis, for example—and storage is always at a premium. It is important to keep such equipment out of sight when not in use, and to isolate treatment areas where patients could be in pain.

Recreation therapy space is often combined with physical therapy, increasing the storage needs. Music, games, and exercise equipment are used to support physical and mental therapeutic goals.

Occupational Therapy

The primary goal of occupational therapy is to restore fine motor skills rather than the gross motor skills that are the focus of physical therapy. Occupational therapy may include driver evaluation and training, hand rehabilitation, and a bracing and prosthetics lab. Space needs vary significantly depending on the scope of services.

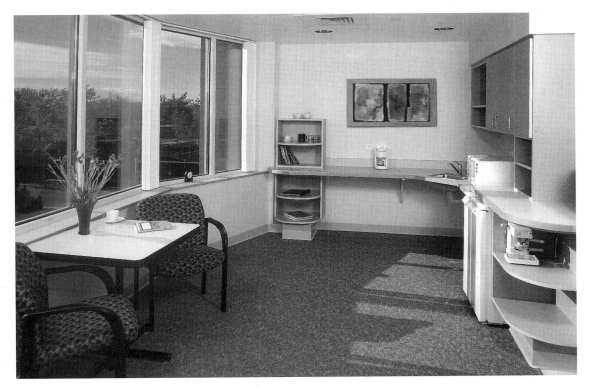

Figure 5-7 ADL apartment. *Courtesy of Dean Birinyi, photographer. Designer: H + L Architecture Ltd., AIA.*

DETAILS
Universal Kitchen Cabinets

- Plan removable base cabinets with an adjustable counter. Each cabinet can be designed as a freestanding unit that is totally removable, as a unit that folds up in place, or as a unit with a removable front and base.

- Base cabinets should be a maximum of 27 in. in height to allow the counter to be lowered for seated users.

- Install upper cabinets on heavy-duty commercial shelf brackets between counter height and the high reach limit of users. Cabinets that lower with the push of a button are also appropriate.

- An open shelf between a cabinet and the counter increases reachable storage space.

- Organize storage by activity—for example, keep the coffee, coffeepot, and filters in the same area. Use high cabinets to store seasonal items and seldom-used equipment.

- Use clear plastic shelves or metal racks in upper cabinets to allow easy viewing by children, shorter people, or those in wheelchairs.

- Lazy Susans or slide-out rotary shelves also improve access. Half-circled pull-out shelves are particularly useful in corners.

- Roll-out shelves must have rims to keep objects from sliding off.

- Removable bins offer access and flexibility on any shelf. Bins and heavy objects slide more easily on smooth surfaces.

- Drawers should be equipped with full-extension roller-type slides, which allow access to deep storage. Pull-out drawers should have one side lowered to allow access from a seated position.

- Cabinets with handles should have extra-long C-pulls. Mount handles vertically on upper cabinets as close to the bottom of the doors as possible. On base cabinets, mount the pulls near the top edge of the cabinet doors.

One of the most popular occupational therapy environments is the ADL apartment (see Figure 5-7), which can be used for training the patient as well as the entire family. It is sometimes used for transitional living between the hospital and home. An activity kitchen is planned with lowered counters so patients may cook while sitting (see Details above and on pages 95, 96, and 97). A large bathroom is provided for training as well (see Research Abstract on page 101). Increasingly, these apartments offer a wide variety of electronic choices, including environmental control systems (see Details on page 97) with accessible controls for all users (see Details on pages 98 and 99).

DETAILS
Universal Kitchen Counters

- People in wheelchairs, children, and shorter people are faced with an awkward angle when lifting heavy objects off and on counters. It is easier to drag a heavy pan of water, for example, along the counter. For this reason, provide a consistent counter height on each surface.

- Alter counter heights when surfaces change. For example, parallel kitchen counters could be at different heights, and a kitchen island could be at a third height.

- Counter surfaces at a variety of heights allow people of all ages, sizes, and abilities to work comfortably. Pull-out breadboards and multiple-height tables should be considered (see Details on page 222).

- Adjustable surfaces offer flexibility for people with strength and coordination differences. Counters can be mounted on recessed heavy-duty shelf standards screwed into studs or solid blocking. If only one adjustable-height counter can be installed, place it next to the refrigerator. This improves reach into the refrigerator for people in wheelchairs and minimizes the inconvenience of counters staggered at different heights. Specify a finish on adjacent counter ends and cabinets, as these are exposed when the counter is lowered.

- Tall people seem prone to lower back pain and may prefer counters up to 42 in. high to prevent bending over tasks.

- The minimum clearance required for wheelchair use under the counter is 27 in.

- A counter no more than 2 in. thick allows wheelchair users to work close to their lap, an advantage when kneading dough or performing other heavy manual work.

- The ideal height for a standing user to perform heavy manual work is about 10 in. below elbow height.[29] Writing and light work can best be done on a work surface 1 to 3 in. below elbow height when standing.

- If the counter has a skirt board, recess it a minimum of 12 in. from the front edge to accommodate a wheelchair user.

- Specify a heat-resistant counter next to the cooktop to prevent burn marks when pans are dragged across it. Ceramic tile does not burn, but it is more difficult to slide pans over tile joints than over a smooth surface. Smooth, heat-resistant solid-surface counters are available for this purpose. Surface burns, scratches, and cuts can be removed from solid-surface counters with a light sanding. These tops are also preferable for people who are allergic to laminate tops adhered to chemically offensive substrates.

- Corners are often difficult to reach from a wheelchair. An L-shaped counter design has only one corner, but a person who uses the counter for support may have trouble leaning into it. Add a straightedge to the corner of the kitchen counter for better support and more workspace.

- Because people in wheelchairs must rest their arms on the edge of the counter while working, bevel or round the edge for comfort. This also protects those who may fall against the counter.

- Elevated rolled edges prevent spills but make it difficult to work directly on the counter from a wheelchair. Rolling out a pie crust, for example, is almost impossible on an elevated edge. Slope the counter slightly to drain toward the sink. This slope also helps people slide heavy pots from the work area to the sink.

- Add a rail to the edge of the counter as a safety feature, as many accidents occur in the kitchen. The rail also protects the surface from chipping and can be used by wheelchair users to pull up to the counter.

DETAILS
Universal Controls

- Switches can be accompanied by warning lights to show that appliances are on. Redundant cuing like this makes controls more noticeable by all people.
- Controls should be large and easy to read.
- Specify push bars rather than pull-out buttons, touch controls rather than dials, and controls that can be operated with the palms up rather than down. Test controls to see if they can be operated with a closed fist.
- Where greatest accuracy is required, hand and arm motion should be applied rather than foot and leg movements. The hand should be held close to the body at approximately elbow level to maximize accuracy when using a control, for example. Locate controls accordingly.
- Avoid controls that can be activated accidentally. Although touch controls are the easiest to use, they are also easiest to turn on by accident. Remember that touch controls can also be easily used by children.
- Specify controls that do not require sustained effort. Some push-type faucets, for example, require sustained holding to operate. Also, keep in mind that it is easier to operate controls in front of the body rather than at the side.

DETAILS
Universal Faucets

- Faucets with a single lever can be operated with one hand. Paddles, blades, and push-type mechanisms are easier to use than knobs. To eliminate controls install faucets that incorporate an infrared sensor to control water flow.
- A gooseneck faucet can be used to fill a pan on the counter without lifting the pan into the sink. One innovative faucet design combines a gooseneck style with a pull-out spray on a retractable hose. Both the faucet and the spray can be installed in an existing sink with a single hole.
- Faucet controls should be located uniformly on all sinks throughout the home to prevent accidental scalding. Hot water taps are normally on the left, cold on the right. Red and blue color coding can be used to differentiate hot and cold taps respectively.

DETAILS 16
Universal Sinks

- Adjustable-height sinks are available in prefabricated models. When customizing an installation, simply change the tailpiece to alter the height. To do so, a flexible supply line must be in place and the trap must be low enough to receive the tailpiece at the lowest position of the sink.

- One sink should be no deeper than 6½ in. From a seated position, the user should be able to place one hand flat on the bottom of the sink. A removable rack can be used to improve reach on deeper sinks.

- If the counter is not adjustable in height, consider installing two sinks in the kitchen. If the cook is standing with arms relaxed, the bottom of the sink should be 2 in. higher than wrist height. For children and seated users, add a bar sink on a lowered counter.

- Specify sinks with the drain to the back and to one side so that connecting pipes are either to the left or right, not in the center, allowing a closer approach from a wheelchair. With a double sink, only one side needs to be accessible.

- It is easier to ease pots and pans out of a sink with a slightly angled side.

- A stainless-steel sink must be insulated to prevent leg burns. Stainless steel is thinner and allows a bit more knee clearance than porcelain, and it does not chip, an advantage for people with differences in coordination.

- Insulate exposed pipes to prevent burns, or add a nonmetallic panel that can be removed for maintenance. The cover also keeps the pipes out of sight.

DETAILS
Environmental Control Systems

- Remote control devices can be used to accommodate a wide variety of abilities. Almost any switch can be changed to a remote control with a transmitter and receiver. Some transmitters are sonic and do not require a battery; others are operated by touch. Some systems do not require manual control but can be operated simply by puffing into the switch or by inhaling or "sipping." When units are operated with a puff-sip switch, tongue switch, rocking lever, communication aid, or small computer, add separate manual controls for use by a guest or aide.

- A series of tabletop rocker switches can serve as a less expensive version of an environmental control system. These units are often used to control a lamp, air conditioner, television, radio, and small intercom. The multiple cords associated with this system, however, are a tripping hazard for many people and difficult for people using mobility aids

Continued

DETAILS
Environmental Control Systems (*continued*)

- Environmental control systems operate many devices, including aide alerts, tape recorders, page turners, televisions, electric beds, lights, and drapery controls. Remote power door openers, for example, can be used in conjunction with bedside environmental controls to let pets in and out of the house and to control lighting.
- Computer-driven systems can run security checks and lower interior temperatures when a room is not in use.
- Specialized devices are available for people with differences in hearing or speech. Examples include text telephones and computers that communicate by telephone. Closed-captioned television provides both audible and written cues, and earphones allow amplification without disturbing others. For people with reduced hearing, doorbells and alarms should be selected in frequencies under 10,000 Hz[22] or wired to vary the level of light in the house.

DETAILS
Electrical Switches

- Locate light switches at the height of the door lever (36 in. for use by people in wheelchairs and by most small children).[30]
- In bedrooms, consider a lighted switch that can act as a beacon in the dark.
- People with differences in sight appreciate rheostats on each switch to control the quantity of light in the room. A rheostat is also helpful for task lighting. For example, it may be necessary to increase lighting over the kitchen sink or in other areas where detailed work takes place.
- Thermostats featuring braille and high-contrast numbers are useful for people with vision differences. Controls that click audibly between settings can be helpful.
- Make sure the main switch box is installed in an accessible area. If the switch box location is not well lighted, attach a magnetic flashlight to the box. Use circuit breakers rather than fuses, which may be more difficult for people with arthritis to handle. Label all circuits and keep the top of the box at a reachable height (54 in.) for a side approach in a wheelchair.
- Wall-mount kitchen fan controls or install a fan on the counter, placing controls within reach.
- Wall-mount the switch for the bathroom light outside the bathroom. It is always helpful to have lighting before negotiating a confined space.
- Specify palm toggle switches, which can be operated with the elbow or a closed fist. Pressure- or rocker-type switches are easier to operate than conventional toggle switches.
- Projecting switch plates are easier to locate in areas with reduced lighting. Self-illuminated trim for switches and levers is also helpful and should be installed at bedroom, bathroom, and entry doors. Color contrast between the plate and the wall makes the switch easier to see. Contrast between the switch and the plate is also helpful.

DETAILS
Receptacle Outlets

- People in wheelchairs and others with mobility problems may have difficulty bending; electric cords on the floor, then, cannot be retrieved easily. Cup hooks next to an outlet can be a temporary solution to the problem, but a face plate that holds an unplugged cord is better.
- Extension cords can pose a tripping hazard and can become entangled in wheelchairs. To eliminate cords, add receptacle outlets to the floor plan after considering furniture, appliance, and lamp placement.
- Determine whether or not additional outlets are needed in the bedroom for medical appliances, communication systems, alarms, and so on.
- An outlet above an exterior door allows a call light or alarm to be added later. A crucial call system should have a backup battery source in addition to the primary power source.
- Electrical outlets must be accessible; a height of 15 in. is preferable.[31]
- In the kitchen, locate multiple outlets on the front of the counter for easiest reach. Some appliances may be served by an outlet under the counter. For example, a mixer could be stored under the counter on a pop-up shelf.

Specialized Services

Rehabilitation units provide specialized services including vocational, social, and neurodiagnostic services. In addition, pain management therapy is often offered, and speech and hearing therapy is provided to increase skills as well as cognition and perception.

One of the newest, most profitable health-care markets is therapy for work hardening (see Figure 5-8). This type of rehabilitation is increasingly needed to return injured workers to the job. Work-hardening therapy stations may include plumbing and electrical simulations, range-of-motion therapy, and a series of shelves to evaluate reach and lifting ability. Services are often offered on an outpatient basis, perhaps in a shopping center. Families may be given pagers and encouraged to wander freely while patients receive treatment. In the past, these services were typically located in the basement of a hospital, a discouraging and inconvenient location for many patients and their families.

As health care becomes more portable, rehabilitation is increasingly offered at home. Emphasis on patient warehousing or maintenance is decreasing, and the inpatient rehabilitation length of stay has been reduced. Those remaining in hospitals tend to have higher levels of need, like patients with quadriplegia or head injury.

Figure 5-8 Reception area for occupational rehabilitation. *Courtesy of Rehabilitation Institute of Chicago. Interior Architecture and Design: Eva Maddox Associates, Inc., 300 W. Hubbard, Suite 300, Chicago, IL 60610; 312/670-0092. Photography: Steve Hall, Hedrich Blessing.*

Design goals for head injury include heightened patient safety, prevention of agitation, and progress toward social integration.[32] Initially, a private room is required, preferably with a gurney-accessible bath. The private room can also be used for sexual training and conjugal visits. The patient room should be located in a quiet area with minimal hospital traffic. Noise should be limited; personal pagers can replace the overhead system.

As the patient progresses, a shared room may be desirable. Patients and their families often learn from one another and increase their social skills when sharing a room.

Because of their extended length of stay, head injured patients have greater storage needs than others do (see Research Abstract on page 229). Space should be provided for storage of a power wheelchair and ventilation must be considered for recharging it. Furniture in patient rooms should be movable to allow the option of adding a Craig bed, a mattress with padded vertical sides designed by Alice Hildebrand (the proud author's mother). This reduces external stimuli and often eliminates the need for restraints.

RESEARCH ABSTRACT
Kohler Demonstration Project[33]

In June 1998, a universal bathroom exhibit was completed at the Kohler Design Center. Designed by Cynthia Leibrock and Mary Beth Rampola, It offers hands-on universal design training to 150,000 participants each year. The universal bathroom addresses a lifetime of needs, the future of each visitor to the Kohler Design Center as well as the future of interior design and architecture. It responds to the diversity of our population and our changing needs in each season of life.

When we design for the average user, we accommodate only a few people well. Universal design acknowledges that one size does not fit all and that a bathroom must meet the needs of children, people who are tall, wheelchair users, and adults of shorter stature. It must accommodate people who use an assistant, a walker, a scooter, or a stroller. It addresses changes in hearing and vision and, compared to standard bathrooms offers older people increased lighting levels, lower ambient noise levels, ergonomically designed products, and safety features that accommodate reduced reaction times. Most important, the universally designed bathroom prevents institutionalization by facilitating home health care and aging in place.

The exhibit demonstrates that universal design is also invisible, never stigmatizing its users or pointing out their physical differences. Listed below are features that were visually integrated into the design:

1. *Turnaround space: (shown by a graphic in the floor).* A 60- by 60-in. turn-around space provides enough room to maneuver with strollers, scooters, crutches, canes, walkers, and guide dogs.

2. *Transfer space.* Clear floor space adjacent to the toilet allows parents room to help children. Attendants use the space to help older family members, and people in wheelchairs use the space to transfer to the water closet.

3. *Lavatory area.* The lavatory and mirror are installed outside of the shower area to keep the mirror from fogging or being sprayed by the handheld shower. For children in wheelchairs, a 36- by 48-in. clear floor space extends under the lavatory. Children have less coordination and actually need more room to maneuver than do adults, who need only a 30- by 48-in. clear floor space. A vanity stool can be used in this space by ambulatory family members who prefer to sit while using the lavatory. A lightweight stool on legs with glides is more stable than a stool on casters.

4. *Adjustable-height lavatory.* With this installation, the counter can be adjusted between 25 in. and 42 in. a.f.f. to meet the needs of tall users, adults of shorter stature, children, and seated users. The flexible waste and supply pipes are positioned to prevent burns. No sharp or abrasive surfaces that could injure a seated user project below the lavatory. Clearance for wheelchair footrests extends the full depth of the lavatory. For people with allergies or chemical sensitivities, solid-surface vanity tops are preferable to laminates adhered to pressboard or particle board, which may offgas formaldehyde. The horizontal finishes were chosen in light colors to

Continued

increase ambient light levels, thereby improving visual acuity. For people with vision differences, the edge of the lavatory area is identified by a handrail. The handrail also provides support for standing users, a grip for people repositioning a wheelchair, and a place to hang towels.

Kohler universal bathroom. *Photo courtesy of Kohler Co. Designers: Cynthia Leibrock, Easy Access, and Mary Beth Rampola, Eva Maddox Assoc.*

5. *Lavatory controls.* The levers can be easily controlled with one hand. They are cued with large markings in red and blue to identify water temperature. Aerating nozzles on taps reduce ambient noise levels; water pressure can be reduced to further quiet the flow. Quieter faucets serve people with a wide range of hearing abilities. People with speech differences who need to be clearly heard and people with reduced vision who depend on their sense of hearing also appreciate lower ambient noise levels.

6. *Mirrors.* The mirror, at 40 in. a.f.f., can be used by a seated user or an adult of shorter stature. A tilted mirror should not be specified because it distorts the image of the user.

7. *Removable cabinets.* Each cabinet under the counter is designed as a totally removable freestanding unit. Removable cabinets make the home easier to sell by offering access to a wider market, including people who use mobility aids. A movable cabinet under the sink can serve as a cart between the counter and tub or toilet, perhaps to store equipment for the bowel and bladder program. When the cabinet is moved out, the space under the counter is clear for seated users and the top of the cart can serve as extra counter space. The cabinet has locking casters and a top rail to prevent items from sliding off. Dividers are added to the cabinet for people who are blind, who are helped by having specific places to put each item. Each storage area is labeled so sighted people can put things back correctly. Medications are stored in a locked drawer that is within reach of wheelchair users but not accessible to children. On all drawers, C-grip handles are horizontal and centered.

8. *Toilet and shower grab bars.* Grab bars are installed at 33–36 in. a.f.f. on all sides of the roll-in shower. For the easiest approach to the toilet, grab bars are located behind it and on one side. The grab bars will not chip or injure users with sharp or abrasive edges. They do not rotate within their fittings. A textured finish is applied for a sure grip.

9. *Bathtub grab bars.* A grab bar is often used by bracing the forearm between the bar and the wall for support. For this reason, install the grab bar exactly 1½ in. from the wall to prevent the entire arm from slipping through the gap. One horizontal grab bar is installed at the foot of the tub when a tub seat is used at the head. Two horizontal grab bars are placed on the long wall, one 9 in. above the tub and the other 34 in. a.f.f.

10. *Shelving.* Upper shelves are of tempered glass or clear plastic to make the contents more visible by children, wheelchair users, and adults of shorter stature. Four heights of hooks are installed adjacent to the shelves.

11. *Accessible shower.* A shower is quicker, easier, and safer to use than a bathtub (see Details on pages 165 and 227). This shower can be used from a shower wheelchair or by a standing user. The corner shower is open on two sides to allow access from more than one direction. The wheel-in shower floor is sloped rather than curbed, as a curb may block wheels or become a tripping hazard. A 2 percent slope to the drain is sufficient; a steeper slope makes it too difficult to maneuver a shower wheelchair or gurney. The many joints of the ceramic mosaic floor tile reduce slippage.

12. *Shower control.* The shower system features temperature and surge controls that ensure a safe flow. The water can be set so that it will not burn a child if the control accidentally bumped. The pressure-balancing feature prevents a surge of hot water that could burn a person with sensation limitations.

Continued

RESEARCH ABSTRACT
Kohler Demonstration Project (continued)

13. *Handheld shower adjacent to the toilet.* The fixture is ideal for use from a shower wheelchair or for cleanup after using the toilet. It can also be clipped to an adjustable-height bracket for use as a conventional shower by a tall standing user, person of shorter stature, or child. The vertical adjustment does not obstruct the grab bars. The valve will not catch the shower hose and requires only one hand to regulate water flow and set the desired temperature.

14. *Towel bars* are offered in four heights and should be reinforced to withstand emergency use as grab bars. Bathroom walls should be reinforced from floor to ceiling with ¾-in. plywood or with wood blocking installed between the studs.

15. *Shower wheelchair.* After one transfer to a shower wheelchair, the user can roll into the shower, under the lavatory, or over a toilet. Multiple transfers to a seat in the shower or to the water closet are not required. With the wheels locked over the toilet, the chair can also be used by a standing person with strength limitations who needs an elevated toilet seat with arms. There is a gap between the two seats and an opening in the front for digital manipulation or for emptying a leg bag. Shower wheelchair storage is also discreetly provided.

16. *Shower curtain.* The shower is planned with curtains rather than doors, which take up floor space. Ceiling-mounted shower curtains have a clean appearance, especially when they curve around two sides of the shower.

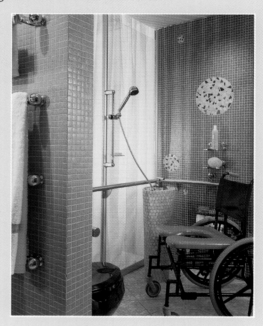

Photo courtesy of Kohler Co. Designers: Cynthia Leibrock, Easy Access, and Mary Beth Rampola, Eva Maddox Assoc.

17. *Shower caddy:* To prevent soap, shampoo, and accessories from slipping out of reach, a shower caddy is used. It drains easily and will not rust. A second caddie is installed at a height suitable for children or people of shorter stature.

18. *Bathtub.* The bathtub has a gently sloping flat (not rounded) bottom for stability. The floor of the tub is slip resistant. The handles can be grasped for entry or exit. The color contrasts with the surroundings to improve visual acuity, and the vertical stripe visually bends at the surface of the water to assist people with vision limitations.

19. *Bathtub controls.* The lever-type faucet and drain control are easy to operate. Controls are installed toward the approach side.

20. *Bathtub seat.* A soak in the bathtub relieves pain for many people, but standard bathtub design can make entry and exit difficult. For this reason, a seat is installed at wheelchair seat height, but a standing user can also transfer from it. The edge of the seat is installed flush with the top of the tub; this makes it easy to slide slowly into the tub from the seat with the help of the adjacent grab bars.

21. *Handheld shower adjacent to the tub.* This shower can be used from the seat for a quick cleanup, to help shave legs and wash hair, and by people who do not have the strength to lower themselves into the tub. It can assist all bathers with washing and rinsing, and can be used to bathe a child in a child seat or on a bathing table.

Photo courtesy of Kohler Co. Designers: Cynthia Leibrock, Easy Access, and Mary Beth Rampola, Eva Maddox Assoc.

22. *Toilet.* An elongated toilet installed at a 17-in. height makes transferring or aligning with the shower wheelchair easier than other toilet types. A wheelchair user can also transfer directly at this height, and the flush lever is on the approach side. The quiet toilet serves people with a wide range of hearing abilities. People with speech differences who need to be clearly heard and people with reduced vision who depend on their sense of hearing also appreciate lower ambient noise levels. For a quiet water flow, specify pipes with as large a cross section as possible.

23. *Toilet seat.* The flat lid is more comfortable to lean against than one that is crowned or dished. The toilet seat is securely installed, but it can always be replaced by an elevated seat if necessary. The seat must not be sprung to return to a lifted position, but it should remain up independently when raised. Men with hemiplegia or one hand only do not have a free hand to hold up the toilet seat while using the toilet.

24. *Toilet tissue dispenser.* One dispenser is installed at least 19 in. a.f.f. and yet low enough so that grab bars do not interfere with its use. It is installed 7 in. in front of the toilet. The toilet tissue holder must permit continuous paper flow and be usable with one hand. Dispensers that require users to reach into a hole to initiate paper flow must be avoided, and no dispenser should have a sharp or serrated edge. A second tissue dispenser is provided for a constant supply and lowered for use by children (2 to 6 in. above the toilet seat). The cover protects the tissue from the handheld shower.

Other design considerations for people with head injury include exit control (see Chapter 2) and wayfinding. Therapy space should be located close to the patient room to reduce confusion. Avoid multipurpose space; keep areas clearly defined for such activities as games, reading, and dining (see Figure 5-9). Limit wayfinding cues to simple geometric shapes and recognizable symbols (see Figure 5-10) These are more easily identifiable by patients with brain injuries.[34] Subtle patterns and muted color reduce anxiety and stimulation.

Figure 5-9 Dining room with view of nature. *Courtesy of James Wilson, Photographer; The Office of James Burnett, Designer.*

Figure 5-10 Geometric shapes used in wayfinding. *Courtesy of Rehabilitation Institute of Chicago. Interior Architecture and Design: Eva Maddox Associates, Inc., 300 W. Hubbard, Suite 300, Chicago, IL 60610; 312/670-0092. Photography: Steve Hall, Hedrich Blessing.*

REFERENCES

1. Martin S. Valins and Derek Salter, eds., *Futurecare* (London: Blackwell Science, 1996): 11.
2. S. DiMotta, B. Dubey, D. Hoglund, and C. Kershner, "Long-Term Care Design: Blazing New Territory—Code Reform and Beyond," *Journal of Healthcare Design* 5 (1993): 198.
3. Janet Reizenstein Carpman, Myron A. Grant, and Deborah A. Simmons, *Design That Cares* (Chicago: American Hospital Publishing, 1986): 228.
4. Robert J. Kobet, "Allergies in Architecture" (paper presented at the regional conference of the American Association of Otolaryngologic Allergists, San Antonio, Tex., 18 May 1987).
5. Elizabeth Brawley, *Designing for Alzheimer's Disease: Strategies for Creating Better Care Environments* (New York: John Wiley and Sons, 1997): 192.
6. Lorraine G. Hiatt. "Breakthroughs in Long-Term Care Design," Journal of Health Care Interior Design 3 (1991): 206.
7. Lorraine G. Hiatt, "Long-Term Care Facilities," *Journal of Health Care Interior Design* 2 (1990): 199.
8. Hiatt, "Breakthroughs in Long-Term Care Design," 206.
9. Hiatt, "Breakthroughs in Long-Term Care Design," 208.
10. B. Colby, *Color and Light: Influences and Impact* (Glendale, Calif.: Chroma Productions, 1990): 15–16.
11. Millicent Gappell, "Hospice Facilities," *Journal of Health Care Interior Design* 2 (1990): 78–79.
12. Lorraine G. Hiatt, "The Color and Use of Color in Environments for Older People," *Nursing Homes* 30, no. 3 (1981): 18–22.
13. Hiatt, "Long-Term Care Facilities," 200.
14. Deborah Allen Carey, *Hospice Inpatient Environments* (New York: John Wiley and Sons, 1986): 223.
15. Leon A. Pastalan, *Aging and Human Visual Function* (New York: Alan R. Liss, 1982): 324.
16. Gary Coates and Susanne Siepl-Coates, "Vidarkliniken," *The Healthcare Forum Journal* (September/October 1992): 27–29.
17. Hiatt, "Long-Term Care Facilities," 200.
18. Carpman, Grant, and Simmons, *Design that Cares,* 228.
19. Walter B. Kleeman, *The Challenge of Interior Design* (Boston: CBI Publishing, 1981): 76.
20. Robert J. Kobet, "The Tight House Syndrome: Causes and Cures" (paper presented at the American Society of Interior Designers National Conference, Washington, D.C., August 1988).
21. *Americans with Disabilities Act Accessibility Standards,* 1991, 4.4.1.
22. L. Trent, "On the Importance of Color," *Interiors and Sources* (September 1994): 48–49.
23. Walter B. Kleeman, *The Challenge of Interior Design* (Boston: CBI Publishing, 1981): 79.
24. J. Streim and I. Katz, "Treating Depression," *Provider* (May 1994).
25. Cynthia Leibrock and James Evan Terry, *Beautiful Universal Design* (New York: John Wiley and Sons, 1999).
26. *ADA Standards,* 4.26.3 (1).
27. V. Regnier and J. Pynoos, eds., *Housing the Aged: Design Directives and Policy Considerations* (New York: Elsevier, 1987): 321–328.
28. Leibrock and Terry, *Beautiful Universal Design.*
29. ADA Standards, A4.32.4.

30. Evan Terry Associates, *ADA Facilities Compliance Notebook Supplement* (New York: John Wiley and Sons, 1995).
31. *ADA Standards,* 4.27.3.
32. Sara O. Marberry, ed., *Innovations in Healthcare Design* (New York: John Wiley and Sons, 1995): 108.
33. Cynthia Leibrock and Mary Beth Rampola, *Universal Design Form #170390-AA* (Kohler, Wis.: The Kohler Company, 1998).
34. Jain Malkin, *Hospital Interior Architecture* (New York: John Wiley and Sons, 1992): 201.

P A R T

T W O

AMBULATORY CARE

HEALTH CARE COST CONTAINMENT

The United States spends more dollars per capita on health care than any other industrialized country. In spite of this, the U.S. is at the bottom of a comparison of health care quality among ten western industrialized nations. Sweden, the Netherlands, and Canada scored the highest. In 1996, the United states was 19th in longevity for women and 22nd for men. In a comparison of 29 countries, we were 24th in infant mortality.[1] Two of the major reasons are that these governments make preventive health care services available to all families, and self-care is encouraged in ambulatory settings. Home health care represents the single greatest opportunity to control health care costs while preserving the quality of care and actually enhancing patients' quality of life. This care is not possible without ambulatory facilities to support it.

More than 90 percent of European citizens take advantage of preventive services. On the other hand, U.S. preschoolers are immunized much less frequently than Europeans.[2] In Europe, most day care is free, and pregnancy and child-rearing leaves are longer than those in the United States even though Europeans spend a smaller percentage of their gross national product (GNP) on health care.

As a cost savings measure, much emergency care in the United States could be replaced by primary care in medical offices. In one year, Americans made 90 million visits to hospital emergency departments.[3] Is it possible that nearly a third of us really needed to go to emergency rooms in one year? Too many people get routine medical care in the emergency room. Because of this overload, emergency care has deteriorated in quality and increased in cost. The problem is complicated by a shortage of nurses, which results in longer waiting periods for patients.

Reimbursement policies are currently reducing the demand for acute care in hospitals and nursing homes and increasing the demand for ambulatory care. Close to 1000 U.S. hospitals have closed in the since 1987,[4] and length of stay in the remaining hospitals is steadily decreasing. Hospitals treat only the most acute cases, with all other patients receiving services on an outpatient basis. In 1965, only 489 medical groups in the United States provided ambulatory services. That number expanded to 16,500 in just 30 years.[5] The hospital is rapidly becoming a small component of the health care delivery system; ambulatory care is the major player.

Consequently, capital investment has shifted into ambulatory care and nonacute facilities.[6] Design opportunities have expanded on the continuum of care; subacute, assisted living, and short-stay ambulatory centers have increased in popularity. Patients are often referred to distant locations; convenience is therefore becoming a major issue. Overall, ambulatory care is growing more complex. Outpatient care is being offered in hospital-based ambulatory care centers, freestanding centers, and on health campuses. Approximately 80 to 85 percent of all surgeries are being done on an outpatient basis.[7]

Ambulatory patients are no longer the "worried well." Sometimes their acuity levels require monitoring and crisis intervention. To accommodate increased acuity, a proliferation of technology in the ambulatory setting is producing massive amounts of patient and administrative information. Clinical systems, automated medical records, and reference information must all be managed. Building codes and regulatory codes are becoming stricter and consumers more demanding.

The successful ambulatory care facility is designed to fit the characteristics of the consumer population.[8] Although the facility must meet the needs of the patient and family, it must also be designed to accommodate the risk group to which they belong—inner city or rural, young or old, mostly well or acutely ill.

Most of our health care system is bimodal, serving primarily sick newborns and the terminally ill. Comparatively little money is spent on other age groups. Our system must change to follow the entire disease cycle, not just the acute episodes of the very young and the very old. This change will be driven by the onset of chronic disease in baby boomers as they move from mature adult status to the Medicare age group. Boomers will live for decades with chronic diseases before they become "elderly." These illnesses will often be diagnosed and treated on an outpatient basis, and boomers will increasingly depend on their family as caregivers. With this emphasis on ambulatory care, we will see an increase in self-health, personal lifestyle training, and education of consumers.

THE MISSING COMPONENT: THE EDUCATED CONSUMER

A growing movement in the United States encourages patients to take responsibility for their own health care. Prevention and wellness plans are everywhere. Our system is becoming dependent on educated patients making responsible choices.

One health-care facility has demonstrated the power of education. Stevens Square patients began by learning a list of acclamations offered by the American Psychological Association.

1. We are responsible for our own health.
2. Illness is a communication from within.
3. Most healing comes from within.
4. Treatment must involve body, mind, and spirit.
5. The caregiver is a consultant, not a miracle worker or an authority figure.
6. Our positive attitude, along with a personalized, caring staff, is essential to change and healing.
7. Our physical and social environments greatly affect health.
8. Nutrition and exercise are the cornerstones of good health.
9. We are uniquely individual and services should be individually tailored with maximum choice.[9]

These acclamations encourage wellness rather than illness and reward preventive behaviors rather than giving love and attention only to those who complain of illness. Stevens Square used a three-part program to implement this philosophy: the teaching of self-responsibility, the development of community instead of isolation, and patient involvement with meaningful activity.

When patients take responsibility for their own health, wellness increases and the pressure on staff is reduced. The Stevens Square wellness program reduced long-term care patient hospital days from 568 per year to 161 per year. In addition, the average length of stay of staff increased from 16.1 months to 63.43 months over a six year period.

The leader of the movement to return responsibility to the educated health-care consumer is the Planetree Project of Derby, Connecticut. Through this project, health resource libraries have been constructed in many U.S. medical centers. Consumers are encouraged to learn about medical technology and services, perhaps finding solutions to their own health-care problems. The libraries provide a free community service with understandable medical information, classes, and support groups. Book delivery and health research services are also available.

In 1986, only 55.3 percent of health care organizations offered community health promotion programs. The figure rose to 77.2 percent in the 1990s.[10] With this emphasis on prevention, attitudes have changed. There is increasing recognition that tragedies can be prevented. Consumers are increasingly demanding information, especially about costs. The health-care system has refocused on health promotion (e.g., fitness and behavior modification), preventive services (e.g., immunization and prevention of transmission), and health protection (e.g., injury prevention and environmental safety).

REFERENCES

1. Gerard Anderson and Jean-Pierre Poullier, "Health Spending, Access, and Outcome: Trends in Industrialized Countries," *Health Affairs* 18 (1999): 189.
2. C. Patrick Charilk, "Preventive Health Care in Six Countries, Models for Reform?" *Health Care Financing Review* 15 (1994)..
3. "Emergency Room Crisis" *USA Today,* 28 August 1991, p. 8A.
4. American Hospital Association, "Historical Trends in Utilization, Personnel, and Finances for Selected Years from 1946 through 1997," *Hospital Statistics* Table 1 (1999).
5. Gloria Austin and Jack Massimino, "Ambulatory Care Design: Emerging Trends," *Journal of Healthcare Design* 5 (1993): 39.
6. Russell Coile, "Keynote Addess: Competing by Design—What You Need to Know About Tomorrow's Business in Healthcare," *Journal of Healthcare Design* 9 (1997): 25.
7. Robyn Dermon, "Ambulatory Care Design: The Integrated Medical Campus," *Journal of Healthcare Design* 5 (1993): 50.
8. Wanda J. Jones, "Ambulatory Care Design: A Patient-Focused Approach," *Journal of Healthcare Design* 6 (1994): 78.
9. John M. O'Donnell, "The Holistic Health Movement: Implications for Consulting Theory and Practice. *Counseling and Human Development* 15, no. 9 (May 1983): 1–12.
10. George R. Pressler, "Ambulatory Care Design: The New Generation," *Journal of Healthcare Design* 5 (1993): 69.

6 DAY CARE AND RESPITE

"What we are seeking to preserve is the spirit of the child. The spirit of the child is a sense of wonder. It is a sense of openness, trust, and responsiveness, an ability to simply be which gets shut down very quickly if the openness and trust are violated."[1] Is it a violation of trust to put a child or elder in day care? Is respite possible for the caregiver without affecting the health and development of the loved one? Sandwiched between two generations, many families desperately need relief from parental and child care but are worried about neglecting their responsibilities.

A comprehensive study by the National Institute of Child Health and Development[2] shows that good day care actually improves skills development in children when compared to those at home with their mothers. The influences of home and family must still predominate, but the study shows that families need not relinquish their responsibilities when children are in day care. In fact, these children scored higher in intellectual and verbal skills than children left with relatives or at home with nannies or sitters.

Another study found that 87 percent of the older people who participated in adult day care programs maintained or improved their level of functioning. Without day care, most of these participants would have been institutionalized; 63 percent had been Medicaid eligible for institutionalization before entering the program.[3]

There are at least 12,000 senior centers in the United States.[4] Most offer day care, meals, adult education classes, health screening, transportation, social services, and other programs, usually at little or no cost. Adult day care provides respite for clients as well as their caregivers, improving the health of older and disabled people and the ability of caregivers to support them.

ADULT DAY CARE AND RESPITE

Respite care centers provide shelter and support for a few hours to several months. Most facilities offer laundry service, meals, recreational activities, and health care. Nurses and physicians are often available. Some programs have even developed alliances with municipalities, industries, and providers to offer a wide range of benefits for their senior guests.

One such organization is On Lok, which began in 1972 as a day care center offering home health care and social services to older residents of San Francisco at risk for institutionalization. The program has been replicated from coast to coast and vertically expanded to offer day health centers, housing, and intergenerational day care. Because of this program, thousands of older people recommended for nursing home placement have remained in their homes.

At On Lok, the design program accommodates all needed medical and social services for the frail older participants. Each day, the health center's multidisciplinary team provides physical as well as psychosocial care. Services include health assessment, respite care, health education, physical therapy (see Figure 6-1), and counseling. Facilities are provided for dining, showering, grooming, toileting, and laundry. Transportation and home care are also offered.

The Hallen respite care center in Solna, Sweden, provides rehabilitation, training, and 24-hour medical intervention to six patients, primarily those residing in the adjacent independent living apartments. The respite center has the feel of a large home, with six bedrooms grouped around a great room. Independent living skills are restored in the training kitchen equipped with an adjustable-height counter, range with front controls, and an island that serves as the nursing station (see Figure 6-2). This project is nicely detailed with plant lights, a fireplace in the living room, and a warm color scheme to improve visual acuity (see Details on page 82). Large windows extend to the floor to increase ambient light and offer a view for wheelchair users. Each bedroom has a private bathroom with an adjustable-height sink. Even the medicine cabinet is lowered for wheelchair users and recessed to prevent injury.

In Copenhagen, the Dronning Anne-Marie Centret provides intergenerational day care as well as housing for older people, single mothers, and their children. The homes are separated by patios rather than com-

Figure 6-1 Physical therapy area. *Courtesy of Kai-Yee Woo & Associates, San Francisco. Photography: Chas McGrath.*

Figure 6-2 Adjustable-height kitchen. *Architect: ETV arkitektkontor AB, Stockholm. Photo: Max Plunger.*

Figure 6-3 Geriatric rehabilitation and work-out center. *Courtesy of Niels Gjerstrup, Dronning Anne-Marie Centret.*

mon walls, and the brick in the corridors of the day care center was laid to absorb sound.[5] The rough texture of the brick also diffuses reflected sound. Poor acoustics have limited the success of intergenerational housing projects in the United States. Most are located in high-density apartment buildings that accentuate the differences in populations.

The Centret provides day care and therapies to the entire community, encouraging interaction and integration. In addition, the Centret offers shared workout facilities (see Figure 6-3) and a commercial restaurant open to all rather than a congregate dining facility for older people.

In the United States, interest in programs offering intergenerational care is growing. Stride-Rite Corporation pioneered the workplace provision of adult and child day care, with mixed results. Providers learned that the two groups have very different energy levels, as do the individuals within the groups. Some older people could not get enough of the children, but the design failed to accommodate seniors who were not comfortable around them. Most successful contact took place at mealtime, but children and elders also worked together on art projects, cooking, and reading. Although each group had its own activity area, the majority of the center was designed for all age levels. Design criteria for intergenerational care include frame chairs that adjust to different heights and abilities (see Details on page 117), and upholstered seating in a variety of sizes (see Details on page 119). Entry seating was planned for layering, offering seniors a chance to observe before joining activities.

DETAILS
Frame Seating

- A comfortable chair allows the user to place both feet flat on the floor. Most of the weight should be on the buttocks, and there should be a space between the thigh and the front edge of the seat. Pressure beneath the thigh over an extended period could aggravate circulation problems.[6]

- The deeper the seat, the more slant is needed on the backrest for comfort. The angle of both the seat and the backrest should be adjustable. Pressure on the spine decreases as the tilt of the backrest increases. A lumbar cushion also reduces pressure and provides support.

- A vertical open space between the seat and the back allows extra room for the buttocks.

- For adults, the back of the chair should be adjustable in height from 8 to 13 in. above the seat surface.

- Plan chairs in a variety of sizes to accommodate both small and large visitors as well as children of all ages. Different styles can also serve as cues for orientation.

- In a chair without armrests, the user is more comfortable if the back of the chair is narrower than the width of the shoulders and lower than the shoulder blades.

- The user should be able to rest naturally on the armrests, although a lower height may be required for wheelchair use. To facilitate transfer from a wheelchair, these must be slightly below the table apron.

- A chair with an armrest that swivels up facilitates transfer from a wheelchair. Make sure that the chair cannot tip forward and that the armrests extend slightly beyond the leading edge of the chair seat.

- Armrests should seldom be higher than 8½ in. above the seat for maximum support and reduction of fatigue. Armrests alone support 12.4 percent of body weight.[7] They offer a sense of security and provide support in rising from the chair. Many people get out of a chair by first sliding forward to the edge and then pushing off.

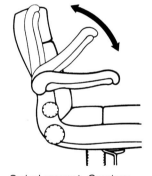

Swivel armrest. *Courtesy of Lux Company, Inc.*

- For adults, the seat may have to be adjusted in height (between 13⅔ and 20⅔ in. a.f.f.).[8] A seat height of at least 18 in. is easier on knees and hips when sitting or rising.

- A high stool may help the user maintain endurance and strength with minimal bending over a task. Mobile stools allow a wide range of motion in places too tight for a wheelchair. Casters should lock for stability. Choose a stool with adjustable seat height, seat angle, armrest, backrest, and footrest.

- On frame seating, the seat cushion should compress no more than 1 in.[9] Firm cushioning is especially important in the area where the spine meets the seat.

- Low bracing interferes with rising from a chair if users tucks their feet under the seat to push off.

Continued

DETAILS
Frame Seating *(continued)*

- Seat stretchers provide extra support and stabilize the chair for transfer from a wheelchair.
- Hard, not padded, arms on chairs offer support for transferring from a wheelchair.
- Choose seating with curved edges, padded corners, and soft surfaces to prevent bruises and pressure on the backs of the knees.
- Welting at the front of the seat may hamper circulation to the legs. Removable cushion covers without welting, ridges, and tufts are easier to maintain.
- Upholstery fabrics that allow the skin to breathe and prevent slipping also make chairs more comfortable. Use nylon upholstery for abrasion resistance, polypropylene for stain and sun resistance (but not resistance to heat or stretching), and wool for porosity and comfort. Remember that vinyl and plastic coverings may become hot, slippery, and uncomfortable when used on upholstery planned for long-term seating. Shiny vinyl is associated with institutional use and makes an interior appear more sterile. Use a vinyl with a slight texture or pattern.

Evaluation Guide: Properties of Fibers

Property	FIBER							
	Wool	Nylon	Modac	Olefin	Cotton	Rayon	Acryl	Poly
Strength	2	4	3	•	4	•	3	•
Flexibility	5	3	3	4	3	3	3	4
Resilience	4	5	5	4	2	2	5	3
Extensibility	4	4	4	•	2	2	4	4
Recovery	3	5	3	3	1	1	3	5
Elasticity	4	4	3	3	2	2	3	4
Absorbency	4	2	2	2	4	4	2	1
RESISTANCE TO:								
Alkali	2	4	4	4	4	3	3	3
Acid	3	2	4	4	2	3	3	4
Solvents	4	4	4	2	4	4	4	4
Sun	1	1	5	3	3	1	5	3
Micro/Insects	1	5	5	5	1	1	5	5
REACTION TO:								
Flame	BS	BS/M	M	B/M	BQ	BQ	BQ/M	BS/M
Flame Removal	SE	SE	SE	CB	CB	CB	CB	SE

Abrasion resistance is a function of strength, flexibility, and resilience.
Dimensional stability is a function of resilience, extensibility, recovery, elasticity, and absorbency.

Legend: • = dependent on formulation, 5 = excellent or very high, 4 = very good or high, 3 = good or medium, 2 = fair or low, 1 = poor or very low.
Modac = modacrylic, Acryl = acrylic, Poly = polyester
B = burns, S = slowly, Q = quickly, M = melts, SE = self-extinguishing, CB = continuous burning

Properties of fibers. *From Virginia Weinhold, Interior Finish Materials for Health Care Facilities, 1988. Courtesy of Charles C. Thomas Publisher, Ltd., Springfield, IL.*

- A high-backed rocker provides head support, but make sure the chair cannot tip.

- Persons seated in groups can maintain eye contact and read lips and gestures most easily from swivel chairs. Semicircular seating arrangements are recommended, perhaps around a table. Make sure swivel chairs, recliners, and other movable seating have locking mechanisms. For some, sitting down in and rising from a swiveling seat is difficult.

- For people who are sensitive to petrochemicals, specify hardwood or metal furniture rather than composite wood or pressboard frames. Choose pieces with mechanical fasteners instead of glue.

DETAILS
Upholstered Seating

- Proper cushioning prevents skin ulcers. Test for proper cushioning by putting the full weight of your closed fist in the center of the seat. You should not feel the springs or supporting boards.

- Soft cushions make wheelchair transfer difficult. Down cushions, for example, are too soft. If the deck itself is too soft, add plywood under the cushion for support.

- Users with strength differences may have trouble rising from the center cushion of a long sofa. A shorter sofa allows more flexibility in furniture arrangement and puts the user closer to an armrest for support when rising.

- Bucket seats and some contour seats make it difficult to shift or change position.

- Rockers aid muscle tone, digestion, and circulation, but they should be locking to aid in transferring.

- To easily rearrange rooms, put casters on all furniture except those pieces used for transfer. Casters allow furniture to be pushed out of the way for wheelchair or gurney clearance and help families rearrange furniture to include all visitors.

- Avoid furniture that involves unusual angles of exertion, like sleeper sofas and some reclining rockers.

- Seats at the same height as a wheelchair (17–19 in. a.f.f.) facilitate transfer and reduce the difference in eye levels for conversation.

Continued

DETAILS
Upholstered Seating (*continued*)

- Recess the base of the seat at least 6 in. for wheelchair footrests.

- Many people lean on upholstered seating for support while standing. The legs of sofas and chairs should be at the corners of the seat. The back legs should extend outward so the feet are even with the top of the backrest.

- Consider a chair with a controlled pneumatic lift. Models with movable seats and armrests are available.

- A high-backed chair can provide protection from drafts and a feeling of security. For users who nap in the chair, look for an adjustable head cushion.

- Unless the chair is very low to the floor, the user also may need a footrest. For users with back problems, choose a footrest that is high enough to keep the knees bent at a height slightly above the waist. Choose footrests that are easily removable. Low ottomans can pose a tripping hazard, however. Keep these well away from high-traffic areas.

- Many users with different abilities are slow in responding to a fire, so fire-resistant furnishings are critical. Most states require testing for flammability. California Technical Bulletin 133 requires that the product as a whole be tested rather than its individual components.

- For stability, avoid slippery fabrics on seating. Textured fabrics with corrugation offer more friction and can help users maintain an upright sitting position for extended periods. (Slicker fabrics on the seat, however, may help weaker users slide into deep booths and auto interiors).

DAY CARE FOR PEOPLE WITH DEMENTIA

The Louis Feinstein Alzheimer's Daycare Center is a hospitable environment built within a community park (see Research Abstract on page 122). Features include a large skylight to increase daylight penetration and a breakfast bar with a view of the kitchen (see Figure 6-4). A changing area with clothing storage and laundry is approachable from both the reception area and the main programming area (see Figure 6-5). Many of the consumers are incontinent, and this plan allows for quick changes without embarrassment.

Figure 6-4 Skylights and breakfast bar. *Project: Louis Feinstein. Photo © Frank Guiliani.*

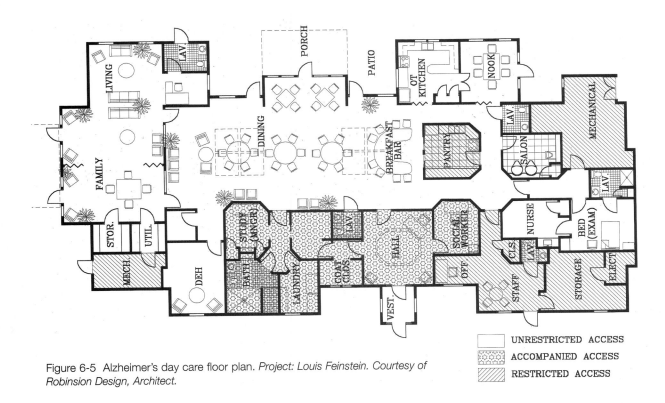

Figure 6-5 Alzheimer's day care floor plan. *Project: Louis Feinstein. Courtesy of Robinsion Design, Architect.*

RESEARCH ABSTRACT
Experiential Research in Detailing Day Care for People with Dementia

John Robinson of Robinson Design, Smithfield, Rhode Island, planned the Louis Feinstein Alzheimer's Center, which offers an extremely inviting, homelike environment for day care. Robinson suggests the following priorities in planning day care centers for people with dementia:

- Involve experienced caregivers, including family members, in the design process. Tour other day care centers with caregivers, recording their responses to the details. Develop a design team that includes environmental gerontologists.

- For client safety, plan three levels of access: participant spaces, accompanied access areas, and restricted access areas.

- Participant spaces should be open to clients for wandering and other activities. Constant supervision should be facilitated by vision panels in doors, see-through dividers, and, perhaps, a breakfast bar separating staff from the dining area.

- Accompanied access areas should be more closely controlled, with client access offered only by staff. These spaces may include the laundry room, front hall, closets, some staff workrooms and offices, the exam room, and nap areas.

- Restricted areas, like maintenance shops and mechanical rooms, should be locked, with entrances planned out of sight of clients.

- Reduce the scale of large spaces by breaking up long lines and planes. Add an alcove to a long wall and break the ceiling line with soffits, coffers, and skylights.

- Activity areas should accommodate small, specialized groups and activities. Provide easy access from most activity areas to secured exterior spaces.

- High light levels are particularly important to minimize anxiety at dusk. In addition to higher ambient light levels, plan light, bright, clear finishes without glare. Finish materials should be free of busy or disorienting patterns or spots (see Details on page 214).

- Provide at least one lavatory for every ten participants; place lavatories in convenient locations throughout the center. Provide at least one shower or tub for every 15 participants.

- Every lavatory and bathroom should provide storage for both clean and soiled garments. Recess a cabinet above the toilet for clean garment storage and conceal an airtight diaper pail in one of the base cabinets. Storage should be secured by a childproof latch usable with one hand.

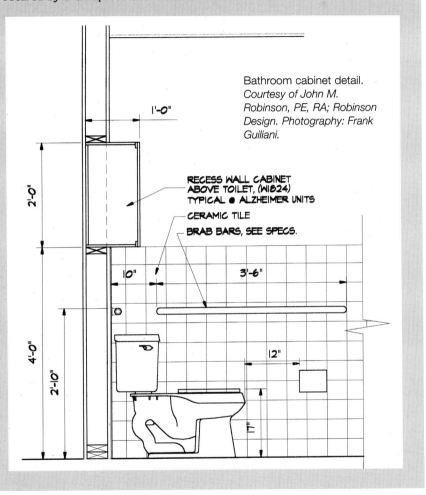

Bathroom cabinet detail.
Courtesy of John M. Robinson, PE, RA; Robinson Design. Photography: Frank Guiliani.

RECESS WALL CABINET
ABOVE TOILET, (W1824)
TYPICAL @ ALZHEIMER UNITS

CERAMIC TILE

BRAB BARS, SEE SPECS.

CHILD DAY CARE

Children need an open place to be themselves, not a closed environment designed for the convenience of adults. For children, the environment is a medium for experimentation and learning. Everything in the environment matters. Child care centers should be filled with artistic, interactive surfaces to explore with the hands and eyes, with movement and activities that a child can enjoy. Children must interact with the environment on a sensory level. Surfaces should softly reflect light, invite touch, offer surprising fragrances, and produce interesting sounds. Children learn through these sensory experiences.

Movement is another way children learn. Children need to move about in the space yet feel comfortable, competent, and in control. Comfort comes from changes in sensory stimulation within a predictable framework, like a flickering fire or a warm breeze.[10] Comfort does not come from maintaining a static position.

Day care learning spaces must accommodate six basic activities: quiet learning, large motor activities, crafts, games, drama, and therapeutic exercise.[11] Quiet areas are used for reading, resting, and time out. These areas must offer security and protection; a corner location or an enclosed space may be best.

The opportunity for change within secure parameters can be offered by the design detail. Dr. Anita Olds designed a play structure with a secure hideaway: a 150-year-old dead maple hollowed out for children to explore (see Figure 6-6). A smaller log was carved into a series of steps leading to a slide built from another log. Halogen lighting created a dappled effect, like light in a forest.

Finishes should be soft and safe, and although this discussion is limited to family-centered design, note that finishes should be planned for ease of maintenance. Craft areas may offer paint, clay, water, and sand. Drama spaces may include a puppet theater, playhouse, and costumes, while games may vary from simple board games to sophisticated computer challenges. Large motor activities include sliding, climbing, swinging, and crawling.

Day care can be much more than babysitting. Innovative day care centers offer therapeutic exercise areas planned to improve a wide range of abilities. Pediatric rehabilitation components can engage children while offering functional restoration. Elements of one system, including stepping stones, logs, cubes, ramps, and toadstools, pop up from the floor. These elements are used in upper-body exercise, fine motor skills development, coordination, and cognitive training (see Figure 6-7).

Day care centers should be designed universally to accommodate children of all ages, sizes, and abilities. Infants need carpeted spaces where they can crawl; toddlers want to practice walking in a soft,

Figure 6-6
Enchanted Forest
play area. *Courtesy
of Gail Collins and
Anita Rui Olds.*

Figure 6-7 Rehabilitation
area. *Courtesy of Guynes
Design Inc.*

enclosed area with changes in level. Teens enjoy cooking, eating, computer games, music, and lounging, perhaps in a separate elevated space where they can remain "above it all."

In summary, child care centers should be planned to create a transition between school and home. Long, disorienting corridors and institutional finishes are not appropriate. A homelike atmosphere must be created, beginning with a warm welcome at the reception area and extending throughout the activity and rest areas. Indirect lighting (on rheostats for naptime) offers an inviting ambience that does not glare in the eyes of children lying on their backs (see Details on page 83). Lighting should support visual access to all areas, including the exterior. Homelike environments offer comfort and security, freeing children to experiment within safe parameters.

REFERENCES

1. Anita Rui Olds, "With Children in Mind: Novel Approaches to Waiting Area and Playroom Design," *Journal of Health Care Interior Design* 3 (1991): 111.
2. Sue Shellenbarger, "Impact of Child Care Is Mixed, Study Says," *Wall Street Journal,* 4 April 1997, p. A5.
3. L. Noelker, "The Impact of Environmental Problems on Caring for Impaired Elders in a Home Setting," (paper presented at the 35th Annual Scientific Meeting of the Gerontological Society of America, Boston, Mass., 1982).
4. Donald H. Kausler and Barry C. Kauslery, *The Graying of America: An Encyclopedia of Aging, Health, Mind, and Behaviour* (Urbana: University of Illinois Press, 1996): 271–272.
5. Victor Regnier, *Assisted Living Housing for the Elderly* (New York: John Wiley and Sons, 1994): 78.
6. Walter B. Kleeman, *The Challenge of Interior Design* (Boston: CBI Publishing, 1981): 94.
7. Ibid., 101.
8. Ibid., 93.
9. Ibid., 265.
10. Olds, "With Children in Mind," 113.
11. Ibid., 114.

7 MEDICAL OFFICES

Nowhere is a person's privacy more violated than in a medical office. Patients and their families are frequently shuffled through a high-volume practice, routinely undressing in front of strangers and submitting to very personal examinations. Even the smallest gestures of support are appreciated: a changing curtain in the exam room, a private area for weighing in (where that impossibly large number will not be broadcast down the corridor), and a covered entry.

Ambulatory care centers treat many patients who are not ambulatory. More and more, patients are using wheelchairs and walkers. In some facilities, the ADA requires 10 percent of the parking spaces to be accessible unless the facility specializes in treating people with mobility impairments (see Details on page 238), in which case 20 percent of the spaces must be accessible.[1] Each accessible space must be located on the shortest route of travel to an accessible entrance (see Details on page 128).

codes

The building entrance should be easily identified and welcoming. The entry should have windows to allow patients and their families a view into the reception area while still offering a layer of protection before entering the space (see Figure 7-1). To help with orientation and to accommodate people with hearing impairments, avoid tall arrangements of flowers and accessories on furniture in the entry. These items block a clear line of vision to the space beyond as well as to interpreters and other people in the room. A tall arrangements in the center of an entry space may make it more difficult to maintain eye contact, to read lips and gestures, to hear, and to be heard.

DETAILS
Parking and Curb Ramps

- All entrances from parking garages, tunnels, and elevated walks must be accessible.

- Provide at least one accessible parking space if 25 or fewer spaces are provided.

- The width of a standard accessible space or van-accessible space is 96 in.

- The access aisle width for standard accessible space is 60 in. with a vertical clearance of 80 in. The width of the access aisle for a van-accessible space in 96 in. with a vertical clearance of 98 in.

- The slope of accessible parking spaces must not exceed 2 percent (1:50).

Total Parking in Lot	Required Minimum Number of Accessible Spaces
1 to 25	1
26 to 50	2
51 to 75	3
76 to 100	4
101 to 150	5
151 to 200	6
201 to 300	7
301 to 400	8
401 to 500	9
501 to 1000	2 percent of total
1001 and over	20 plus 1 for each 100 over 1000

Accessible parking requirements.
Americans with Disabilities Act Standards.

- Curb ramps located where pedestrians must walk across them or where they are not protected by handrails or guardrails must have flared sides. The maximum slope of the flare must be 1:10 on a 48 in. accessible route. If the route is less than 48 in., use a 1:12 maximum slope.

- Curb ramps with returned curbs may be used where pedestrians would not normally walk across them.

- Keep all curb ramps within marked crossings (excluding flared sides).

- If diagonal (or corner-type) curb ramps have returned curbs or other well-defined edges, the edges must be parallel to the direction of pedestrian flow.

- The bottom of diagonal curb ramps must have 48 in. minimum clear space. If diagonal curb ramps are provided at marked crossings, the 48-in. clear space must be within the markings.

- If diagonal curb ramps have flared sides, they must also have at least a 24 in. long segment of straight curb located on each side of the curb ramp and within the marked crossing.

- Raised islands in crossings must be cut through level with the street or have curb ramps at both sides and a level area at least 48 in. long between the curb ramps in the part of the island intersected by the crossings.

- For security purposes, the parking lot should include audio communication to security guards and parking attendants, video cameras, and appropriate lighting.

Side lights and vision panels in doors also help with orientation, allowing patients to look inside to see if they have reached their destination. The bottom of the panel should be mounted no higher than 36 in. a.f.f. to allow an adult of shorter stature, a child, or a person in a wheelchair to see and be seen before the door is opened. The panel should not

Figure 7-1 Entry as a social layer. *Courtesy of Watkins Hamilton Ross Architects.*

Figure 7-2 Divider walls moving patients and their families into suites. *Courtesy of Mackey Mitchell Associates.*

extend to the floor; people with vision differences can mistake such panels for door openings. Vision panels should always be made of safety glass (unless fire codes require wired glass).

Entry walls angling into the corridor help with circulation, moving patients and their families into the suites (see Figure 7-2). If the suites are not located on the ground floor, elevators are required.[2] There is no elevator exception in the ADA standards for an office of a professional health-care provider, even if the building is less than three stories in height or less than 3000 sq. ft. per floor. If a physician has offices just on the first floor of a multistory building, an elevator to the other floors in not required (see Details on page 130).

DETAILS
Elevators

- In some existing buildings, the ADA permits an accessible elevator to be a minimum interior size of 48 by 48-in.,[3] but an interior of 54 by 68 in.[4] is much more usable. Dimensions must even be larger to accommodate a gurney including a clear opening of at least 48 in.

- Consider separate elevators for public and staff use, especially if staff transports patients on gurneys.

- The elevator should be automatic and self-leveling (within a tolerance of ½ in.).[5] Leveling should be tested with a full load as well as without a load.

- The elevator should start and stop smoothly, and a fold-down seat and stationary handrail should be provided for use by people with differences in balance and strength. A seat on each floor outside of the elevator is also helpful.

- A visual indicator on each elevator control button should light when touched and extinguish when the command is completed.

- All car controls, as well as the car platform, landing sill, and car threshold, should be illuminated to at least 5 fc.

- Position indicators should incorporate redundant cuing, offering both visual and audible cues.

- In the corridor, an audible signal should sound once for the up direction and twice for the down (or use a spoken announcement of up or down).

- Call buttons should be installed at a maximum height of 42 in., with the up button on top.[6] Consider installing a second call button at a height of 36 in. for use by short people and children.

- Any object placed or installed beneath the call buttons should not project into the space more than 4 in.

- A call button should be a minimum of ¾ in. in diameter.[7]

- Hall lanterns indicating which car is answering the call should be a minimum of 2½ in. in diameter.[8]

- A 2 in. high raised floor designation should be mounted on each side of the hoistway entrance. It should be installed at a height of 60 in.,[9] and a second designation should be installed at 48 in. a.f.f., when appropriate, for children.

- Interior control panels should be installed within reach from a wheelchair. Controls for children should be installed at a height of 36 in. Some panels are designed to be mounted horizontally to improve reach. Arrange the numbers in ascending order, reading from left to right. A floor number or other raised designation should be installed to the left of the button and should contrast with the background.

- Numerals above the door should light and a signal should sound as the car passes or stops at a floor. A spoken announcement may be substituted for the signal.

- The elevator should have a sound signal to indicate that it is safe to enter or exit.

- If the door becomes obstructed, it should reopen without requiring contact and remain open for at least 20 seconds.[10]

- The ADA standards and the Uniform Federal Accessibility Standards (UFAS) require only that a door remain open for as little as five seconds in response to a call.[11] This is insufficient time for many people to respond, even if forewarned of arrival by redundant cuing.

- An emergency communication system inside the car should comply with ADA standards in height, hardware, and length of cord, if any. A vocal system (like an intercom) should be incorporated in addition to an alarm system. Intercoms are easier to use and tougher to vandalize than systems requiring the use of a handset. Only the nonverbal alarm system is required, however. Instructions for use should be both tactile and visual.

RECEPTION

Patients and their families judge a clinic by small design details and visual impressions. Sensibly designed and maintained reception areas show respect for patients as people and contribute to humanizing the experience of visiting a medical office. Dusty plants, old magazines, dirty finishes, and burned-out lightbulbs indicate to patients and their families that a poor quality of medicine is practiced. On the other hand, thoughtful design detail magnifies the impression of competence. Provide a secure place for coats, boots, and umbrellas. Plan a public telephone in the waiting room and drinking fountains at different heights (see Details below). Offer large-print magazines on a lowered rack. Locate a children's area away from door swings and traffic areas but within sight of the receptionist. At reception, the computer screen should swivel to allow patients and their families access to their information. These design details are appreciated by patients of all ages, sizes, and abilities.

HIPPA

DETAILS
Drinking Fountains and Water Coolers

- Blind people who use canes cannot detect water coolers with floor clearances exceeding 27 in. People in wheelchairs require a clearance of at least 27 in. for a front approach, so this must be the exact clearance to meet the needs of both populations.[12]

- A second fountain should be mounted at standard height. When children frequently use the space, a third fountain should be considered with a spout no higher than 30 in. and a clear knee space of 24 in.

- The spout of a water fountain for shorter adults and wheelchair users should be no higher than 36 in.[13] It should be located close to the front of the unit with a water flow parallel to the front edge.

- The flow must be at least 4 in. high to facilitate use with a cup.[14] A paper cup dispenser adjacent to the water fountain allows use by many people who have differences in reach and coordination.

- A recessed fountain or cooler for wheelchair users optimally should be 17 to 19 in. deep.[15] The recess should be a minimum of 30 in. wide and a maximum of 24 in. deep for a front approach. For a side approach, the alcove must be 60 in. wide if the depth exceeds 15 in.[16]

- Controls on all fountains should be located near the front edge. They should be operable with one hand without pinching, tight grasping, or twisting of the wrist. An automatic sensor is most easily operated by people of all sizes and abilities.

Each counter should provide a surface for writing (at 42 in. a.f.f.) and a lowered surface (30–34 in. a.f.f.) for wheelchair users, children and shorter adults (see Figure 7-3). At the check-in counter, the window should be open and welcoming so that patients and their families do not feel closed out. Locate the receptionist's telephone away from the check-in window (to maintain privacy) and plan a telephone for patient and family use, perhaps at a seated desk. Provide space for a telephone and laptop or TTY. For typing, the desk surface should be 5½ to 7 in. above seat height. For wheelchair use, the top should be 30 to 34 in. a.f.f. with clearance of 27 in. below.[17] An accessible width of 36 to 42 in. should be allowed.[18]

A checkout counter opening to the business office should be placed adjacent to the exit. It is thoughtful to plan a separate exit so that

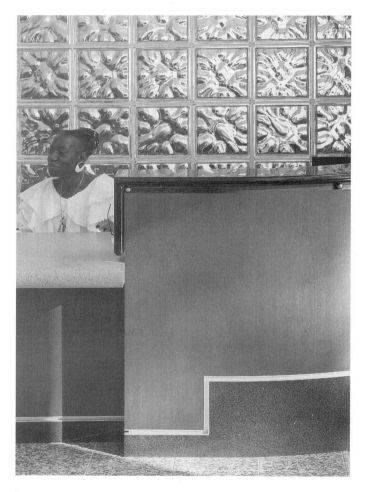

Figure 7-3 Lowered surfaces. *Designer: The S/L/A/M Collaborative, Architects & Engineers. Courtesy of Esto Photographics.*

Figure 7-4 Alternate exit. *Courtesy of Watkins Hamilton Ross Architects.*

patients need not walk through the reception area after a procedure (see Figure 7-4). This door may also be used as an alternate entrance for emergencies, signed with instructions to ring the adjacent bell for service (see Details on page 240 and Research Abstract on page 242).

These considerate details advertise the sensitivity of the providers and their awareness of the patients' needs. A view of the street connects the center to the neighborhood. The decor should be in context with the location of the center (see Figure 7-5).

The center must also acknowledge American cultural norms. Unlike people of other cultures, Americans do not like to be touched. They appreciate more personal space, maintaining a distance at least of 8 ft. from strangers.[19] Place seating groups accordingly, planning some single seating so strangers need not sit together. Also provide an intimate grouping of chairs and tables for families (see Details on pages 117, 119, and 222).

Figure 7-5 Mexican decor in context with the location. *Project name: Scripps Ambulatory Surgical Center. Interior architecture: Jain Malkin Inc. Photography: Steve McClelland Photography.*

Patients and their families sometimes wait for hours, especially in obstetricians' and gynecologists' offices. Seating must be comfortable and easily used by pregnant women and older adults. Seated users should be able to rest their entire weight on one arm of the chair without tipping. Plan individual chairs with arms; sofas are difficult to exit and force strangers to touch.

Patients and their families feel more comfortable when provided access to nature and sunlight. The waiting area can be planned in an atrium or adjacent to a courtyard (see Figure 7-6). The sound of running water relieves stress (see Figure 7-7). Natural light can be provided via a solarium or skylight (see Figure 7-8). With a high ceiling, mirrors can be added to the skylight to increase the lighting levels (see Details on page 83).

Figure 7-6 Courtyard for waiting. *Designer: The S/L/A/M Collaborative, Architects & Engineers. Courtesy of Wheeler Photographics.*

Figure 7-7 Relaxing waterfall. *Courtesy of H + L Architecture/Rob Davidson. Dean Birinyi, photographer.*

Figure 7-8 Skylight. *Courtesy of Mary Jean Thompson, ASID, Thompson Design Assoc.*

Figure 7-9 Natural light. *Courtesy of Chambers Lorenz Design Assoc.*

DAYLIGHT   +BIRD

Natural light deinstitutionalizes and humanizes the reception area
(see Figure 7-9). Artwork, aquariums, and puzzles are other elements
that help make the office less threatening (see Figure 7-10). In addition
to permanent art, staff should be encouraged to personalize each space,
perhaps with a changing display of collections or crafts. Room dividers
and wall systems can be used to exhibit these works, to house an entertainment center, or to store patient and family education materials (see
Details on the next page).

Figure 7-10 Positive distractions. *Courtesy of Watkins Hamilton Ross Architects.*

DETAILS
Room Dividers and Wall Systems

- Avoid partitions with legs that extend into traffic areas. The legs can pose a tripping hazard and can limit access by wheelchair users.
- Ventilation to control heat buildup and odor is an important feature if the room divider is used to conceal a television, computer, or appliance.
- Heavier items, like televisions, can be more easily managed on swing-out shelves or turntables. Deep shelves and clothing racks should roll out.
- Pull-out shelves and drop-lid desks are available on many wall systems, offering the option of lower work surfaces for use from a wheelchair.
- For people in wheelchairs, cabinets and drawers must be raised at least 9 in. from the floor to allow footrest clearance.
- Keep drawers in wall systems at a reachable height (under 32 in.). Patients in wheelchairs may have trouble reaching to the back of drawers that are installed any higher.
- When planning shelf heights and depths, consider the maximum reach of the patient in a wheelchair.
- If a phone is placed in the wall system, plan a shelf for phone books, a clip on the shelf to secure a note pad, and space for a text telephone (also known as TDD and TTY). This telephone requires 6 in. of vertical clearance[20] and an outlet within 48 in.

Figure 7-11 Resource library. *Courtesy of Lowell General. Designer: TRO. Photography: Ed Jacoby.*

Education is an important component of the program for all ambulatory centers. A niche in the reception area could be dedicated to patient and family education and house a video monitor and VCR. Consider an adjacent reading room (see Figure 7-11), lending library, or computer station with Internet access to current medical research (see Details on the next page). The office of the provider and the examination rooms may also house educational materials.

> **DETAILS**
> **Computer Stations for All Abilities**
>
> - Voice recognition systems (which accept spoken commands) are commonly available. These work well for many patients, even those with vision limitations, if the system provides audio feedback of each choice and command. Software is also available to enlarge text and images.
> - For people who are blind, braille systems and optical readers are helpful add-ons. A braille display orally "reads" the information from the screen and also presents it in braille. Printed information can be scanned, reprinted in braille, or "read" by the speech synthesizer.
> - Keyboards should be placed on a surface 5½ to 7 in. above seat height.[21]
> - Consider large keys for people with differences in coordination.
> - Membrane keyboards are available for people who cannot depress keys.
> - A speech synthesizer offers voice output for a person who cannot use the screen or who has a speech impairment. The computerized voice lets the user hear the information printed on the screen. It provides immediate audio feedback as data are entered on the keyboard, so mistakes are easily identified.
> - When used with a telephone interface, a synthesizer can serve as a speaker phone, allowing two-way conversation without the use of voice.
> - Computer peripherals are becoming more user friendly for people with varying abilities. A printer system, for example, can be operated with a mouth stick, by voice, or by hand without requiring manual dexterity. One excellent example of a user-friendly device is a disk-loading system that can be fully operated with a mouth stick.
> - People with learning differences benefit from the immediate feedback offered by computers. Learners see, hear, and feel information (on a touch screen) to reinforce the message and allow for a variety of learning styles.
> - Plan an adjacent shelf with at least 6 in. of vertical clearance for text telephone use of the computer. Locate an outlet within 48 in.[22]

EXAMINATION AND CONSULTING ROOMS

In a consulting room, every effort should be made to remove communication barriers. The provider should sit across a table from the patient and their family instead of hiding behind an imposing desk. The patient should be fully clothed and seated at the same level as the provider. If the practitioner's office is not located on site, a family consulting room should be planned within the examination suite (see Figure 7-12).

The family consulting room is normally adjacent to three or four exam rooms and a nursing station. In a decentralized plan, these few rooms form a pod with a provider team assigned to each. Each team may be composed of two doctors, one assistant, one receptionist, and one

Figure 7-12 Private
consultation rooms.
*Courtesy of Ellerbe
Becket. Photography:
Koyama Photographic.*

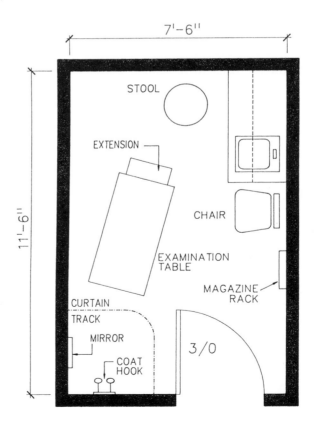

Figure 7-13 Exam room plan.
Courtesy of Jain Malkin Inc.

billing person. Patients and their families work with the same receptionist, assistants, and doctors on each visit, maintaining a sense of intimacy even in a high-volume practice.

Large practices run the risk of appearing to be a medical factory. A series of pods reduces the anonymity of one large clinic with 50 exam rooms. Pods may be organized around a central courtyard with access to light and nature. Windows in exam rooms, however, should not extend to the floor, compromising the privacy of the patients and limiting wall space for storage and seating.

For privacy, horizontal blinds can be angled to offer good light and a view (see Details on page 54). The foot of the exam table should be angled away from the door opening, and the door swing should also be planned to offer a degree of privacy (see Figure 7-13). For acoustical privacy, the door should have solid core (see Details on pages 68 and 70). The walls could feature staggered stud construction with insulation (see Figure 7-14).

Exam tables should be adjustable in height for shorter people, children, people in wheelchairs or on gurneys, and older people (see Figure 7-15). The exam room should be furnished with a chair, hooks for clothing, and a mirror. A makeup mirror, perhaps in a cabinet with lighting, is always appreciated.

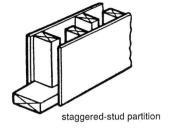

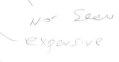

staggered-stud partition

Figure 7-14 Staggered stud construction. *Courtesy of C. Harris, Dictionary of Architecture and Construction, 1995, reproduced with permission of The McGraw-Hill Companies.*

Not seen
expensive

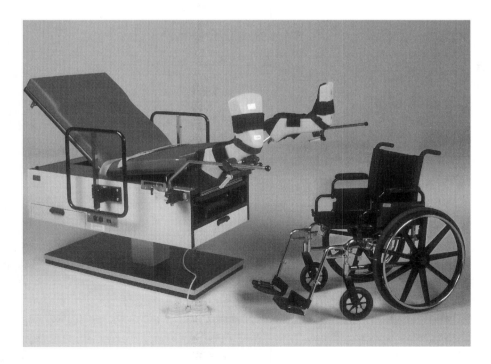

Figure 7-15 Adjustable exam table. *Courtesy of Hausmann Industries, Inc.*

If the dressing room is separate from the diagnostic area (as in a radiology suite), lockers should be provided for valuables (see Figure 7-16). Exam rooms and dressing rooms can be named instead of numbered for a less institutional approach (see Figure 7-17). These rooms should include an emergency communication system, perhaps a buzzer or light to call for assistance. Carpeting in these areas is more comfortable on bare feet and, with today's technology, there are few places where carpet cannot be used (see Details on page 24 and Research Abstract on page 23).

Adjacent to the exam rooms, provide a toilet room. A specimen pass-through should be planned (see Figure 7-18). In many practices, the staff-controlled toilet room replaces the public rest room so patients can be reminded by staff if a urine sample is needed.

Figure 7-16 Dressing room with lockers. *Courtesy of Chambers Lorenz Design Assoc.*

Figure 7-17 Dressing room signage.
©Al Payne. Designer: Orcutt/Winslow
Partnership. Project: Scottsdale
Healthcare's Breasthealth Center.

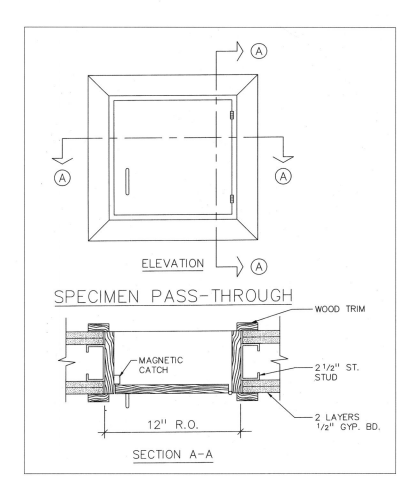

Figure 7-18 Specimen pass-through.
Courtesy of Jain Malkin Inc.

SPECIALIZED PRACTICE

This discussion is limited to family-centered design detail in four of the most common medical specialties: allergy clinics, pediatrics, ambulatory surgery, and diagnostic centers. For comprehensive design direction on these and on at least 40 other medical specialties, I recommend *Medical and Dental Space Planning for the 1990s* by Jain Malkin.[23]

Allergy Clinics

Petrochemicals, toxic finishes, adhesives, and phenols are but a few of the hundreds of irritants commonly found in building materials. In addition, common house dust, dust mites, mold spores, cigarette smoke, and animal dander frequently cause problems. Toxins typically build up in closets and storage areas, so good ventilation is critical in these spaces.

In wall construction, a light gypsum plaster wall finish on metal lath may be the best choice. It should be left unpainted but may be tinted with hypoallergenic, nontoxic dyes. A water-based sealant or a hard-finish polyurethane may also be a good choice. Avoid cellulose, fiberglass, and rock wool insulation. Specify vermiculite and perlite, which are also resistant to moisture, mold, and mildew.[24]

To prevent reactions to interior finishes and furnishings, avoid common allergens such as wool and products that offgas formaldehyde. Heavy drapery, horizontal louvers, and carpet may harbor dust mites. Seamless hard-surfaced flooring eliminates leakage in the seams that promotes bacterial growth. Monolithic high-density vinyl floor coverings are acceptable to most people with allergies if installed with wood baseboards that are nailed rather than glued (see Details on page 181).

Pressboard cabinets and plastic lampshades frequently offgas. Laminate tops are often adhered to chemically offensive substrates. Specify paper shades and solid wood cabinets with solid synthetic tops. Cabinets and furnishings used to store televisions, VCRs, and other electronic devices may have to be vented outdoors to eliminate carbonized dust and odors. Unprotected bulbs and radiant heating also carbonize dust, a common irritant. Dehumidifiers that do not rely on air conditioners may be helpful in minimizing mildew, mold, and dust mites. These common allergens are minimized when the relative humidity is below 50 percent.

Air can be cleaned with an uncoated paper filter system and good HVAC design with ventilation that allows at least one air change per hour. Air-to-air heat exchangers can minimize energy waste as fresh air is brought in.

An ounce of flexibility is worth a pound of remodeling. Construction dust can have a profound effect on patients, especially those with immune deficiencies.

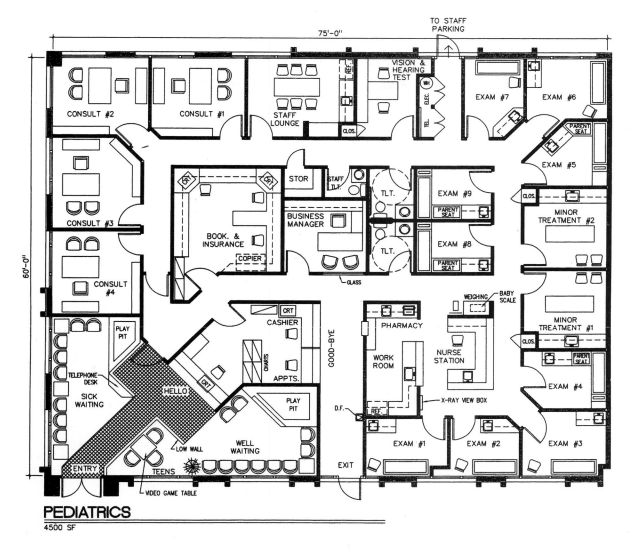

Figure 7-19 Separation between incoming and outgoing patients and their families. *Courtesy of Jain Malkin Inc.*

Pediatrics

Pediatrics is a high-volume specialty where physicians sometimes see six to eight patients per hour. Arriving and departing patients and their families should be separated (see Figure 7-19). Some clinics also separate sick children from well children in reception to prevent contagion.

In pediatric offices, a public rest room should be planned adjacent to the waiting room. Parents need to change their babies without the inconvenience of requesting access to a private bathroom in the back. Equip the bathroom with disposable diapers and a wall-mounted

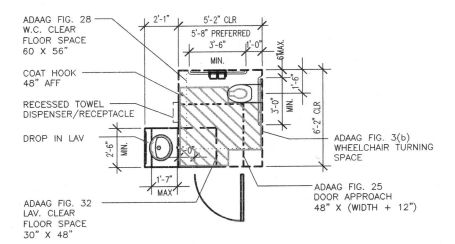

ADAAG FIG. 28
W.C. CLEAR
FLOOR SPACE
60 X 56"

COAT HOOK
48" AFF

RECESSED TOWEL
DISPENSER/RECEPTACLE

DROP IN LAV

2'-1"   5'-2" CLR
5'-8" PREFERRED
3'-6"   1'-0"
MIN.

6"MAX.

3'-0"
MIN.

1'-6"
MIN.

6'-2" CLR

2'-6"
MIN.

1'-7"
MAX

ADAAG FIG. 3(b)
WHEELCHAIR TURNING
SPACE

ADAAG FIG. 25
DOOR APPROACH
48" X (WIDTH + 12")

ADAAG FIG. 32
LAV. CLEAR
FLOOR SPACE
30" X 48"

Figure 7-20 Minimum-size unisex bathroom. *Courtesy of Evan Terry Associates, P.C.*

Figure 7-21 Private registration. *Courtesy of Phoebe Putney. Designer: TRO. Photography: George Cott.*

counter for diaper changing. A unisex bathroom allows an adult or aide to accompany children of either sex without concern. All toilet areas and exam rooms need to be large enough to accommodate several siblings at once. Properly planned, these larger rooms also accommodate parents, strollers, and children who use wheelchairs, walkers, or guide dogs (see Figure 7-20 and Figure 10-2 in Chapter 10).

Ambulatory Surgery

Outpatient surgery, also called *same-day surgery* because patients are discharged on the day the procedure takes place, offers patient and family convenience and reduces the fear of entering a hospital. Ambulatory centers are not filled with patients arriving on stretchers or attached to equipment. Most patients are candidates for elective procedures.

There are seven stages of patient flow: preadmission, arrival, patient preparation, induction, recovery, postrecovery, and discharge.[25] Preadmission and arrival take place in the reception area (see Figure 7-21), although a private entry may be necessary for patients who do not wish to advertise a procedure like plastic surgery.

In outpatient surgical facilities, families wait for much longer periods than in other practices, sometimes most of the day. Every detail of the interior is noticed and every benefit appreciated. Choices should include comfortable seating of all sizes, a place to conduct business with a telephone and a grounded outlet for computers, and an entertainment center. These design details reduce stress, a necessary consideration even though stress levels are typically lower in outpatient areas than in hospital waiting rooms.

Plan areas for patient preparation, induction, recovery, and postrecovery where the family can stay with the patient (see Figure 7-22).

Figure 7-22 Preoperative/postoperative recovery suites. *Courtesy of Ellerbe Becket. Photography: Koyama Photographic.*

Figure 7-23 Grooming area. *Courtesy of Watkins Hamilton Ross Architects.*

Some thoughtful practices plan a space for help with hair and makeup before discharge (see Figure 7-23). Plastic surgeons typically use gray mirrors and low-level lighting in these spaces to minimize the immediate impact of bruises.

Most patients are discharged in wheelchairs and should be met by transportation near a private discharge area. Outdoor seating in this area is helpful for those waiting for a ride. Plan a slip-resistant surface that drains away from the door. The exit should be protected from wind to allow the door to be easily opened (see Details on the next page).

Oncology

When physicians suggest radiation therapy, patients hear, "You're going to die." They don't need to hear, "We're sending you underground for treatment." But treatment machines are usually placed in the basement because of the 400,000 lbs. of lead shielding required.

DETAILS
Passenger Loading Zone

- The passenger loading zone should be visible from the entry door.
- At a minimum, the passenger loading zone must be 5 ft. in wide and 20 ft. long parallel to the vehicle space.[26]
- The zone must be slightly sloped for drainage, not to exceed 1:50.[27]
- A minimum vertical clearance of 114 in. is needed by some vans.[28]
- From the access aisle or passenger loading zone, an accessible route should be provided to all buildings on the site. The route should be free of auto traffic and protected from adverse weather elements. It should be well illuminated and maintained.
- The minimum clear width for a single wheelchair is 36 in., but a universal route is 44 in. wide (except at tight turns).[29] For two wheelchairs to pass, the route must be 60 in. wide.[30]
- To improve visual acuity, use color and texture on sidewalk intersections leading directly into the street or parking lot.
- A covered entrance with a passenger loading zone is required by the Americans with Disabilities Act (ADA) only in health-care facilities where the stay may exceed 24 hours,[31] but ideally, all medical offices should provide one. In addition to a cover, a doorman or greeter is helpful to patients. Valet parking, on the other hand, poses problems. Many patients do not like to trust their vehicle to valet parking, especially if the vehicle has hand controls or special accommodations.

The New York University Medical Center (NYUMC) Radiation Oncology Center is designed to conceal the basement location. Backlighted murals serve as windows to the world of nature, and hot air balloons float into the "sky" above the treatment rooms. A 155-gallon fish tank placed in the simulator room subliminally says that these radiation levels are harmless to living things. Interior spaces communicate either positive or negative messages to patients and their families. Murals of sunsets or fall and winter scenes may unintentionally remind people that life is winding down; clouds on the ceiling could lead to concern about going to heaven.

Patients with cancer feel out of control. At the NYUMC treatment center, family-focused design detail tells patients and their families that they are the center of the practice, that they are in charge. Patients have access to their own records and can bring a friend or family member with them everywhere except the treatment room. Treatment tables move up and down to make it easier for patients to get on and off. Patients are

REFERENCES

1. *Americans with Disabilities Act Accessibility Standards,* 1991, 4.1.2 (5)(d).
2. Ibid., 4.1.3 (5).
3. Ibid., 4.1.6 (3)(ii)
4. Ibid., 4.10.9.
5. Ibid., 4.10.2.
6. Ibid., 4.10.3.
7. Ibid., 4.10.3.
8. Ibid., 4.10.4.
9. Ibid., 4.10.5.
10. Ibid., 4.10.6.
11. Ibid., 4.10.7.
12. *ADA Standards,* 4.15.5.
13. Ibid., 4.15.2.
14. Ibid., 4.15.3.
15. Ibid., 4.15.5 (1)
16. Ibid., 4.2.4.2
17. Ibid., 4.32.3
18. North Carolina State Building Code Council, *North Carolina State Building Code,* vol. 1-C (Raleigh: NCSBCC, 1989).
19. Jain Malkin, *Medical and Dental Space Planning for the 1990s* (New York: John Wiley and Sons, Inc., 1990).
20. *ADA Standards,* 4.31.9 (2)
21. Walter B. Kleeman, *The Challenge of Interior Design* (Boston: CBI Publishing, 1981): 99.
22. *ADA Standards,* 9.3.1.
23. Malkin, *Medical and Dental Space Planning.*
24. Robert J. Kobet, "The Tight House Syndrome: Causes and Cures" (paper presented at the American Society of Interior Designers National Conference, Washington, D.C., August 1988).
25. Malkin, *Medical and Dental Space Planning,* 270.
26. *ADA Standards,* 4.6.6.
27. Ibid., 4.5.2.
28. Ibid., 4.6.5.
29. Department of Justice, "ADAAG for Buildings and Facilities, Children's Facilities, Proposed Rules," *Federal Register* (22 July 1996).
30. *ADA Standards,* 4.2.2.
31. Ibid., 1991, 6.2.

8 WELLNESS CENTERS

There is a small town in central Florida called Celebration, a town that looks like a peaceful village from the turn of the century. But the traditional homes have been equipped with some very nontraditional options.

The homes are wired with fiber-optic cable to support an interactive multimedia network which can be used to connect the entire community. This network can offer unlimited possibilities for education, recreation, and home health care. Each home can be linked to a 750,000 sq. ft. health and wellness center so physicians can monitor pulse, blood pressure, EKG, body weight, and pulse oximetry of patients at home. Teleradiology can be used to transmit digitized images from the home to radiologists at the center. Teleconnective cable can allow physicians to diagnose from the center using video camera transmission from the patient's home. Even without the cable, the provider can conduct a visual assessment and listen to real-time heart and lung sounds over a standard telephone line (see Figure 8-1).

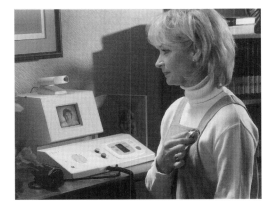

Figure 8-1 Heart and lung sounds transmitted from home. *Courtesy of American Telecare.*

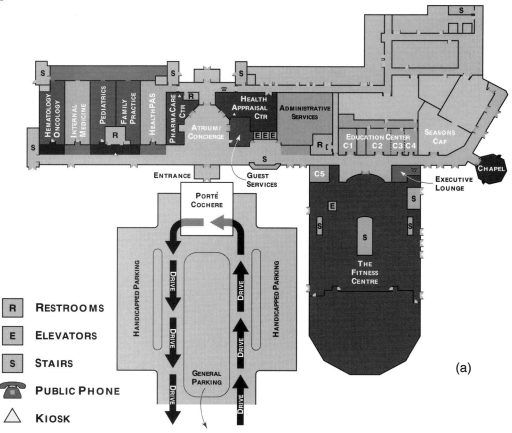

RESTROOMS

R RESTROOMS

E ELEVATORS

S STAIRS

☏ PUBLIC PHONE

△ KIOSK

Figure 8-2 (above and on facing page) Celebration Health floor plans. *Courtesy of Florida Hospital Celebration Health.*

From a home computer, residents will also eventually be able to receive training, schedule appointments, check the menu at the health center restaurant, check their medical records, and e-mail questions to doctors (see Details on page 139).

Primary, secondary, and tertiary care are offered at Celebration Health, a 60-bed center, which bears little resemblance to a traditional hospital. Equipment and staff are hidden behind the scenes, an idea borrowed from the adjacent Disney World. Who would guess that the building houses an emergency department (ED), an obstetrics unit with oversized Labor, Delivery, Recovery, Postpartum (LDRP) rooms (see Chapter 9), a dental center, a surgical unit, and a state-of-the-art imaging center (where children can watch their favorite video inside the MRI) (see Figure 8-2).

Located on a 60-acre campus, this center is housed in a low-rise building for maximum light and air penetration. Members (not patients) and guests approach on a tree-lined drive (see Figure 8-3) and enter an atrium resembling the lobby of an upscale hotel. The atrium is filled with sunshine and flowers rather than the fluorescent light and institu-

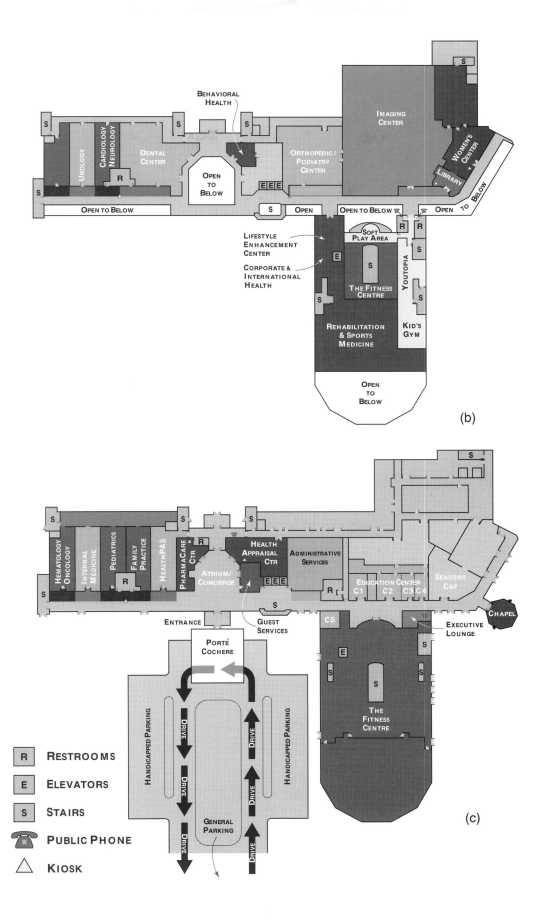

(b)

(c)

R RESTROOMS

E ELEVATORS

S STAIRS

📞 PUBLIC PHONE

△ KIOSK

Figure 8-3 Celebration Health entrance. *Courtesy of Florida Hospital Celebration Health.*

tional finishes found in most hospitals. The atrium and galleries connect to all major destinations in the building, offering easy wayfinding (see Details on pages 251 and 252).

Each health and wellness center member or guest is greeted by a receptionist in a polo shirt and khakis, not an institutional hospital uniform. There are few traditional waiting rooms. In the ED, for example, members and guests with minor emergencies wait separately from those with major trauma, shielding patients and their children from disturbing situations. Telephone and electric outlets are planned so that visitors can work on laptop computers before *and* during any delays in the examination or treatment.

The computer system allows physicians to instantly update medical charts, view X-rays, and access lifelong medical histories. They transmit prescriptions directly to the pharmacy. Computers with touch screens are located throughout the center. Visitors use the computers to find the answer to medical questions or receive nutritional information. They might join the fitness classes on-line or browse through medical library. They can learn about a wide range of subjects including self-care, caring for older parents, stress management, and choices in complementary medicine. Members and guests can determine their "health age," a chronological age based on physical, emotional and spiritual condition. In the pharmacy, they can access information about products and services to enhance their overall health plan.

Doctors offer fitness prescriptions to address individual health needs. The fitness center is used by both the healthy and healing. Rehabilitation and therapy are integrated into the fitness center, removing the fear associated with checking into a hospital. For the athlete, biomechanical assessments, sports psychology, sports nutrition, and performance enhancement prescriptions are available. Electronic notebooks are attached to the training equipment to evaluate progress. If a member slacks off, the equipment "tattles" to the staff, triggering a friendly follow-up note.

The surgery center incorporates state-of-the-art technology, including endoscopic diagnosis, which is performed by inserting a tiny camera and scope into the body via small incisions. Aesthetic surgery is offered. Celebration Health is also an international telesurgery site: there is videoconferencing in real-time to specialists in remote locations. Acute care is delivered in oversized, private rooms of universal design that can be converted for intensive care, pediatric, and obstetrical service provision. Suites feature sofas, a 30-in. television, a data link, in-room dining, and other amenities.

The health and wellness center at Celebration embraces creativity. In fact, members and guests are taught wellness from the acronym CREATION.

C reminds each member that *choice* is the cornerstone of wellness. Patients are encouraged to become their own primary care physicians. With this authority must come the personal responsibility for one's own health. Physicians treat members and guests as partners, not as obedient patients. To educate members and guests about their choices, the center offers a 2,200 sq. ft. library with current medical resources of the sort normally accessed only by physicians. Books are also sold in a retail store, along with a large choice of self-care products.

R prompts the need for *rest* and *relaxation*. The facility is designed to promote a peaceful atmosphere. Large windows and balconies offer access to nature and fresh air, and music plays softly in the garden (see Details on page 234). The restaurant provides a place to get away from concerns, relax with friends, and enjoy healthy meals.

E stands for the importance of *environment*, modeled by the design of Celebration Health. The center is illuminated by large windows that fill the space with sunshine. Water features surround the facility. In addition to natural beauty, environmental priorities include safety and cleanliness. For example, special attention is paid to air quality.

A represents *activity*, everything from box aerobics to spinning, tai chi, and stretching. Adult-supervised child care frees parents to participate. Adolescents are intrigued by the virtual-reality workout area.

T symbolizes *trust* in a divine power. The chapel is the heart of the facility, a perfect octagon symbolizing the eight principles of creation of good health.

I reminds members and guests of the importance of *interpersonal relationships*. The behavior center creates an atmosphere of support, confidentiality, and concern. Treatment includes marital and family counseling.

O emphasizes the importance of a healthy *outlook.* Personal discovery and growth are encouraged through support groups and classes offering understandable medical information. The behavioral health center also provides treatment for depression and chemical dependency. In addition, classes are offered to help eliminate smoking, modify dangerous habits, and reduce consumption of fat, salt, and sugar.

Finally, *N* stands for *nutrition.* Nutritionists are available for individual consultation as well as group training in a classroom format.

The goal of the health and wellness center is to maximize the healing potential of patients through risk reduction and health promotion. Members and guests are encouraged to learn about medical technology and services, perhaps finding solutions to their own health-care problems and, in the process, taking responsibility for their own health.

TRANSFORMING HOSPITALS INTO WELLNESS CENTERS

With a $130 million budget for new construction, innovation at Celebration is practically a given. But can these wellness ideas be applied to the small hospital with a limited budget?

A wellness approach is truly the logical choice for the small hospital. Hospitals are looking for healthy ways to expand services (and revenue). They must encourage daily use by the well, not occasional use by the acutely ill. Traditionally, 80 percent of our health-care dollars have been spent on disease care, not health care.[1]

As hospitals age, the demographics of their location changes. They often find themselves in low-growth areas in need of a new market. With shorter lengths of stay and restrictions on fees for services, hospitals find it increasingly difficult to maintain census. Competition for existing services forces them to market new services and differentiate themselves from their competitors. For a hospital to remain competitive, it must capture the outpatient market. A wellness center may be the answer.

Reimbursement drives design, and insurance companies are increasingly promoting the wellness philosophy. It is in the best interest of managed care providers as well as patients to prevent illness rather than just cure it. In addition, many private companies are now self-insured, and they pay if employees are not proactive in their health care. Those companies that cannot afford an in-house wellness program are increasingly using hospital-based prevention services. Patients at hospitals are seldom required to use the wellness services. Membership in the wellness center is viewed as a choice, not a "need," and it is rarely reimbursed by third parties. As membership is optional and market driven, the center must truly be consumer oriented.

Figure 8-4 Track elevated over a basketball court. *Courtesy of OWP&P Architects and Paul Schlismann Photography.*

The wellness center must be conveniently located with ample parking and extended hours (see Details on page 128). Members must be comfortable and secure, but the design must go beyond meeting basic needs; it must motivate people to change. For example, the member may become bored running in a circle with no diversion, so the track can be elevated over another activity area (see Figure 8-4) or designed in an unusual configuration offering a variety of visual stimuli. If it winds over or through the other exercise areas, the track can provide a positive distraction for those involved in all the programs of the center. Lighting under the handrail on the track is a nice design detail.

Hospital wellness centers must accommodate diversity and a wide range of abilities. It is a mistake to target youth exclusively when the market can be expanded to include older users as well. Wellness should be a lifetime commitment, and design should reflect the needs of the entire human lifespan. For example, equipment must be selected to meet a variety of needs and appeal to members of all ages. Low-speed treadmills and low-weight training machines should be offered. Both must feature user-friendly controls. Private areas for training can be provided for those who do not want to advertise their body profile.

Just as hospitals profit from a wellness component, wellness centers also profit from offering services traditionally provided in hospitals. Health-care services provide backup for the wellness program. For example, if the personal trainer encounters difficulties, a physical therapist can be consulted. If a weight control program is unsuccessful, it can be adjusted by a dietitian. Sports injuries can be prevented by educa-

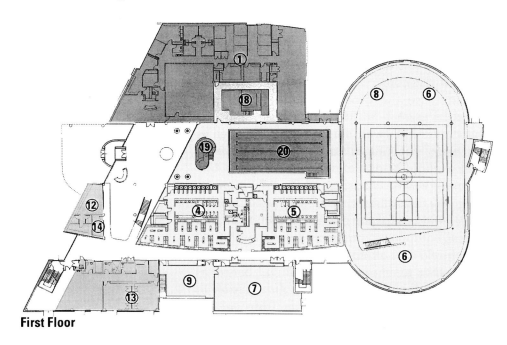

First Floor

Second Floor

Floor Plan Legend

Clinic Functions
1 Sports Medicine
2 Cardiac Rehab
3 Cardiac Rehab Equipment Area

General Fitness Activities
4 Women's Lockers
5 Men's Lockers
6 Exercise Equipment
7 Aerobics
8 Free Weights
9 Exercise Equipment
10 Manicure & Massage
11 1/12 Mile Running Track

Community Services
12 Boutique
13 Children's Activities
14 Administration
15 Lounge/Cafe
16 Conference
17 Multi-Purpose

Pools
18 Warm Water Therapy
19 Spa
20 Lap Pool
⬤ Open to Below
○ Circulation

Figure 8-6 Floor plan showing athletic courts. *Courtesy of OWP&P Architects and Paul Schlismann Photography.*

Adjacent to the fitness area, provide space for warm-up and stretching. Courts for tennis, racquetball, squash, volleyball, and basketball should also be considered (see Figure 8-6). In addition, consider a retail space for fitness clothing and supplies (see Figure 8-7).

The fitness assessment area is considered the heart of the wellness center. Each member begins with an evaluation that leads to creation of an individual treatment program. Special equipment may be integrated into this area to evaluate cardiovascular fitness, pulmonary function, aerobic work tolerance, strength, and flexibility. It may also be necessary to take blood samples and assess body fat percentage.

Nonmember Spaces

Wellness centers frequently lease space to health-care providers offering services to the entire community. Many wellness centers now offer cardiac rehabilitation with stress testing, sports medicine, occupational

Figure 8-7 Retail space. *Courtesy of Ohlson Lavoie Corporation, Denver, CO. Photo: Brian Fritz Photography.*

therapy, physical therapy, and industrial rehabilitation. These day services seldom conflict with a fitness club schedule, which is crowded before and after work. To encourage use by nonmembers, diagnosis and treatment areas should be accessed from the main entrance (see Details on pages 63 and 149). Examination rooms may needed (see Chapter 7). A community day spa can also be planned, offering massage therapy, herbal wraps, facials, sauna, and steam.

Many wellness centers successfully incorporate a restaurant. The restaurant location should indicate clearly that it is open to all, not just the members of the center. Heart-healthy cooking classes may be offered by the restaurant staff. A mobile cooktop can be wheeled into classrooms for this purpose, or a demonstration kitchen can be planned.

Child day care services may also be planned for use by nonmembers. Give special attention to acoustics to prevent noise transmission. Include an adjacent bathroom for children (see Chapter 10).

Locker Rooms and Wet Areas

There is a lack of flexibility, almost a planned obsolescence in the design of many wellness centers. This is especially true in the wet areas. Without a plan for expansion, there is no way to adjust to changing user needs. Movable walls can be specified in these areas, allowing modification to meet the needs of shifting gender populations. Movable therapy pools, showers, and lockers are other examples of flexible elements.

Personal lockers are a real convenience to members. The locker room should provide some separation from the wet and dry areas as well as proper humidity control. Private changing areas should also be provided; curtains are easier to use than doors, especially for those using mobility aids. Seating in the locker room is helpful for expectant mothers, older people, and wheelchair users who transfer to a bench to change clothes. Benches should be planned in several seat heights ranging from 11 in. for children to 19 in. for people in wheelchairs. It may be helpful to wall-mount a handrail (at 34–38 in. a.f.f.)[3] next to one bench (see Details on page 254). Hooks and shelves are also helpful. A full-length mirror that can be viewed from the bench is also useful to people of all heights and abilities. It should be installed no lower than 9 in. a.f.f. to prevent damage from wheelchair footrests.[4]

At a minimum, a 36 in. wide accessible route should be planned through the locker room and wet area, including the lavatories, stalls, showers, and pools.[5] The shower area is frequently planned between the locker room and the pool area (see Details on the next page). The public bathroom must be usable by people of all sizes, ages, and abilities (see Details on pages 166, 167, and 168).

DETAILS
Showers

- Provide a shower wheelchair. After one transfer from the wheelchair to the shower wheelchair, the user can roll into the shower, under the sink, and over a toilet without additional transfer.

- A universal shower can be used by all members, including shower-wheelchair users and those on gurneys. It must be 30 in. by 60 in. minimum to comply with the ADA Standards.[6] Grab bars should be installed on all sides (33–36 in. a.f.f.).[7]

- The shower floor should be sloped rather than curbed, as a curb could block wheels and become a tripping hazard. If the entire floor of the room cannot be sloped to a drain, a flexible curb is another solution.

- A steep floor slope (exceeding 2 percent) makes it difficult to maneuver a shower wheelchair.[8]

- Water can also be contained by recessing instead of sloping the floor of a wheel-in shower. Use a grating to raise the floor height to that of the bathroom. A grating and ramp can also be used to access an existing shower with a lip (see Details on page 247).

- A second shower with a seat should be provided for ambulatory users who need to sit and people in wheelchairs who can transfer to a seat. This shower must be small so wheelchairs users can reach the grab bars for transfer. Shower controls should be mounted on the wall opposite the seat and offset to the shower entrance.

- Specify a fold-up shower seat to clear the space for standing users. The seat should be slip-resistant, with small openings for good drainage. Make sure the corners are rounded.

- Small transfer-in showers require a ½-in. curb to contain the water.[9] During transfer to a shower seat, the front wheels of a wheelchair are placed over the curb to prevent the chair from sliding backward.

- Shower stalls should have rounded corners inside and out for safety and ease of maintenance, and the floor should be slip-resistant.

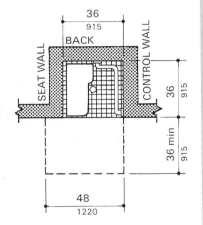

Transfer-in shower. *Uniform Federal Accessibility Standards.*

- Plan all showers with curtains, not doors. An open shower that requires neither curtains nor doors is easily accessible and helpful for people with allergies. Shower frames and curtains retain moisture and encourage mold growth; furthermore, plastic shower curtains may release irritants when heated.

- Equip each shower with an adjustable handheld shower fixture. This system is ideal for wheelchair users. The fixture can be clipped to a bracket for standing users.

- The valve should not catch the shower hose and should require only one hand to regulate water flow and set the desired temperature. An integral thermometer and surge control provides a safe flow of hot water.

Continued

DETAILS
Showers (*continued*)

- The flexible hose should be at least 60 in. long,[10] but some users may require a hose as long as 72 in.
- Choose a model with a water-volume control in the shower head.
- Specify a shower head bar for vertical adjustment that does not obstruct the grab bars.
- A shower shelf or caddy can prevent soap, shampoos, and accessories from slipping out of reach. Choose one in solid brass, plastic, or stainless steel to prevent corrosion and rust; make sure that it drains easily.
- Plan multilevel soap dispensers.
- For convenience, store towels in a cabinet close to the shower.
- Consider planning a separate shower for children with controls at a height no greater than 36 in. and with the grab bars at 27 in. a.f.f. maximum.[11]
- A sensor could be used to automatically start the children's shower upon entering. The temperature can be preset to prevent burns.
- Some lever controls prevent burns by maintaining temperature if the control is bumped by accident. This feature is also helpful to children just learning to use the controls. Another option is an integral thermometer, which allows the temperature to be preset.

DETAILS
Toilet Stalls

- The approaches to accessible toilets should alternate throughout the building, as some people are stronger on one side than the other.
- Accessible stalls of minimum size must have toe clearance of 9 in. a.f.f.[12] (12 in. for children). Larger stalls are preferable. Florida requires a minimum size of 68 in. by 68 in.
- In larger stalls, a partition to the floor can provide a positive stop for a person using a mobility aid.
- In an accessible stall, the door must swing out.[13] Actually, this is a convenience on all stalls.
- Stalls should be equipped with gravity-closing hinges and hardware that does not require tight grasping, pinching, and twisting.[14]
- A lavatory in the stall allows for additional privacy for cleanup.
- A tissue dispenser should be at least 19 in. a.f.f. and yet low enough so that grab bars do not interfere with its use. It must be installed on the side wall 7 to 9 in. in front of the toilet.[15]
- The dispenser must permit continuous paper flow and be usable with one hand.[16] Do not use a dispenser that requires users to reach into a hole to initiate paper flow or a dispenser with a sharp or serrated edge.
- Consider two tissue dispensers for a constant supply, with one at a lower height for children (2 to 6 in. above the toilet seat).
- The tissue dispenser should be recessed so it does not interfere with mobility aids.

DETAILS
Lavatories

- Wall-mounted lavatories are easy to wheel under if properly installed. Deeper wall-mounted lavatories must be supported by extra bracing.

- Water supply and drainpipes can be plumbed in a horizontally offset position to free knee space. Sharp or abrasive edges around or under the lavatory may injure a seated user. Insulate pipes under approachable lavatories or add a removable cover to prevent burns. Plastic pipe may not require insulation if the maximum hot water temperature does not exceed 120°F.[17]

- Thermostatic controls limit maximum temperature and prevent sudden changes.

- The height of the lavatory is critical in accommodating the needs of people with varying ranges of motion. People in wheelchairs need a rim no higher than 34 in. with knee clearance of 29 in. at the front edge.[18] This height is also usable by most standing adults and many children. Children in wheelchairs require a rim that is no higher than 30 in. and knee space of at least 24 in.[19]

- A clear floor space of 30 by 48 in. should be provided, extending under the lavatory a maximum of 19 in.[20] Children in wheelchairs require a clear floor space of at least 36 by 48 in. extending under the lavatory a maximum of 14 in.

- For people with differences in vision, identify the edge of the lavatory area by contrasting with a color. Color-coded hot and cold water controls are also helpful.

- A single-lever faucet can be easily controlled with one hand; spring-loaded faucets take more strength to operate.

- Mount faucets and controls on the front apron of the counter or to the side of the lavatory to improve reach.

- A universal faucet control is operated without use of hands. It senses any object underneath and flows at a safe, preset temperature. These valves can be programmed to open and close the flow at preset intervals, without the use of external controls. If a self-closing valve is used, the faucet should remain open for at least 10 seconds.[21]

- A temperature control prevents burns. Set the mix valve at a temperature of 115°F to start; do not exceed 120°F.[22]

- The corners of the vanity should be rounded if they extend into the room around the lavatory.

- The bathroom mirror must be low enough to reflect the wheelchair user's image. In most cases, it must be installed to the top of the splash. The bottom of a permanently installed mirror should be no higher than 40 in.[23] (34 in. for children).[24] A tilted mirror distorts the image but provides a fuller view than a flat mirror.

- Wall-mounted paper towel and soap dispensers must project no more than 4 in. into the clear floor space.[25] They must be mounted no higher than 36 in. for children. The preferred installation is on the surface of the counter.

DETAILS
Toilets and Urinals

- Elongated toilets are easier than standard size to use when transferring or aligning with the shower wheelchair for toileting.

- Use a toilet with a seat adjustable to wheelchair height for adults and children (11 to 19 in.). Most accessible toilets are too high to easily empty a leg bag into. The lip of the toilet needs to be below the level of the drainage tube since the leg must be elevated to this level to empty the bag.

- A low toilet with a high seat leaves a gap between the two. For the bowel or bladder program, it may be necessary to reach into this gap. Specify a seat with an opening in the front.

- Firmly attach a toilet seat with a wide bench for ease in transferring from a wheelchair.

- The toilet seat must not be sprung to return to a lifted position, but it should remain up independently when raised. Men with hemiplegia or only one hand do not have a free hand to hold up the toilet seat while using the toilet.

- The clearance below a wall-mounted toilet provides extra floor space for wheelchair footrests.

- The flush valve lever should be on the wheelchair approach side.[26] The toilet should be easy to flush, requiring no more than 5 lbf for operation. A portable toilet flush lever extension may be needed. The universal design is a sensor for automatic flushing.

- For people with differences in hearing, the noise created by water flow should be reduced. Consider low-pressure cisterns instead of high-pressure heads. Reduce ambient noise by specifying pipes with as large a crosssection as possible.

- Accessible urinals must be specified with a maximum rim height of 17 in. a.f.f., but a floor-mounted urinal is more accessible to small boys and others who need a lower rim.[27]

- A clear floor space of 30 by 48 in. must be provided in front of each urinal.[28]

- A urinal in a stall is preferable for privacy in emptying a leg bag. In public urinals, the privacy shields must not extend past the front edge of the urinal into the clear floor space.

- The accessible urinals should be wall mounted a minimum of 14 in. from the wall.[29]

At a minimum, a 4 ft. wide route should be planned around the pool. A ramp into the swimming pool provides easy access for children, older people, and wheelchair users (see Figure 8-8). It should not exceed a slope of 1 in. of rise per 10 in. of length.[30] It should be 36 in. wide and have railings on each side, which can be used to guide a shower chair on entering and exiting. Both the ramp and the route should have a nonslip surface.

A portable lifting device can be used in place of a ramp. A series of steps can also be used to access a pool or spa, with the highest step planned at wheelchair seat height (17–19 in.). After transferring to the top step, wheelchair users slide down from step to step.

A pool can be used for aquatic exercise classes, which may require underwater treadmills. Lap pools can be used for swimming, aquatic exercise, and to teach infants to swim. For security purposes, the swimming pool should be located where it is easily observed.

A hydrotherapy spa is an important addition to the wet area, but it presents acoustic challenges. The pump should be placed in an isolation closet and the spa location should be carefully planned to prevent noise transmission to other areas. Members appreciate the privacy of a gender-specific spa in each locker room.

In conclusion, wellness centers are exploring the entire continuum of care, from illness to wellness. Most provide information to the community in the form of health education programs. Wellness centers also encourage their members to apply this information to holistic self-care, going beyond care of the body to encompass the mind and spirit as well.

Figure 8-8 Ramp into a pool. *Courtesy of Healthcare Environment Design.*

A holistic approach treats the person, not the disease, using mild, natural methods whenever possible. Finally, the continuum leads to a high level of wellness that combines traditional and complementary medicine with a lifestyle approach. The result is optimal physical health, emotional serenity, and mental clarity.[31]

> Today, most of the diseases we encounter are lifestyle diseases with influencing factors we can control.... The future is the extension of quality of life, dying as old as we can as young as possible.
>
> Des Cummings, Jr., CEO,
> Florida Hospital Development

REFERENCES

1. Laura Bailey, John Purdy, Gijs Van Oort, and Thomas Wills, "Wellness Centers," *Journal of Health Care Interior Design* 2 (1990): 108.
2. Ibid., 113.
3. *Americans with Disabilities Act Accessibility Standards*, 1991, 4.8.5.
4. Cynthia Leibrock and James Evan Terry, *Beautiful Universal Design* (New York: John Wiley and Sons, 1999).
5. *ADA Standards*, 4.3.3
6. Ibid., 4.21.2
7 Ibid., 4.21.4
8. Ibid., 4.3.7
9. Ibid., 4.21.7
10. Ibid., 4.21.6
11. *Americans with Disabilities Act Accessibility Guidelines for Buildings and Facilities: Building Elements Designed for Children's Use*, 4.17.7(5).
12. *ADA Standards*, 4.17.4.
13. Ibid., 4.22.2.
14. Ibid., 4.13.9.
15. Ibid., 4.16.6.
16. Ibid., 4.16.6.
17. North Carolina State Building Code Council, *North Carolina State Building Code*, vol. 1-C (Raleigh, N.C.: NCSBCC, 1989).
18. *ADA Standards*, 4.19.2.
19. *ADAAG for Children's Use*, 4.24
20. *ADA Standards*, 4.19.3.
21. Ibid., 4.19.5.
22. *North Carolina State Building Code.*
23. *ADA Standards*, 4.19.6.
24. *ADAAG for Children's Use*, 4.19
25. *ADA Standards*, 4.4.1.
26. Ibid., 4.16.5.
27 Ibid., 4.18.2
28 Ibid., 4.18.3
29 North Carolina State Building Code
30. Robert Sorensen, *Design for Accessibility* (New York: McGraw-Hill, 1979): 158.
31. Teresa Peck, James R. Van Vorst, and Jane A. Root, *Wellness: The Revolution in Health Care* (St. Louis: Catholic Health Association, 1983): 4.

INPATIENT HOSPITALS

Our current health-care system is a product of the industrial age, a place where technology is valued and people are sometimes treated like machines. Health-care providers are considered the technicians who work on the machines. But in the information age, patients and their families are learning about other choices and beginning to take action.

Informed patients are maintaining decision-making authority and increasingly seeking a collaborative relationship with providers. Patients are becoming partners, taking responsibility for their own health. Providers are becoming teachers, and the facility is evolving into the classroom.

This new paradigm puts patients and their families in charge. It concedes that people are more important than technology and that patients deserve more than treatment of the physical machine. This holistic approach provides treatment for both the mind and spirit. Illness is viewed as an opportunity to learn, to discover a healthier lifestyle.

On entering the hospital, patients and their families should be greeted as welcome members of the team. Following a direct visual path to the greeter, all members should be received with comfort, consideration, and efficiency. In consideration of privacy, waiting space should be planned away from the very ill and out of the traffic pattern for staff and visitors. The initial interview should be conducted in a private place but, surprisingly, the need for privacy may not be a priority in the patient's room.

Some patients progress more rapidly by learning from other patients in a shared room. One study revealed that a majority of patients actually preferred a shared room, even when cost was not a factor.[1] The success of a shared room is often limited when the age discrepancy between the roommates is large or when privacy is destroyed by noise, odor, or unwanted visitors. In other words, membership can-

not be at the expense of privacy. Throughout the hospital, stress is caused alternately by a lack of privacy and too much isolation. Privacy and membership must be balanced to create a low-stress environment.

When patients and their family enter a hospital, they are suddenly adrift, floating between two worlds, not knowing on which shore they will eventually land.[2] If you were going to another world, what would be important to you? Wouldn't it be the little things—the memories of family and friends, the taste of a great dessert, the fragrances of baking bread, the feel of your pet's fur, the voice of a loved one, the rhythm of the ocean?

At the hospital, patients need to stay in touch with the world they just left, their home. A shelf for family pictures would help. Indirect lighting can set the mood and windows can reconnect patients with the rest of the world (see Details on page 49). Design detail can help preserve the independence enjoyed at home: a table in the room where a meal can be shared, a private space for family meetings. Design detail keeps one's life under control. Nonslip flooring conveys the confidence needed to exercise and regain health (see Details on page 181). Environmental cues keep patients oriented. Empowering design is flexiblel; bathrooms are adaptable to people of all sizes and abilities (see Details on pages 166, 167, and 168 and Research Abstract on page 101) and flexible policies are in place with regard to rooming-in, cooking, and visiting hours. Flexibility contributes greatly to a home-like atmosphere in the hospital.

Several interesting research studies evaluated homelike features. Furniture position was the single most highly correlated feature in deinstitutionalizing the environment. According to this study, the middle of the room should be furnished and several styles of seating should be provided. Chairs with arms and cloth covers were highly rated, but many styles were perceived as institutional. The study suggested an increase in horizontal surfaces and a decrease in seating. Elements perceived as less institutional included wood casement windows, decorative wood trim, more than one doorway to a room, movable incandescent floor lamps, and sheer window treatments.[3]

This is not to say that the hospital should be decorated to look like home. The environment must walk the line between institutional sterility and homelike grubbiness. Patients and their families are looking for competent health care in a professionally planned environment.

Today's hospital is a sensory hub where specialized treatment takes place. The hospital frequently receives patients from a network of satellite hospitals and ambulatory care facilities. While most people in ambulatory care are basically well, the acute care hospital is increasingly a place for people who are very sick and where the most critical care takes place.

The hospital can also be a high-touch hub integrated with such high-touch elements as massage, music, relaxation techniques, nature, and sunlight. Individual spaces can be small and clearly differentiated to support wayfinding (see Details on pages 251 and 252). Large spaces are perceived as institutional, fostering dependence, while smaller, intimate spaces are associated with more independent behavior. One study specifically found that smaller rooms (of 199 sq. ft. or less) with lower ceilings (90–102 in.) were considered less institutional.[4] Surprisingly, this study also found that fire extinguishers, sprinklers, and exposed heating systems were not perceived as institutional. So much for formula design.

Patient and family perception is increasing in importance as hospitals are forced to compete for patients. According to Russell Coile, leading health care futurist, customer satisfaction ratings will be made public and managed care inspectors will check facilities to see if providers meet their design expectations. Managed care has arrived at one simple conclusion, "If we don't keep the patient first, we're dead."[5]

Many hospitals have already died. As stated earlier, close to 1000 hospitals have closed since 1987. Many hospitals are downsizing to accommodate a lower census. In Colorado, half the hospital beds are frequently empty.[6] Primary care is taking place in ambulatory facilities rather than inpatient hospitals. Real estate agents have been trying to dispose of deserted properties. The remaining hospitals are looking for ways to differentiate from the competition, ideas that will attract patients and their families.

The irony of this situation is that the existing competition is so easily surpassed. In many existing hospitals, patients expect to be hurt and to be treated as numbers rather than as individuals. Patients are stressed by confinement and lack of exercise. Patients must deal with institutional surroundings, a loss of independence, and separation from the family. Existing hospitals provide little access to information while patients face financial concerns, the threat of illness or death, and problems with medication or pain.[7]

With competition like this, a winning strategy is elementary. The following chapters are filled with solutions that will differentiate caring hospitals from their competition. Family-focused care is the entry point for a brighter health-care future, and that future will be exciting indeed.

REFERENCES

1. E. A. Reed and E. M. Feeley, "Roommates," *American Journal of Nursing* 73 (1973): 104
2. Laura Gilpin, "Acute Care Design: A Workshop on Patient-Centered Environments," *Journal of Healthcare Design* 8 (1996): 44.
3. T. Thompson, J. Robinson, M. Graff, and R. Ingenmey, "Home-Like Architectural Features of Residential Environments," *American Journal of Mental Retardation* 95, no. 3 (1990): 328–341.
4. Ibid.
5. Russell Coile, "Competing by Design: What You Need to Know About Tomorrow's Business in Healthcare," *Journal of Healthcare Design* 9 (1997): 26.
6. Richard Lamm, "Futurizing America's Institutions," *The Futurist* 30, no. 5 (September/October 1996): 23–26.
7. B. J. Volicer, M. J. Isenberg, and M. W. Burns, "Medical-Surgical Differences in Hospital Stress," *Human Stress* 3 (1977): 3.

9 BIRTH CENTERS

Hospitals know that if a woman is pleased with her birthing experience,f she will return for her family's future health care needs. For this reason, birth centers are viewed as a marketing tool and are frequently designed as the showpiece of the hospital. Today's woman is interested in a high-quality birthing experience. She is having fewer children, often waiting until her 30s or 40s to have her first child, who may turn out to be her only child. She wants the event to be special. From the initial examinations to the actual labor and delivery, design detail can determine the quality of this unique experience.

INNOVATIONS IN BIRTH CENTERS

Today's mother is no longer required to move from a labor room to an operating theater, into recovery, and back to a patient room where she is separated from the newborn. Quality care can be provided in an LDRP suite, which supports labor, delivery, recovery, and postpartum care in one room. Another choice is the LDR suite, which can accommodate up to 350 births per room per year versus 120 births in an LDRP.[1] The LDR suite is sometimes less expensive but little postpartum care is provided in the room; the mother and infant must be separated after birth.

In an LDRP suite, the mother and child are not delivered to the services; the health care is delivered to them. Although our discussion is limited to family-centered design, it should be noted that the LDRP suite reduces the staff time required to clean multiple rooms and to move the occupants. More important, it minimizes the risks associated with moving mothers or separating them from their infants. Couplet care encourages maternal bonding and reduces the infant's exposure to disease, noise, and the extreme lighting levels present in some nurseries. It also increases the security of infants and reduces infant theft. For this reason, separate labor, delivery, recovery, and postpartum units are declining in use.[2]

Although the mother and infant remain together in a LDRP, an optional respite nursery is a good idea for short, intermittent use. Temporary nursery care is appreciated if the mother does not feel well or if she requires a sedative. She may also choose to place the infant in the nursery while she is bathing or if she is having difficulty sleeping.

An acute-care hospital provides support for obstetrical complications, often in a comfortable setting. Many hospitals offer a cesarean birth suite. In high-risk cases, the mother may need to be moved to a maternal-fetal intensive care unit. The room must provide mechanical ventilation, invasive hemodynamic monitoring, and other life support interventions. After the birth, the infant may need to be placed in a neonatal intensive care unit (NICU) (see Chapter 14). Market research reveals that special infant care services are most frequently requested by patients in birth centers.[3]

A standalone birth center is a safe choice for women at low risk for obstetrical complications, especially for women who have previously delivered safely. These centers are designed for primary care, not the acute care provided in hospitals. They are focused on the entire family, which often participates in the birth.

Only 1 percent of births occur at home, and the home is not expected to become the birthplace of choice.[4] As technology improves, birthing may eventually take place in outpatient centers, but today, most births occur in hospitals or in standalone birth centers not affiliated with hospitals.

THE BIRTH ROOM

In hospitals and standalone birth centers, the mother's room should be designed to treat the birth as a gratifying experience rather than as a disease. In one study, a soothing environment, numerous maternal choices, and a caring staff reduced labor to an average of 7.5 hours for 37 percent of first-time mothers, who generally labor 12 to 16 hours.[5]

Maternal choices may include walking, sitting, or even soaking in a tub to relieve discomfort. The mother can choose her own food or allow her family to provide comfort and support by preparing a meal for her in a kitchen available for family use (see Details on pages 94, 95, 96, and 97). She may be offered a choice of rooms with soothing colors and themes (see Details on page 82). Hospitality (not hospital) furniture includes a larger bed to accommodate a spouse, often raised to gurney height. The height can be minimized visually with a short coverlet and a long skirt. The coverlet can be stored in a window seat.

The birthing bed is aligned with a full-length mirror so that the mother can watch the birth and reach down to receive the baby as it is born (see Details on page 228). This represents a major paradigm shift; 20 years ago it was not uncommon to strap the mother's arms to the bed and instruct her not to touch the baby.

High-tech equipment and medical gases are now stored out of sight, either behind a piece of art on a hinged frame or concealed in cabinets (see Figures 9-1 and 9-2). Other details in this room include a tailored bedspread which won't catch in a wheelchair or gurney, wainscoting that doubles as a handrail, and a sleeping chair for rooming-in.

Equipment is planned to allow mothers to monitor fetal blood pressure and heart rate. Three sets of medical gas outlets are needed, one on the head wall for the mother and two located on the side wall for use with twins. Each set must include one suction outlet and one oxygen outlet.[6] Three emergency power four-lex outlets must be placed near the head of the bed; monitoring an epidural anesthesia requires 12 outlets. Two additional emergency power outlets must be planned at another site in the room.[7]

The birthing bed must not block the path between the infant stabilization area and the door. A sink should be available in the room, planned for hands-free operation by staff (see Figure 9-3). A shared equipment room (between two LDRPs) is not a good idea; it contributes to a lack of privacy and an increase in ambient noise (see Details on pages 265 and 266). A shared bathroom (between two LDRPs) generates the same problems. In each room, plan a private bathroom with a second sink and a place to store a hair dryer and cosmetics (see Details on page 228).

Optional amenities include a candlelight dinner to celebrate the birth, perhaps served in a private dining area in the room. There may be an entertainment center with a VCR to replay the birth tape (see Details on page 137). Lighting should be soft and indirect. Infants and mothers should not be forced to constantly stare into direct lighting sources, like overhead fluorescents. Task lighting must be available when needed, including a surgical light recessed in the ceiling over the bed. Color and lighting selection must not interfere with the perceived color of the newborn's skin.

One excellent study found significant difference in the reaction of neonates to light frequency. Those exposed to high-frequency (blue)

Figure 9-1 "Before" LDRP. *Courtesy of Wheeler Photographics. Designer: The S/L/A/M Collaborative, Architects and Engineers.*

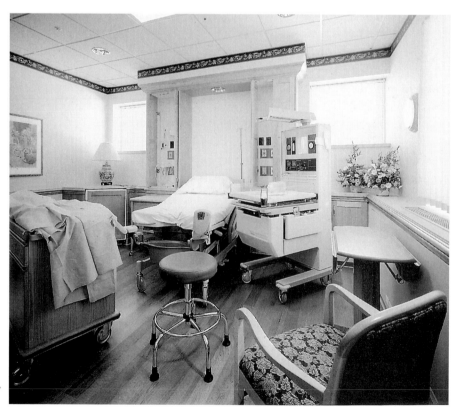

Figure 9-2 "After" LDRP. *Courtesy of Wheeler Photographics. Designer: The S/L/A/M Collaborative, Architects and Engineers.*

Figure 9-3 In-room sink. *Courtesy of Woodruff/Brown Photography. Designer: The S/L/A/M Collaborative, Architects and Engineers.*

light waves awoke more often and had a greater variability in sleep-wake frequency than infants experiencing low-frequency (red) light waves.[8]

HOSPITABLE ENVIRONMENTS

Lighting alone can transform an institutional environment into a welcoming space (see Details on page 83). The institutional association with the hospital can also be minimized by planning a separate entrance to the birthing wing. Nursing stations can be eliminated and charting completed in the birthing rooms. Point-of-care technology allows the same information to be accessed throughout the facility, not just at a nursing station. Laboratory and medication areas may also be decentralized, with satellite units located in each birth unit for family conve-

RESEARCH ABSTRACT
Experiential Research in Detailing Birthing Centers

The firm of Smith Hager Bajo is nationally recognized for expertise in planning and managing women's and children's health-care facilities. They provide the following Top Ten ideas:

1. Provide private rooms, from testing and triage to discharge.
2. Position the birthing bed and door to the corridor for acoustic and visual privacy.
3. Provide self-medication packets in bedside table drawers.
4. Specify comfortable queen-size beds for postbirth couplet care.
5. Provide family access to fax and e-mail for notifying other family members and friends of the birth.
6. Supply a family kitchenette.
7. Supply portable or fixed whirlpool baths.
8. Plan adequate lighting for newborn examinations in a Murphy bed in each room.
9. Plan a respite nursery versus traditional admission to a term nursery.
10. Provide ample parking and easy access from the parking lot.

nience. Even the hospital gift shop can be family centered, offering a choice of christening gowns or a book with of for children.

Privacy may be the most requested feature in birth centers, and private rooms should be planned for all levels of care (see Research Abstract above). A private lounge is greatly appreciated for physician conferences, family education, breast-feeding by visiting mothers, prayer, and grieving. Family members may use the lounge for sleeping when they cannot be provided overnight sleeping arrangements in the mother's room. The lounge may also provide secure storage for personal belongings, an adjacent bathroom, and access to phones and vending machines. Some feature a small kitchen or a coffee and espresso cart.

Finishes throughout the birth center should be selected for aesthetics, maintenance, and infection control. Appropriate choices include paint, vinyl wall covering, and sheet materials with fused seams (see Details on the next page). To limit microbial growth, specify casework and countertops with the fewest possible seams. According to a national perinatal survey, most LDRPs used carpet, at least in the corridors.[9] Hard-surfaced floors are not safer than carpet for controlling fungal or bacterial growth in health-care environments (see Research Abstract on page 23).

DETAILS
Flooring

Microbial Growth

- Sealed sheet goods prevent leakage from spills and protect the subfloor better than vinyl tiles, especially if the seams are chemically or heat welded. Leakage in the seams promotes microbial growth.

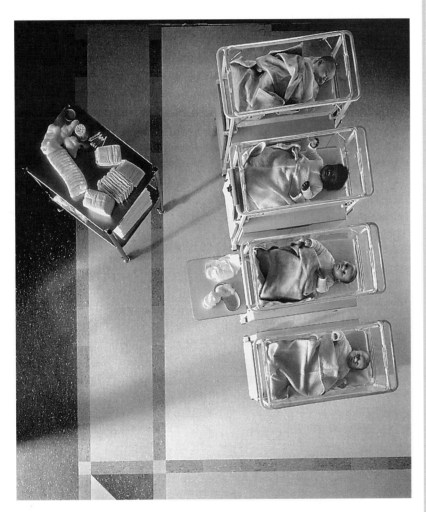

Sealed flooring. *Courtesy of Polyflor XL 2000, distributed in the U.S. by Bonar Floors. Manufactured in the U.K. by James Halsted, Ltd.*

- Acrylic-impregnated wood floors can be safely treated with gamma radiation to harden surfaces and prevent dents and chips. The acrylic saturation process also helps improve flame spread ratings and resistance to bacterial growth.

Continued

DETAILS
Flooring (continued)

Design Intervention

- For people with allergies, adhesives and leveling compounds must be avoided. Monolithic high-density vinyl floor coverings are acceptable to most people with allergies if fastened with wood baseboards.

- Avoid high-contrast patterns in floor coverings, which can make small objects on the surface difficult to locate, especially for people with low vision.

- Contrast the floor color with the wall color to highlight the edges of the room. Also, contrast the floor with the furniture to prevent collisions and accidents when sitting. To improve visual acuity, the contrast should exceed 2 on the gray scale.[10]

- Ceramic tile, impregnated wood, rubber, and solid vinyl floor coverings (with nonskid polish) are easily used with carts, gurneys, and wheelchairs.

- Deep joints in a width greater than ¾ in. may hold the wheel of a wheelchair, gurney, cart, or stroller. Protruding joints may produce a washboard effect, which can cause extreme discomfort, pain, or spasticity for the wheelchair or gurney user.

Appearance

- Floors with a high percentage of vinyl resin are the most resistant to stains.

- Rubber and solid vinyl floors are the most resilient and dent resistant.

- Self-shining synthetics eventually need touch-up and should not be used in high-traffic areas. Solid vinyl floors or floors with a large proportion of vinyl resins are the best choice for abrasion resistance in such areas. Solid-colored vinyls and inlaid patterns are more resistant to abrasion than vinyl prints or rubber.

- Solid colors appear soiled more quickly than do patterned floors. Soiling is also exaggerated by both very light and dark colors. Midrange to darker values help to hide marks left by wheelchairs, but unpatterned dark floors show dust and footprints. Dark colors also absorb light, a consideration for clients with vision differences who require increased lighting.

- Cushioned floors can be permanently dented by braces, canes, high heels, and other sharp objects, but they do reduce such high-frequency noises as footsteps. They are not durable enough to be used in high-traffic situations, however.

Slip Resistance

- In bathrooms and other potentially slippery areas, specify sheet vinyl impregnated with corundum chips. The seams can be chemically or heat welded to prevent leakage. This surface is easier to maintain than some other nonslip floors.

- Self-shining synthetics may be too slick for many people. Rubber and vinyl floors provide better traction and are often self-waxing, requiring only occasional maintenance with a commercial buffer.
- A rubber floor polished with a water emulsion provides better traction for wheelchairs than does a smooth quarry tile. A rubber floor in the bathroom is a good choice for slip resistance.
- Textured wood floors offer surprisingly good traction. Avoid wood floors with shiny polyurethane finishes, which offer limited traction. They are especially difficult for people in power wheelchairs.
- Textured quarry tile and ceramic mosaic tile, especially in small sizes with many joints, offer better traction (and less glare) than do shiny ceramic tiles. When greatest traction is needed, select a tile with an abrasive face, such as silicon carbide, carborundum, or grit.
- A slightly raised pattern reduces slipping, but cobblestones and uneven surfaces may impede rolling traffic. Irregular paving and flooring materials look as if they provide good traction, but they may cause tripping, especially for users of mobility aides.
- A nonskid surface must have a friction coefficient no less than 0.6 (0.8 for ramps), whether wet or dry.[11] A rubber floor often exceeds this criterion and is a good selection, especially in a design with a slightly raised disk or strip. Rubber floors also lightly cushion falls.
- Rubber flooring is resistant to wear, slippage, abrasion, cigarette burns, and most oils, acids, and alkalis. It shows fewer scuff marks than does solid vinyl, but rubber surfaces are not recommended for commercial kitchens, operating rooms, or spaces subject to heavy rolling loads and grease stains. Patterned vinyl can be substituted because it resists grease and oil and does not easily show scuff marks.
- Hard surfaces must be slip resistant or treated with a nonskid wax. Test slipping with a crutch angled at approximately 70 degrees from the horizontal.

REFERENCES

1. Joyce H. Vogler, "Birthing Centers," *Journal of Health Care Interior Design* 2 (1990): 121.
2. Judith A. Smith, *The Family Birthplace: Planning and Designing Today's Obstetric Facilities* (Chicago: American Hospital Publishing, 1995), 2.
3. Ibid., 41.
4. Ibid., 89.
5. Jain Malkin, *Hospital Interior Architecture* (New York: Van Nostrand Reinhold, 1992), 238.

6. Smith, *Family Birthplace,* 57.
7. Vogler, "Birthing Centers," 124.
8. B. W. Giradin, "Lightwave Frequency and Sleep-Wake Frequency in Well, Full-Term Neonates," *Holistic Nursing Practice* 6, no. 4 (1992): 57–66.
9. Smith, *Family Birthplace,* 16.
10. Lorraine G. Hiatt, "Long Term Care Facilities," *Journal of Health Care Interior Design* 2 (1990):200.
11. *Americans with Disabilities Act Accessibility Standards,* 1991, A4.5.1.

10 CHILDREN'S HOSPITALS

The single most important aspect of child health design is facilitating the involvement of parents.[1] When a child is hospitalized, the entire family becomes the patient.[2] Unfortunately, children's hospitals have traditionally been system centered rather than family centered. Hospital policies have forced family members to leave after visiting hours. Parents have been prohibited from using the physician's library to learn about their child's health. They have been limited in the care of their child and discouraged from changing a child's clothes, giving a sponge bath, accessing simple hospital equipment, and delivering the child to therapy. Research has shown that 24-hour open involvement of families, information sharing, and family participation with care can decrease the length of stay for babies by 30 to 50 percent.[3] The same study demonstrated that repeat hospitalization and the use of emergency services can be reduced.

Family participation also reduces costs and increases patient satisfaction with care. The child may be much more comfortable with a parent as the primary caregiver. The hospital should consider the parent a provider. Both children and families should be empowered with choice. Design can empower, providing efficacy, comfort, positive distractions, and a sense of belonging. Efficacy is exemplified by a nursing station equipped with a computer that swivels to provide parental access to medical records. A stool can be added inside the nursing station to provide a place for the parent. Comfort can be offered by a chair or sofa that opens into a bed for parents who wish to stay with the patient. Some hospitals even provide

Figure 10-1 Alligator play sculpture. *Courtesy of Zimmer Gunsul Frasco © Eckert & Eckert.*

overnight guest suites. Positive distractions are exemplified by destinations where parents and children can get away: a garden, a chapel, children's art gallery, and a family lounge.

The family lounge provides a place to read, relax, watch television, or cook a child's favorite meal, all within view of the nursing station. A play area for siblings should be planned in the family lounge (see Figure 10-1). Sometimes a family kitchen is planned (see Details on pages 94, 95, 96, and 97 and Research Abstract on page 59). Be sure to specify an automatic off switch on the cook top and keep controls out of the reach of small children. The lounge should also provide lockers, telephones, and a family bathroom (see Details on pages 166, 167, and 168 and Research Abstract on page 101).

The unisex or family toilet room is another good example of a design element that provides efficacy and control and helps to keep parents in charge (see Figures 7-20 and 10-2). The design allows a family member to accompany an older child of the opposite sex, providing care without clearing out the bathroom or embarrassing others. The family bathroom also provides a private place to change a baby. A counter or fold-down shelf should be provided for this purpose.

The remainder of this chapter is dedicated to empowering children and their families via design. Perhaps the most important goal is efficacy, keeping children and their families effective in the hospital environment.

EFFICACY

Children and their families seek independence, competence, and control. For a child in a health care facility, competence means being able to choose to play, to continue to go to school in the hospital, to care for themselves.

Children and their families need to be effective in their environment. They want to be able to see over desks, drink from water fountains, open doors, and use the bathroom with or without a wheelchair (see Details on pages 188 and 191). Illness can restrict movement, yet children have a need for movement without assistance.

Treatment areas should be planned so children can walk or wheel to them on their own, but young patients are frequently disabled by forgotten design detail (see Details on page 188). The route requires a second set of signs lowered to 48 in. a.f.f. to meet the needs of children (see Details on page 240 and Research Abstract on page 242) In elevators, braille and raised lettering must be mounted on both jambs at 48 in. a.f.f., below the 60-in. cues required by the ADA. The elevator call button should be installed at 3 ft. a.f.f.; redundant elevator controls should also be specified inside the cab at or below this height.

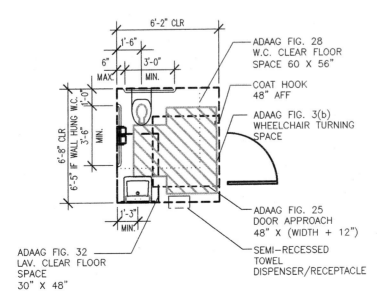

Figure 10-2 Family toilet room. *Courtesy of Evan Terry Associates, P.C.*

> **DETAILS**
> **Accessible Routes for Children[4]**
>
> - Maintain a clear width of 44 in. on the accessible route (instead of the 36 in. required for adults). Children require more maneuvering space.
> - Objects should not protrude more than 4 in. on the route. Protruding objects as low as 12 in. a.f.f. could be a hazard to a blind child.
> - Clear floor space at controls along the route should be increased to 36 by 48 in. For example, this larger clear floor space must be provided at elevator call buttons, drinking fountains, and telephones. Each control must be within reach. Clear floor space should extend no more than 14 in. under objects.
> - Door levers should be mounted 30 to 34 in. a.f.f.
> - Signs should be centered no higher than 48 in. a.f.f.
> - Eliminate all ramps on the accessible route. The maximum slope of an accessible route for children is 1:20. Ramps are not required at this slope.
> - A second set of handrails at stairs should be mounted 20 to 28 in. a.f.f. It is also recommended that the vertical clearance between handrails be at least 9 in. in order to reduce the risk of entrapment. Some health-care standards are more stringent than ADA.
> - The diameter of the handrail should not exceed 1¼ in.
> - Drinking fountains and telephones cantilevered from walls or posts must provide knee clearance (24 in. minimum) and toe clearance (12 in. minimum) below the unit for a forward approach. The knee space should extend 14 in. under the fountain or phone. The spout on drinking fountains must be no higher than 30 in. a.f.f.

Paradoxically, the accessible route must be wider for children than for adults (44 in. versus 36 in.). Children in wheelchairs require more maneuvering space and larger clear floor spaces at controls like elevator call buttons (36 by 48 in. versus 30 by 48 in.). The slope of the route should not exceed 1:20, making ramps unnecessary. If ramps and stairs are used, a second set of handrails should be provided (20 to 28 in. a.f.f.). (see Details on page 252). Handrails should be no larger than 1¼ in. in diameter, a universal dimension that works well for both children and most adults (see Details on page 254).

Drinking fountains, telephones, and counters along the route should be lowered for access by children in wheelchairs (30 in. a.f.f.). Knee space of 24 in. a.f.f. should be provided under all three. When public telephones are lowered for use by children, a flip-down seat can be added to facilitate use by adults as well. Text telephones can be located in these lower accessible telephone booths when a seat is added. As in any health-care facility, provide at least one accessible text telephone adjacent to the emergency rooms, recovery rooms, and waiting rooms, as required by ADA.[5]

Glass block serves as a nice transition at the entrance to each waiting room. Children and their families can see through from the corridor for orientation. Entrances can be recessed for additional spacial differentiation.

Treatment rooms should provide seating at a variety of seat heights ranging from 11 to 19 in. for children (see Details on pages 117 and 119). A full-length mirror should be provided in the dressing space, installed no lower than 12 in. a.f.f. (to protect it from wheelchair footrests); it should be viewable from the seat or bench. A grab bar adjacent to the bench is helpful for wheelchair users and for those who have difficulty bending and stooping (see Details page 88). Heights vary from 18 to 27 in. a.f.f. depending on the ages of the children served. A zigzag grab bar may be the best solution.

All public spaces in the hospital must be planned to empower children and their families. Restaurants must provide accessible seating and lowered service counters. Tray slides at 34 in. a.f.f. are helpful to adults using wheelchairs, adults of shorter stature, and some children, but most children in wheelchairs need a section lowered to 30 in. a.f.f. Tableware, condiment areas, self-service shelves, and dispensing devices must be approachable and within reach.

Many hospitals provide a family reference library. Books for children in wheelchairs should be stored 20 to 36 in. a.f.f. The library should include 44 in. wide access aisles, lowered checkout counters, and accessible fixed seating, tables, and study carrels (26 to 30 in. a.f.f.). Most important, libraries must provide children and their families access to computers, software, scanners, and copiers. In this information age, universal design of libraries is increasingly found in electronic access (see Details on page 139).

In the patient room, the door levers should be lowered to 30 to 34 in. a.f.f. The patient bed should be placed so that the child can face those entering the room, providing visual control. Specify a mattress with a firm edge at 11 to 19 in. a.f.f. to help in transferring (see Research Abstract on page 229).

Windows should be planned low enough for children to see out but high enough to prevent damage from wheelchair footrests (12 in. a.f.f.). Casement windows with controls on the bottom are easier for children to reach. Sliding, hopper, and awning windows can also be reached. Double-hung windows can drop unexpectedly and are difficult for everyone to open (see Details on page 54).

Make sure all controls can be operated with a closed fist. Touch controls that do not require tight grasping, pinching, or twisting should be installed. As a test, try to operate window controls, lighting switches, call systems, and telephones with a closed fist. Light switches should be installed no higher than 36 in. a.f.f. (see Details on page 98). Cords on roller shades and wands on blinds must be long enough to be reached by older children and wheelchair users, about 44 in. a.f.f.

Hooks, hangers, and shelves should be redundantly planned at a variety of reach ranges. Also consider installing pegs or wall-mounted racks between the counters and cabinets for storage within reach of children in wheelchairs. An adjustable-height counter or table can accommodate a variety of ages and abilities.

In the patient bathroom, accessible detail becomes critical for use. The height of the tub should match the height of the wheelchair seat. The height that serves most adults and children is 17 in. a.f.f., but the needs may vary from 11 in. for children to 19 in. for adults. A handheld shower helps all kids, not just those in wheelchairs. It also makes it easier for a parent to rinse a child's hair without getting shampoo in their eyes. Children can also be bathed in a child seat or on a bathing table that fits in the tub (see Figure 10-3).

Install a bathroom window to the side of the lavatory to allow children, people of shorter stature, and wheelchair users to reach window controls and to open the blinds and see out the window. Lavatories, toilets, and grab bars must also be carefully placed (see Details on the next page).

COMFORT AND SAFETY

Children are visually more comfortable with reduced scale. The children's hospital should not be a monumental building establishing power and authority. It should be the scale of a village—smaller, quieter, and more manageable. Large windows can be divided by mullions that snap out for

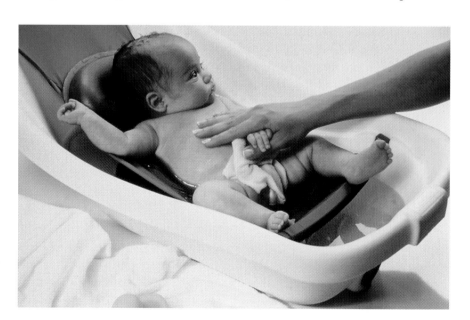

Figure 10-3 Infant bathing seat. *Courtesy of Century Products, Inc., Photo: Stehpen Ciuccoli. Design: Anderson Design, Inc.*

DETAILS
Accessible Bathrooms for Children[6]

- Maximum and minimum mounting reach heights should be specified for three age ranges: 36 in. (high) and 20 in. (low) for ages 2 through 4, 40 in. (high) and 18 in. (low) for ages 5 through 8, and 44 in. (high) and 16 in. (low) for ages 9 through 12. These ranges are the same for forward and side reaches. Door levers should be mounted 30 to 34 in. a.f.f. Signs should be centered no higher than 48 in. a.f.f.

- The centerline of the water closet must be 12 to 18 in. from the side wall or partition. A centerline placement of 12 in. is recommended for children ages 3 and 4, 15 in. for children ages 5 through 8, and 15 to 18 in. for children ages 9 through 12.

- The height of water closets must be 11 to 17 in., measured to the top of the toilet seat. A seat height of 12 in. is recommended for ages 3 and 4, 12 to 15 in. for ages 5 through 8, and 15 to 17 in. for ages 9 through 12.

- Urinal rim height should be a maximum of 14 in. a.f.f. Privacy shields must not extend past the front edge of the urinal.

- Mount grab bars 18 to 27 in. a.f.f. instead of 33 to 36 in., as is specified for adults. The rear toilet grab bar is required to be at least 36 in. long. A grab bar height between 18 to 20 in. is recommended for ages 3 and 4, 20 to 25 in. for ages 5 through 8, and 25 to 27 in. for ages 9 through 12.

- The maximum diameter of the grab bar must be 1 ¼-in.

- The flush valve must be mounted on the wide side of the toilet. The flush valve should be mounted no higher than 36 in. at water closets serving children ages 2 through 4, 40 in. at those serving children ages 5 through 8, and 44 in. at those serving children ages 9 through 12.

- Toilet paper dispensers should be mounted 14 to 19 in. a.f.f., measured to the dispenser centerline. A dispenser height of 14 in. is appropriate for ages 3 and 4, 14 to 17 in. for ages 5 through 8, and 17 to 19 in. for ages 9 through 12.

- With a wall-mounted toilet, plan a minimum depth for standard stalls of 59 in.

- In standard stalls, the front partition and at least one side partition should be at least 12 in. above the floor to provide toe clearance.

- Provide a rim clearance of 27 in. a.f.f. minimum and knee clearance of 24 in. a.f.f. minimum under lavatories, provided that the rim or counter surface is no higher than 30 in. Lavatories used primarily by children ages 5 and younger need not provide these clearances if space for a parallel approach is provided.

- Provide clear floor space of 48 by 36 in. extending no more than 14 in. under lavatories.

- Sink depth should not exceed 5½ in.

- Faucets should be located within 14 in. of the front of the bowl.

- The bottom edge of the mirror should be no higher than 34 in. a.f.f.

Continued

DETAILS
Accessible Bathrooms for Children[6] (*continued*)

- Knee space at least 24 in. high, 30 in. wide, and 14 in. deep must be provided under accessible tables and counters.
- Plan a surface height of 26 to 30 in. a.f.f. on vanities, tables, and counters.

A choice of counter heights. *Courtesy of Spector Group with Guenther Petrarca.*

easy maintenance. Etched patterns can also be used to visually reduce the scale (see Figure 10-4). Monumental doors should be eliminated. Children are more comfortable with a lower ceiling height, especially children in wheelchairs. It is most important to keep the scale manageable in transition spaces like entries, porches, and elevator lobbies where decisions are made. This keeps the child in control.

A child may need more tactile, auditory, and visual stimulation than an adult. Provide an environment that encourages fantasy, a space that gives children permission to act out their fears and relieve their anxiety (see Research Abstract on the next page). Carpeting provides a tactile, quiet, and comfortable surface for play. Padding adds additional comfort, but it is difficult for use with carts, gurneys, and wheelchairs. Properly

RESEARCH ABSTRACT
Experiential Research in Design Detail for Children

Award-winning interior designer Barbara Huelat, ASID of, Huelat Parimucha Ltd. in Alexandria, Virginia, has 30 years of experience in health design for children and their families. Following are seven of her favorite ideas:

1. One of my favorite play-rooms encourages the fantasy of being in an aquarium to entice children to use health education computers. The underwater blue color and reflective ceiling with neon waves creates a great ambience. This room was so carefully planned that even the neon lighting is positioned to reduce glare on the computer screens.

Encouraging fantasy. *Courtesy of Electronic Playroom at Kidsville, Children's Hospital of Hillcrest Baptist Medical Center, Waco, Texas. Designer: Huelat Parimucha.*

2. Plan nutrition centers accessible to children and their families. These centers can become a gathering place, offering juice, coffee, and snacks in a fun atmosphere complete with a jukebox filled with popular children's music.

3. Many hospitals provide health reference libraries, but placement of the library determines whether it is used. The elevator lobby is a good location, with the library entrance in sight as one exits the elevator. This entrance must be planned to invite people in to read a book or watch a video. Add a book drop and a computer monitor just outside of the library for after-hours research.

4. Children and their families need extra storage in their room. We include a day bed for rooming-in with storage drawers below. Frightening equipment can be stored behind artwork or in closets. We plan closets with double access so equipment can be maintained or used elsewhere without disturbing the patient.

5. A healing garden makes a great meeting place at the time of discharge or admission. The sound of running water beckons people to sit and stay for awhile (see Details on page 234).

6. To improve wayfinding, use consistent lighting details at all major decision-making points. Repeat a hospital icon or logo at these patient decision points (see Details and on pages 251 and 252).

7. Children need something to do while waiting or they can become disruptive to others. We add "kids' corners" throughout our health-care projects, identifying them with distinctive landmarks so kids can look for their own area of fun.

Figure 10-4 Etched
glass windows.
*Courtesy of Zimmer
Gunsul Frasco ©Timothy
Hursley.*

maintained carpet is not a negative factor in infection control. In a comprehensive test of carpeting in pediatric patient rooms, it was found that hospital-acquired infections were not associated with organisms found as contaminants of the carpet.[7] In fact, properly specified carpet can actually reduce microbial growth in the space (see Research Abstract on page 23). Research has also shown that negative pressure ventilation in the patient rooms can also reduce the incidence of disease transmission (in the case of this study, nosocomial chicken pox).[8]

HVAC also plays an important roll in the comfort of children and their families. Children, wheelchair users, and adults of shorter stature are religated to the lower, colder part of the space and may require higher ambient temperature levels. Individual HVAC controls are the solution. These should be installed at a reachable height (44 in. a.f.f. for older children).

A fetus develops in a warm, dark, quiet environment, and when children are very ill, they need to return to more subdued surroundings.[9] Carpeting, wall fabric, and acoustical tile can be used to reduce ambient noise levels (see Details on pages 265 and 266). One unique tile provides a surprising positive distraction—stars on the ceiling (see Figure 10-5). Quiet telephones at the bedside light instead of ring, a detail helpful for children with hearing impairments as well.

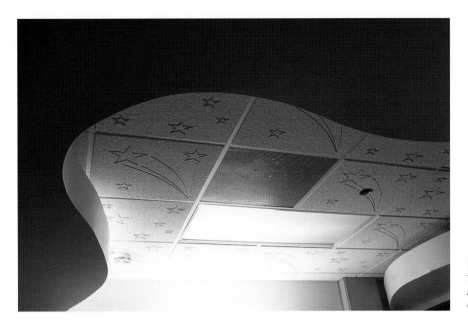

Figure 10-5 Stars on the ceiling. *Courtesy of Desert Samaritan Medical Center, Phoenix.*

For children with reduced vision, objects that protrude more than 4 in. are a real hazard. A child using a cane will miss any protruding object installed as low as 12 in. a.f.f. Examples of low protruding hazards include wall-mounted ashtrays at elevators, open stairways, and extensions on handrails. Corners of windowsills and other millwork should be rounded to prevent injury.

Hyperactive children may experience a shortened attention span and nutritional problems triggered by fluorescent lighting.[10] Use indirect tungsten lighting without glare in patient rooms, even over the patient's bed. Task lighting can be moved to the bed to increase lighting levels when necessary (see Details on page 83).

Specify heavy footboards in a height of 20 to 28 in. a.f.f. to provide stability when walking around the bed (see Details on page 225). Other patient room safety features include nontoxic plants and controlled access to HVAC registers, receptacle outlets, and exposed plumbing (see Details on page 99).

In the bathroom, select a faucet control that prevents sudden temperatures changes when bumped by accident. This feature is also helpful to children just learning to use the controls. Another option is an integral thermometer, which allows the temperature to be preset. Both systems should include a pressure-balancing feature that prevents surges of hot and cold water. As an alternative, a sensor could be used to automatically start the shower when children enter. The temperature can be preset to prevent burns.

Fire safety is critical for children and their families, but fire codes do not adequately address their needs. Adults of shorter stature and children are often unable to use heavy fire doors, particularly those equipped with panic hardware and door closers (see Details 6 and 7 on pages 68 and 70). Codes require some doors to remain open, inviting children to wander out of the hospital.

To increase the child's response time to a fire, specify flame-retardant fabrics, furnishings, and carpet. Furniture should comply with California Technical Bulletin 133, which tests the entire piece rather than the individual components.

On interior doors, vision panels provide warning and prevent accidents. Use safety or wire glass and keep the glass higher than a child's wheelchair footrests (12 in. a.f.f.). Avoid interior folding doors, in which children can pinch their fingers.

A SENSE OF BELONGING

Children never feel like they really belong in a hospital. In an attempt to soften the blow, many children actually bring more belongings to the hospital than the average adult patient. They therefore need more storage space than do adults (see Research Abstract on page 229). They also need a safe place to secure and display personal possessions. A lockable drawer should be planned in the patient room. A deep windowsill can be used to display toys. Open shelving and labeled bins may encourage kids to put things away.

Children and their families need a way to personalize their space. Plan a large bulletin board with magnets that can be used to display cards. A poster frame allows children to mount their own posters, perhaps selected from an "art cart." White boards allow children to draw decorations for their own room.

Each room should be clearly differentiated by shape, ceiling heights, color, and pattern (see Details on pages 82 and 214). Children are more comfortable with a large variety of social and private spaces on a residential scale (rather than one or two large adaptable spaces). Residential scale and spacial differentiation improve wayfinding and encourage activity, mobility, and exploration (see Details on pages 251 and 252).

POSITIVE DISTRACTION AND DIVERSION

This is the fun part of designing for children and their families; almost anything goes to provide a positive distraction (see Figure 10-6). The creative juices start flowing and before you know it, you've planned a mapped constellation on the ceiling with little telescopes along the railings (see Figure 10-7). You can build an aquarium into the front of the reception counter or

Figure 10-6 The diversion of a fountain. *Courtesy of Ewing Cole Cherry Brott. Photographer: Matt Wargo.*

Figure 10-7 Constellation on the ceiling. *Courtesy of NBBJ.*

add a fountain with foot-activated pads to turn on jets of water (see Figure 10-8). Some hospitals have a petting zoo and others offer entertaining animals with none of the associated maintenance (see Figure 10-9). At the Hasbro Children's Hospital, the multilevel playhouse (see Figure 10-10) was so popular that parents were delaying appointments because they couldn't get their children out of the playhouse! Playrooms provide a place to escape from treatment and the isolation of the patient room.

Children's art is effective in creating a whimsical, distracting environment (see Research Abstract on page 230). Art can be transferred to ceramic tile or recreated in stained-glass windows. Neutral-colored walls maximize the visual impact of the art and provide a background for personalization in the patient rooms. Strong colors may be appropriate on less permanent finishes and furnishings (see Details on page 82).

In *Hospital Interior Architecture,* Jain Malkin provides an excellent summary of the appropriate color choices for children in each developmental stage.[11] Although most of the hospital must remain neutral and flexible to accommodate a changing population, this color research is particularly useful on floors dedicated to specific age groups.

Figure 10-8 Fountain controlled by children. *Courtesy of Shepley Bulfinch Richardson and Abbott.*

Figure 10-9
Entertaining animals.
*Courtesy of Ellerbe
Becket. Photo:
Walter Smalling.*

Figure 10-10
Playroom.
*Courtesy of
Shepley Bulfinch
Richardson and
Abbot.*

RESEARCH ABSTRACT
Experiential Research from NBBJ

How can we determine what families really want when children have to go to the hospital? NBBJ, a Seattle-based architecture firm, asked young patients to draw their ideas and to assist in the design of Rainbow Babies and Children's Hospital in Cleveland.

Kids drew windows and beds first, windows so big that they didn't fit in the rooms. Rainbow Babies installed windows in the patient rooms that actually go past the ceiling line. Each window represents something other than the hospital, and the kids camp out there. The oversized window brings light far into the room, controlled by blinds inside double-paned glass.

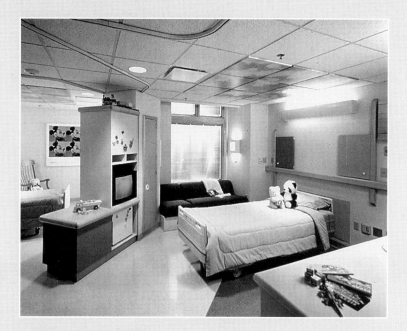

Windows larger than the room. *Courtesy of NBBJ.*

Because windows and beds were the priorities, NBBJ provided two beds for each child, one below the window. This sofa bed is used for rooming-in, but it becomes each child's favorite place in the hospital. Even in double rooms, each child gets a window and a couch detailed with a reachable personal reading light.

From the childrens' drawings, themes were established for each of the seven floors. On the "technology" floor, wayfinding symbols like computers, beakers, and cell phones are repeated on the marquee, nursing station, and corridor. The elevator lobby has fiber optics in the floor with backlighted technology icons that reinforce the theme. Each floor is additionally distinguished by one of the seven colors of the rainbow, and each patient room is differentiated by an acrylic panel on the door to display patient drawings. Children and their families can additionally personalize their rooms on magnetic crescent-shaped white boards for drawing and display.

Discovery was a recurring theme in many of the children's drawings, so the hospital is filled with surprises. The corridor overlooks a performance space with theatrical

Slide to the lower story. *Courtesy of NBBJ.*

lighting. Medical gases to support recovering children during the performances are hidden in the corridor columns. A slide from this level travels through a canyon of stone that provides needed access to a daylight basement. Although children in wheelchairs cannot use the slide, they have access to a pond at wheelchair height at the bottom of the slide.

Discovery is what childhood is all about. Electronic games provide interactive information at many locations. An interactive television provided in the lobby refers to all areas of the building and scheduled events. The lobby also has a voice-activated "people finder" with redundant cuing. An adjacent research library makes it easy for parents and children to discover answers about health.

Abstraction encourages curiosity and keeps children searching for answers while in the hospital. Abstract forms were taken from the children's drawings and incorporated into the building. Many of these forms reflect Cleveland's priorities: steel, shipping, and religion (not necessarily in that order). The hospital structure features applied white porcelain panels reminiscent of sails. The entry incorporates a stretched fabric canopy that looks like another sail. The top of the building sports flags reminiscent of ships. A steeple acknowledges the importance of worship.

The ethnic diversity of the community is represented by the multiple colors used in the building. Rainbow colors attract people to the hospital and make the building less frightening. Even the bright exterior lighting makes people feel safe.

The importance of family is another recurring theme. Family members are provided with their own areas for storage, a place to cook and store food, a laundry, and even a rocking chair in each child's room. Each floor has medical equipment accessible to parents and private conference rooms available for grieving. A family playroom on each floor is equipped with table football and a pool table. A glass wall in the playroom brings light in from the courtyard, and another glass wall carries this light into a private parents' lounge.

Color can intensify feelings. Children remember, color, places, and sensations more than they remember people, and they remember unpleasant experiences more than pleasant ones.[12] Unpleasant places are truly memorable. Pleasant places planned specifically for children indicate that someone cares. Children begin to feel that they will be dealt with as human beings, not as just another patient. Positive distractions help children to develop confidence that the hospital will deal with them honestly as children.

Music is one of the best examples of a positive distraction that makes a difference. In a study of the impact of music on children's anxiety levels, it was found that music caused a significant reduction of anxiety.[13] In a unique rehabilitation application, music is used to reward children for successful therapy (see Details below).

DETAILS
Therapy as Play

A life-size game board called Rehab 1,2,3 rewards children with music when a therapy sequence is completed. This is just one of the pediatric rehabilitation components designed to engage children while providing rehabilitation. During therapy, rocket ships take off, ping-pong balls go crazy, and confetti flies. Some elements of the system pop up from the floor. Stepping-stones, logs, cubes, balls, ramps, and toadstools are used in upper-body exercise, fine motor skills development, coordination, and cognitive training. A climbing wall, a Velcro wall, and a cognitive wall make therapy fun. Other optional components include a puppet theater, a funhouse mirror, and a technology center complete with computers and video games.

Rehab. 1, 2, 3. *Courtesy of Guynes Design Inc.*

Figure 10-11 Garden getaway. *Courtesy of Anshen + Allen, Architects.*

Children also have a universal attraction to water, and therapy seems easier in a swimming pool. A ramp into a swimming pool should not normally exceed a slope of 1 ft. of rise per 10 ft. of length,[14] but the slope may need to be more gradual for children. It must be 44 in. wide with edging and handrails on each side, which can be used to guide a shower wheelchair during entry and exit. Children in shower wheelchairs become buoyant (and lose control of their wheelchairs) at a depth of 30 in.[15]

Water elements are frequently integrated into play areas as well (see Details on page 204). An outdoor play area or garden can serve as a strong reference point to help with orientation to the building. It offers a child the energizing fragrance of spring. It meets the child's need to be active, breathe fresh air, soak up some sun, and get away from the hospital (see Figure 10-11).

Windows also provide a temporary visual escape to nature. Children spend so much time in the windows of the New York Foundling Hospital that the hospital installed radiant heating panels above the windows to warm them. Shutters on the windows can entertain the children with a light show of changing pattern.

DETAILS
Outdoor Play Areas for Children with Disabilities

An element of fun and mystery must be balanced against the functional requirements of children with disabilities. Heavy vegetation may surround a path that is barely accessible, but to a child in a wheelchair, it becomes a fun ride through the jungle. Running or wheeling through a fountain can be an adventure or an unwelcome surprise to a blind child when there is no tactile warning. Play areas may allow children of all abilities to develop their skills or prevent them from participating. Designers must tread the fine line between creating exciting challenges and creating barriers.

Accessible fun often involves a degree of challenge, but the risk must be based on anthropometric data and existing safety standards. When safety and accessibility conflict, err on the side of safety. Accessible routes must be stable, firm, and slip resistant, with surfaces like decomposed granite, asphalt, wooden boardwalk, resilient mats, and concrete. Platforms can be used by children in wheelchairs to safely transfer to play structures. Sand play areas can be provided in a variety of heights for play on the ground or in a wheelchair. Boulders or posts can provide back support in the play area. Accessible benches in a variety of heights should provide back support as well.

One exciting installation allows children to control the flow of water. By pressing on a bollard, children cause the water to flow at ground level on one side (for wading) and at a raised height on the other side (for access by children in wheelchairs). This installation also features a mastodon rib cage as a climbing structure. A missing rib provides access by children who use wheelchairs and walkers. The "archeological dig" features a fossil discovery, a stimulating tactile experience for sighted and unsighted children. Native American

Missing rib. *Courtesy of Moore Iacofano Goltsman, Inc.*

drums provide auditory stimulation at a variety of heights for standing and seated users. The swing area provides an accessible ground surface and a bucket swing for younger children or those with balance limitations. The play area integrates all children, improving their physical, social, and intellectual abilities.

Fossil discovery. *Courtesy of Moore Iacofano Goltsman, Inc.*

Signage and audible cues for orientation provide perceptible information about the play area. A wind chime can provide a sense of direction to all users, not just to people with low vision or reduced cognitive skills, who depend on redundant cues. Caterpillar pull handles on the exterior doors entice children out of the garden to the indoors.

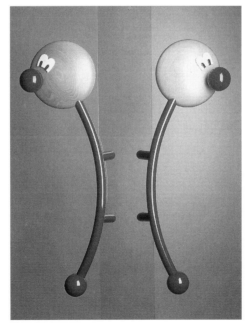

Caterpillar pull handles. *Courtesy of HEWI, Inc.*

REFERENCES

1. Jill H. Hall, "Healing Environments," *Journal of Health Care Interior Design* 2 (1990): 67.
2. Jain Malkin, *Hospital Interior Architecture* (New York: John Wiley and Sons, Inc., 1992), 127.
3. Lloyd Acton et al., "Children's Health Design: Designing for Family-Centered Care," *Journal of Health Care Interior Design* 9 (1997): 130.
4. *Americans with Disabilities Act (ADA) Accessibility Guidelines for Buildings and Facilities; Building Elements Designed for Children's Use.*
5. *Americans with Disabilities Act Accessibility Standards,* 1991, 4.1.3 (17)(c)(iii).
6. *ADA Guidelines.*
7. R. L. Anderson, D. C. Mackel, B. S. Stoler, and G. F. Mallison, "Carpeting in Hospitals: An Epidemiological Evaluation," *Journal of Clinical Microbiology* (March 1982): 408–415.
8. J. D. Anderson, M. Bonner, D. W. Scheifele, and B. C. Schneider, "Lack of Nosocomial Varicella in a Pediatric Hospital with Negative Pressure Ventilation Patient Rooms," *Infection Control* 6, no. 3 (1985): 120–121.
9. Malkin, *Hospital Interior Architecture,* 155.
10. Walter B. Kleeman, *The Challenge of Interior Design* (Boston: CBI Publishing, 1981), 79.
11. Malkin, *Hospital Interior Architecture,* 133 and 164.
12. Hall, "Healing Environments," 65.
13. S. F. Parkin, "The Effect of Ambient Music upon the Reactions of Children Undergoing Dental Treatment," *ASDC The Journal of Dentistry for Children* (Nov./Dec. 1981): 430–432.
14. Robert Sorensen, *Design for Accessibility* (New York: McGraw-Hill, 1979), 158.
15. National Center for Accessibility, 1997, "Swimming Pool Accessibility Project," Martinsville: NCA.

11 INPATIENT PSYCHIATRIC UNITS

Ohe third of all Americans are likely to suffer from mental illness or substance abuse sometime during their lives, and almost every American family will be touched by mental illness.[1] Fortunately, great progress has been made in medical treatment; most people with chronic mental illness can be stabilized with medication and remain in the community. Institutions and addiction recovery facilities are being replaced with treatment-adherence clinics providing medications that correct genetically based addictions and diseases.[2] Most clients receive treatment on an outpatient basis, remaining in their homes with the support of ambulatory care facilities (see Part Two)

For those requiring inpatient care, psychiatric facility design has a tremendous impact. The design program must support a normalized lifestyle, patient independence, integration of the family, mental therapy, and physical healing.[3] Design detail can make a significant contribution to achieving these goals.

NORMALIZATION

Some of the most interesting design research on normalization has been conducted by Mayer Spivak. Jain Malkin provides an excellent illustrated synopsis of this research in *Hospital Interior Architecture*.[4] Spivak maintains that clients "are told by their environment to misbehave," to stay out of the norm.[5] He discusses "standing behavior" elicited by a space. For example, a bedroom induces escape (through sleep) to most users. Access to the bedroom is not always desirable during the day when patients are being encouraged to face reality, not to escape from it.

Each room makes a statement about the client. Does the hospital think enough of patients and their families to provide and maintain a supportive environment? Are the spaces planned for important clients who are treated with respect? What is the message communicated by bars on the windows of hard, institutional spaces filled with indestructible furnishings? Does this convey trust or fear?

Humphrey Osmond, as reported by Spivak,[6] divides space into sociopetal and sociofugal areas. Sociopetal space brings people together while sociofugal space keeps them apart. Sociopetal space encourages people to discuss personal feelings. For example, personal space is easier to establish around the perimeter of the room, so most socializing takes place in this sociopetal space. The center of the room is less protected; furniture arrangements, area rugs, and lighting, and low partitions can be used to redefine it as sociopetal space. These "behavior markers"[7]— architectural elements supporting specific behaviors, offer a wider range of choices to the patient, articulating the space and maintaining a sense of personal identity.

In one fascinating study at a maximum-security hospital, furniture was rearranged from nonsocial patterns into group seating. The wards with the rearranged furniture had a lower rate of patients requiring seclusion and a lower rate of casualty incidents. In addition, the nurses reported improved attitudes and social interaction.[8]

Room size also determines sociopetal space. The smaller the room, the greater the social interaction. Research has shown that there is less isolation and less passive behavior in small rooms.[9] Private bedrooms and smaller spaces produce more frequent and appropriate social interaction.[10]

Privacy and confidentiality can also be supported by design detail, including sound-absorbing finishes like nonaccessible acoustical ceiling products. Limit sound transmission and place windows and doors away from sources of noise (see Details on pages 265 and 266). Carpet can be effective in deinstitutionalizing the space, reducing the ambient noise while protecting patients from falls. Carpet borders may be problematic for people with compulsive behavior disorders; they may be unwilling to step on the edge or move into a space defined by a border.

Intimacy can be encouraged by soft natural lighting and variety in the color and texture of finishes (see Details on pages 82 and 83). A quiet, soft environment can help the patient to stabilize and return to everyday life.

PATIENT INDEPENDENCE

Just 20 years ago, people with mental illness were confined in hostile environments featuring bars on the windows, harsh lighting, medical furnishings and equipment, and sterile finishes. These facilities provided custodial care with very little treatment or hope for recovery.

The best facilities return control, efficacy, and independence to their clients. Individuals may select their own artwork, choose a room in their favorite color, and regulate their environment with individual HVAC and lighting controls. Piped-in music is replaced with personal choice of music in each room, and spaces are differentiated to support individual activity choices. Clients should be able to choose between smoking and nonsmoking areas, quiet and noisy rooms, private and public spaces.

A public day room is ambiguous space, difficult for patients to understand and control. These rooms provide little or no privacy, which is especially problematic when this is the only space available to patients and their families. Rather than a large, flexible space, several rooms should be planned to support various activities. A lounge for reading may be furnished with large, overstuffed chairs. Another activity area may provide seating around tables for games, hobbies, or study (see Details on page 223). Boundary definition may be improved by using square tables[11]; round tables make personal space more difficult to define.

Abnormal behavior can be reduced with careful attention to design detail. A therapeutic environment must be understandable, not filled with confusing finishes or furnishings that can be mistaken for something else. Faux finishes or even plastic imitations of metal or wood can be visually confusing. Optical illusions can be caused by glare in the environment (see Details on page 80). In addition, ramps can cause the illusion of a foreshortened space; users appear to rapidly increase in size as they come down the ramp.

One study of adolescents documented that most aggression takes place in corridors, entries, and other areas of transition.[12] Patient ownership must be clearly defined in these spaces. Caregivers should assume a hands-off approach, allowing patients and their families to care for themselves. The public phone should be tucked into a private alcove where others are less likely to invade personal space. In the entry, the doorbell and staff phone may be answered by a patient. Patients are encouraged by these details to take ownership and responsibility for their lives.

INTEGRATION OF THE FAMILY

Family-centered design softens the blow of admitting a family member to the hospital and encourages family members and friends to visit. A family activity area for socializing, dining, and entertaining can be planned, perhaps with a small kitchen for preparing snacks and meals (see Details on pages 94, 95, 96, and 97 and Research Abstract on page 59).

For the safety of patients, controlled access should be planned for the kitchen. Of course, all sharp utensils must be locked away, and the temperature of hot water should be controlled. Small appliances should be permanently installed; perhaps a refrigerator, a toaster oven, and a microwave (which is considered safer than a range). Cabinets should be within reach without using stools or chairs.

Overnight accommodations for family use may also be provided, perhaps in an apartment in the complex. Patients can also stay in the apartments with their families as a transition to home care.

Families may also be granted access to patient recreation areas, encouraging community interaction with the facility. Public educational centers are becoming more popular; these offer space for seminars and perhaps a community library for information about mental illness. These resources are particularly appreciated by families trying to come to terms with these diseases.

Family therapy rooms should also be considered. These spaces are planned for privacy but are sometimes used by therapists for observation of family dynamics. Acoustics are a primary consideration; assure control of both ambient and transmitted noise.

TREATMENT AND THERAPY

Therapeutic design is driven by reimbursement. Before the Community Mental Health Center Act of 1963, most chronically mentally ill patients were warehoused in institutions with little treatment. Isolation and unvaried routine lured these clients into total dependence on the institution. After the act was passed, many of these dependent patients ended up on the street with no medications, mental health services, or means of living independently.

This Act required institutionalized patients to be treated in their own communities, and Hill-Burton funds were to be used to build community treatment centers. Funding of these centers was contingent on the provision of free care to indigent clients being released from institutions. Little care was ever provided, however, and many people with mental illness ended up homeless with no treatment. Few acute-care beds were available at this time, and Medicaid funds were available to mental health patients in acute-care hospitals only, not freestanding psychiatric facilities.

In the early 1980s, much of health-care treatment was effectively capped with the advent of the DRG reimbursement system (diagnosis-related groups). Because mental disorders were exempt from this cap, it finally became financially advantageous to treat mentally ill people. According to Williams as reported by Malkin,[13] between 1970 and 1986, the number of beds in psychiatric hospitals increased by 75 percent, and the market experienced a boom in construction.

Unfortunately, little was known about therapeutic design for people with mental illness. Only institutional models existed, examples of poorly defined flexible spaces. Research has shown that when expected behavior patterns are not clearly defined by space, all behavior feels out of place and random.[14] Signage must be clear, consistent, and redundantly cued (see Details on page 240 and Research Abstract on page 242). Provide landmarks every 20 ft.; memorable personal cues like collections and client art are more effective than unfamiliar cues in improving orientation. Even a client bulletin board can serve as a personal cue. For safety, use tape on the bulletin board, not pins or tacks. Orientation can also be improved by posting the day and date on the bulletin board. Crossing off days on a calendar can be discouraging, reinforcing a sense of lost time.

Space must be clearly defined. Flexible space can be disorienting at best and lead to inappropriate behavior at worst. Orientation to unfamiliar and changing surroundings is problematic for people with mental illness.

Unfortunately, flexible space is often justified as a response to ever-changing therapeutic techniques. Dayrooms have multiple uses and are filled with too much furniture or equipment, confusing and discouraging patients, forcing them to escape to the security of their bedrooms. Lightweight furnishings are used in flexible spaces because they are easily rearranged, but they are also easily used as weapons.

Today, inpatient facilities are planned with clear spatial differentiation. Dayrooms have been replaced with clearly defined treatment space, individual seclusion spaces, and auditoriums with sophisticated audiovisual equipment.

When patients are acting out, a quiet room may be necessary. Generally the room is used to calm the patient, but it may also be used to protect patients from harming themselves or others. The patient may be observed in this room, either through safety glass, plastic, or by video camera. Because the patient may be on the verge of suicide, the room may contain nothing more than a bed bolted to the floor, a mattress, and an inoperable window with a view. The bottom of the door must be secured to prevent razor blades, matches, or pills from being passed under. A locked bathroom should be close, if not connected.

Access to nature and natural light is critical to treatment. In one excellent research study, length of stay for depressed patients in sunny rooms averaged 16.9 days, while those in dull rooms required 19.5 days of care.[15] Sunshine can be incorporated into the interior with skylights, solariums, atriums, and courtyards. Light must minimize shadows, exaggerated images, and sensory distortion.

THE BODY-MIND CONNECTION

Today's psychiatric facilities recognize the link between a healthy body and a healthy mind. Treatment should include recreational, physical, and occupational therapy as well as psychiatric treatment. Activity is critical. Many patients are restless and have difficulty with inactivity, especially waiting. Time management is frequently an issue, and this is exacerbated by reactions to psychotropic drugs that reduce the ability to sit for long periods. Provide furniture that rocks, bounces, or swivels safely. Gymnasiums with running tracks, weight rooms, racquetball courts, aerobic dance, spas, and swimming pools are planned in many facilities.

In addition to encouraging physical fitness, facilities must protect patients from physical harm, especially self-induced injury. Specify breakaway closet rods and hooks and use flush door hardware to prevent suicidal patients from hanging themselves. Recess plumbing, lightbulbs, and sockets. Diffusers, switches, light fixtures, and grilles must be installed with tamper-proof screws that require a special tool to remove.

Sharp objects must be eliminated. Fixtures and artwork must not have glass components; mirrors must be specified in laminated glass. Razor blades can be hidden behind baseboards; glue and screw the base to the wall and eliminate the base in closed units. Windows blinds should be sandwiched between layers of safety glass.

Some patients develop a sensitivity to bright light as a side effect of their medications. Draperies should be installed on ceiling-mounted rods and attached with Velcro, not hooks. They should be controlled by wands, rather than cords.

For security, emergency windows should be operated from the exterior with special keys and elevators should have a key-only option. Fire door locks should be alarmed. Doors for patient use should have contrasting frames, while doors to dangerous areas or rooms for staff-only use should be visually blended with the wall. Each door must have double-swinging hinges so it cannot be blocked with furniture or by a patient who has fallen. Exposed furniture and door hardware can be tied to another object with belts, stockings, or shoelaces; to prevent barricading, injury, and escape, hardware must be recessed and installed with security screws.

Movable furnishings also must be planned to discourage injury and suicide attempts. Furniture must be heavy and difficult to throw. Sharp edges must be eliminated. Furniture must not be placed near the entrance to the room, where it could be used in a surprise attack. A tall piece of furniture can be tipped on an attendant or another patient, and some hardware can be disassembled and used as weapons. Patients can be injured by rocking on chairs and tabletops until they come loose. A sled base stabilizes a chair and the tabletop should be permanently attached to the base. Edging, like vinyl T-moldings, can be picked apart and removed.

In the patient room, the bed should be placed on a platform rather than on a metal frame that could be disassembled (see Figure 11-1). The mattress should be nonspring for the same reason. Avoid zippers and pockets that could be used to hide dangerous objects. Drawers in the nightstand should be difficult to remove and soundly constructed. The wardrobe should have a lockable door or drawer for grooming supplies that require staff supervision during use (see Details on pages 267 and 269).

Finishes should be tamper-proof and virtually indestructible, but not institutional. Color and pattern can make a tremendous contribution if carefully selected. Some patterns are too distracting for clients who have difficulty maintaining concentration for long periods (see Details on page 214). Many have problems screening out external stimuli. Excess clutter, overhead announcements, noisy pedestrian traffic, and vacuum cleaner noise are examples of negative distractions.

Figure 11-1 Bed on platform. *Courtesy of the Menninger Foundation.*

DETAILS
Pattern, Texture, and Contrast

- Converging lines created by contrasting baseboards, wainscoting, valances, and handrails are perceived as a confusing pattern to people with concentration differences.[16] This problem is most apparent at the end of a corridor. Blend these elements together into a monochromatic color scheme. This technique can also visually reduce the appearance of a long institutional corridor.

- A lower ceiling helps a room appear cozier and less institutional. In addition, many people in wheelchairs or on gurneys are more comfortable with a lower ceiling height. Pattern can be used to visually lower an existing ceiling, and warmer colors can reduce the perceived ceiling height as well. Orange and red tones come to focus behind the retina and cause the surface to visually advance or lower, while blue and green tones come to focus in front of the retina and appear to recede.[17]

- Contrast between the wall and the floor helps to define boundaries. A contrasting door frame draws attention to the doorway. Because most doors are left open, the molding should contrast with the walls, not necessarily with color of the door. In the bathroom, provide contrast between the countertop and bowl. Contrasting toilet seats may help in seeing the edge of the toilet.

- Visually confusing mirrors produce patterns that are distracting and can make concentration and orientation difficult (see Details on pages 251 and 252)

- For people with schizophrenia and others who suffer from distortion of perception, keep colors and textures as unambiguous and understated as possible.[18]

- Limiting textures and colors in interior decor is helpful for the many people with mental illness who are susceptible to sensory overload. Low-intensity colors, especially for background surfaces, are most appropriate for this population.

- People who spend much of the day in bed may grow tired of facing a patterned or highly textured wall covering. Use strong patterns only on walls adjacent to or in back of the bed. Even in these locations, texture and pattern may produce a response of stimulation rather than relaxation.

- Perforations and other ceiling patterns may be visually confusing. Allowing clients to control the ceiling pattern can actually reduce stress. Clients may choose to project videotapes on the ceiling or suspend artwork, a technique frequently used in doctors' examination rooms.

- Stripes on the wall can appear to be bars and wavy patterns can appear to be in motion, affecting mobility.[19]

- Texture makes tones appear darker,[20] absorbing important ambient light.

- Value contrasts of more than two digits on the gray scale are adequate to increase the imagery of objects.[21] (The gray scale consists of 10 increments from black to white and can be found illustrated on the back of many printer's rules.)

Figure 11-2 Warmth of wood. *Courtesy of the Menninger Foundation.*

Wood adds warmth without excessive distracting pattern (see Figure 11-2). Although our discussion is limited to family-centered design, it should be noted that wood is easily maintained and repaired. Lightly patterned wall covering is also easily maintained. It should be specified in commercial weight and 108 in. widths for a seamless installation. Wood guards prevent patients from picking at the edges.

Bathrooms are particularly dangerous and difficult to detail. Excessive thirst is a common reaction to psychotropic drugs, resulting in increased demand for bathrooms. Exposed plumbing could be disassembled and used as a weapon; it must be covered in each bathroom. Use toilets with flush valves that cannot be disassembled rather than toilets with tanks. Shower heads must be recessed and activated by a sensor with thermostatic control. A patient can easily block the drain in the shower, sink, or toilet. Install a central drain in each bathroom to handle the overflow.

Ground-fault circuit interrupters and fail-safe touch controls must be specified. Bathroom shelves and toilet paper holders must have collapsible connectors. Shower curtains must have breakaway Velcro to foil suicide attempts. Curtains must be ceiling mounted to prevent the rod from being used as a weapon.

It is difficult to motivate some mentally ill people to physically care for themselves. Medication frequently slows metabolism to the point where each motion requires extraordinary effort. It feels like each task is being performed in a vat of molasses. In addition, psychotropic drugs reduce manual dexterity, making tasks like bathing especially difficult.

Design elements can be used to increase motivation, providing positive incentives to participate in healthy behaviors. This goal requires imagination; the key is to make each activity fun. For example, a hot tub is more fun than a bath. An active game is more motivating than a scheduled exercise regime. With a little creativity, clients can be encouraged to exceed their physical and mental limitations to achieve better health.

REFERENCES

1. Tama M. Duffy and Barbara Huelat, "Psychiatric Care Units," *Journal of Health Care Interior Design* 2 (1990): 90.
2. Richard L. Miller and Earl S. Swensson, "New Age Public Won't Settle for Old-fashioned Facilities," *Health Facilities Management* (March 1995).
3. Duffy and Huelat, "Psychiatric Care Units," 92–93.
4. Jain Malkin, *Hospital Interior Architecture* (New York: John Wiley and Sons, 1992).
5. Mayer Spivack, *Institutional Settings* (New York: Human Sciences Press, 1984), 89.
6. Ibid.
7. W. Ittleson, H. Proshansky, and L. Rivlin, "Bedroom Size and Social Interaction of the Psychiatric Ward," *Environment and Behavior* 2, no. 3 (1970): 255–270.
8. S. Baldwin, "Effects of Furniture Rearrangement on the Atmosphere of Wards in a Maximum-Security Hospital," *Hospital and Community Psychiatry* 36, no. 5 (May 1985): 525–528.
9. Ittleson et al., "Bedroom Size," 255–270.
10. C. Holahan and S. Saegert, "Behavioral and Attitudinal Effects of Large-Scale Variation in the Physical Environment of Psychiatric Wards," *Journal of Abnormal Psychology* 82 (1973): 454–462.
11. Malkin, *Hospital Interior Architecture*, 296.
12. John Boerger and Mardelle Shepley, "Mental Health Design: A Case Study," *Journal of Healthcare Design* 3 (1991): 155.
13. Malkin, *Hospital Interior Architecture*, 269.
14. Spivak, *Institutional Settings*, 87.
15. K. M. Beauchemin and P. Hays, "Sunny Hospital Rooms Expedite Recovery from Severe and Refractory Depressions," *Journal of Affective Disorders* 40 (1996): 49–51.
16. JoAnn L. Shroyer and J. Thomas Hutton, "Alzheimer's Disease: Strategies for Designing Interiors," *American Society of Interior Designers Report* 15, no. 2 (1989): 10–11.
17. Walter B. Kleeman, *The Challenge of Interior Design* (Boston: CBI Publishing, 1981), 61.
18. Ibid., 152.
19. Lorraine G. Hiatt, "The Color and Use of Color in Environments for Older People," *Nursing Homes* 30, no. 3 (1981): 21.
20. Ibid., 18–22.
21. Lorraine G. Hiatt, "Long-Term Care Facilities," *Journal of Health Care Interior Design* 2 (1990): 200.

12 MEDICAL HOTELS

The medical hotel model emerged in the 1980s, when hospitals started to view patients as guests and families as health-care partners. Some guests used the hotel in lieu of a hospital stay, but most were transferred from acute care for the last few days before discharge, generally to reduce costs. Depending on the amenities, a medical hotel may cost as little as one third as much as the same care in a hospital.[1]

Today, the medical hotel serves as a luxurious transition between hospital and home, allowing the patient to recuperate in a comfortable environment under physicians' care. Nursing, therapy, radiology, and laboratory services are often available in the medical hotel. A medical technician generally serves as the concierge on each floor.

Although some amenities, such as the concierge, have been successfully integrated, conflicts in the merger of the hospitality and health-care models do exist. For example, hotels replace finishes every 3 to 5 years and purchase products accordingly. Health-care facilities refurbish every 10 to 15 years[2] and evaluate products on this basis. They resist hospitality products that will not withstand the health-care environment for this length of time, leaning toward institutional products that are incompatible with hotels.

COOPERATIVE CARE MODEL

The Rhode Island Hospital is one of the first successful mergers of hospital and hotel—with a twist. With one simple change, the hospital lowered operating costs by 30 percent and construction costs by $70.00/sq. ft. It increased market share and reduced its daily rate by $200. Treating the same illnesses as a traditional inpatient hospital does, its acute-care length of stay was reduced by 50 percent. The hospital also reduced its readmission rate and improved patient outcomes and satisfaction with care. Medication errors dropped to 79 percent below the expected rate, and slips and falls were reduced by 41 percent. In addition, the hospital improved both job satisfaction and staff retention rate. What was this simple change?

All of this was accomplished by asking patients to bring a care partner with them when they check into the medical hotel. The partner stays with the patient in a room that features the comforts of home, the amenities of a hotel, and the security of a hospital. The partner provides much of the routine care and is taught to take vital signs, to chart the results, to take the patient to and from treatment, and to give medication. On discharge, patients have to take their own medication anyway, so it is best to start in the hospital, where help is available if a medication error is made. The partner also monitors the patient, providing comfort and support. In the process, both patient and partner learn to collect data about the illness. They deal with discharge realities while they build skills and confidence to manage at home.

In the cooperative care model, the patients wear street clothes. They have the security of locked private rooms (each with a safe), which they share with a partner who cares about them. Dependence on strangers is less than in traditional hospitals; nurses do not enter the rooms without permission. Patients and staff are given beepers in lieu of an overhead paging system. Patients have access to a resource center providing computer searches and current medical research (see Details on page 139). They order their own food in the dining room. They stay in control.

Patients and their partners know what to anticipate. As they retain responsibility for health care, patients heal faster. The reduction in medication errors and slip and fall is the direct result of an educated patient and a caring partner. The home care training reduces the readmission rate. The increased patient satisfaction with care reduces litigation and insurance rates.

When patients and their families care for themselves, pressure on staff is reduced. High staffing levels are no longer needed. Only three night nurses are required in this 74-bed facility, greatly reducing operating costs. The facility has fewer nursing stations, simpler mechanical systems, and fewer rooms with oxygen, which translates into lower construction costs.

Figure 12-1 Medical
hotel reception area.
*Courtesy of the
Robinson Green
Beretta Corporation,
Providence, RI.*

The daily charge at the Rhode Island Hospital Cooperative Care Center is
$420, compared with $620 at the main hospital.[3]

Rhode Island Hospital is uniquely designed, dividing service zones
into patient care and patient support areas.[4] The patient care zone
includes admission, discharge, patient and family education, and treatment. The patient support zone houses administration, food services, dining, and housekeeping. Admission and discharge are designed along the
hotel reception model (see Figure 12-1). After admission, the patient-
partner team receives training on cooperative care in the education center.

Adjacent to the center are eight exam and treatment rooms where the
patient-partner teams see the physician daily. The lounge is also used for
treatment by patients with IVs, perhaps taking chemotherapy. A nine-bed
postoperative observation area is used to stabilize patients who are not
coping well in their own rooms. Some of the patient rooms are equipped
with medical gases, and all have amenities including television, VCR,
refrigerator, and coffee maker (see Research Abstract on page 59). All of
the patient bathrooms are accessible (see Research Abstract on page 101
and Details on pages 165, 166, 167, and 168).

For a successful cooperative care unit, physician buy-in is a key component. Not only must providers be willing to refer patients to the unit,
they must also change their thinking to a family-centered paradigm from
the traditional staff-centered model.

The cooperative care unit of the Tisch Hospital of the New York University Medical Center has achieved these goals. Tisch offers 104 cooperative care patient rooms in a homelike setting; about half are dedicated to outpatient care. For admission, patients must be mobile. They must arrive with a care partner, who is not charged for room and board. Patients are never required to share a room with another patient, only with their care partner. Each patient has an individual living area on a floor separated from the area of core services. Nursing units were not placed outside of the patient rooms because cooperative care patients typically do not need extremely close supervision. But one provider maintains, "If we had it to do over again, we would use a circular or square plan with a central core. Like most buildings in New York, our building is tall and skinny, not providing the sprawling plan that would be best."

With the help of their partner, patients travel to the centralized core which offers clinical, educational, and dining services. The education center is staffed by providers of nutritional guidance, nursing education, pharmaceutical services, and social work. Here patients and partners complete a skills assessment and receive training in the tasks they will perform in the hospital and at home. They are trained in toileting techniques, transferring skills, and the selection of a nutritional diet. To reinforce the training, all of the food they receive in the hospital is labeled with nutritional qualities: fat, salt, calories, and so on.

Clinical care is handled in the therapeutic center. Following the initial assessment at the education center, a clinical assessment is completed. The provider then prepares the patient and partner to participate in care, including the dispensing of medications. This center includes a six-bed observation unit for clinically unstable patients.

In summary, the design program for cooperative care emphasizes the following priorities:

- Patient and partner convenience is a higher priority than staff convenience. People also take priority over machines and process. Clear circulation routes and wayfinding systems are provided for guest convenience (see Details on pages 251 and 252). Treatment and diagnostic areas must be located close to patient rooms.
- The unit's distinct identity is based on hospitality, which is very different than a medically intensive identity. Arrival and departure areas should reflect the standards of a fine hotel.
- Costs, including construction and operations, are controlled. About 85 percent of the time, patients call for a nurse because they are cold, hot, thirsty, or have to go to the bathroom.[5] A partner can easily address these needs, saving nursing time and resulting costs.

VIP SUITES

The medical hotel is an emerging market-driven model where guests are treated like VIPs rather than hospital patients. Some medical hotels offer VIP suites that are typically selected by guests; hospitals are often selected by physicians. In the past, patients and their families seemed to be willing to accept a lower-quality health-care environment based on a physician's referral, but that attitude is changing. With more choice in facilities and more competition for market share, consumers are offered hospitable rather than hospital models.

These medical hotels are actually more exclusive than hotels. They typically restrict the type of patient that can be admitted. Most do not accept critical care, telemetry, obstetric, pediatric, psychiatric, or chemical dependency patients. These restrictions may be based on the amount of equipment needed to care for these patients or the distance to treatment spaces they required. Transportation between hospitals and VIP suites is critical.

Although the VIP medical hotel must be adjacent to the hospital, a separate VIP entrance is normally provided (see Details on pages 63 and 149). Some patients check in with their entire family (see Figure 12-2)—even the dog! Staff and equipment are kept out of sight and a separate traf-

Figure 12-2 Family lodging. *Courtesy of Shepley Bulfinch Richardson and Abbott. Photo: Steve Rosenthal.*

fic pattern is established. A dedicated service elevator and pneumatic tube system reduce employee traffic.

The policies of a medical hotel differentiate it from a hospital. The guests are not awakened for baths, medication, maintenance, examinations by interns, or meals. Room service is provided, and the meals are sometimes served with alcoholic beverages (with physician approval). For snacks, refrigerators and juice bars are provided. Customized menus are available and small ovens provided to keep food warm.

A drop-leaf dining table in the room may accommodate two or three people, although it does not provide strong support. A wall-mounted table that folds flat against the wall may be more stable. Be sure the space between the legs is wide enough (30 in.) for approach in a wheelchair. When not in use, it folds up to clear the space for wheelchair or gurney passage (see Details below).

DETAILS
Tables

- A sturdy table may be necessary for support. When evaluating table construction, look for blocking in the leg joints. The joints should also be glued and screwed. Consistency in the type of wood used is a sign of high-quality construction.
- Specify a stable base that will support a person who leans on the edge of the top.
- Table and desk surfaces should reflect 30 to 50 percent of light. Darker woods, including rosewood and walnut, reflect as little as 9 percent. A white top reflects too much light and can tire the eyes. Shiny and glossy surfaces also produce too much glare. Select dull greens and beiges or light oak, maple, cherry, and teak for proper light reflection.[6]
- A round or oval top on a pedestal base allows a wheelchair user to approach from all directions, but is less stable than a table with legs.
- Select a table with a border clearly identifying the edge. A raised edge keeps spills off the floor.
- Specify a round table or a table without sharp corners to prevent bruising.
- Adjustable-height tables accommodate detailed projects and reading. High tables (32–36 in.) offer a closer approach for a wheelchair user. High tables also facilitate use of the shoulders and upper arms. If too high, however, such tables may put pressure on the back.
- Children require a knee space of 24 in.[7] from the underside of the table to the floor (see Details on pages 188 and 191).
- Low crossbars between table legs may prohibit wheelchair access. Crossbars should be recessed a minimum of 19 in. from the front edge of the table.
- Skirt boards should be recessed a minimum of 12 in.[8] Rubber or upholstered legs resist wheelchair abrasion.
- Tables with a minimum clearance of 27 in. allow a wheelchair user to slide under the table apron.
- Sleigh legs are easier than traditional legs to move over textured surfaces.
- Specify locking casters so that tables can be moved for storage.

Gourmet meals may be served with special china and linens (see Figure 12-3). Other room amenities may include terry-cloth robes, fresh flowers, a daily newspaper, and secretarial help upon request. Many medical hotels feature a gift shop, conference center, fitness center, solarium, and chapel. Most provide round-the-clock security. One even serves high tea from 2:00 to 4:00 P.M.

In the guest room, luxurious design details abound. Etched glass doors, walnut and maple inlaid floors, and polished granite finishes may be used (see Figure 12-4). The guest room may open onto a balcony or terraces. Bay windows provide expansive views. Draperies can be remotely controlled from the bed, as can the television and VCR, which are concealed in an armoire (see Details on page 269). The desk may offer an outlet and telephone jack for a computer modem, sometimes in the base of the desk lamp (see Details below). In planning reachability, consider the shape of the desk. With a 60 × 30 in. rectangular desk, only 68 percent of the surface can be easily reached.[9] A person with mobility differences can use even less of the surface. An L- or U-shaped surface can bring all items within reach for many people, although the corners may still be difficult.

Desk accessories like staplers, scissors, paper clips, tape, pencils, and pens may be redundantly placed on the nightstand as well as on the desk to save the energy required for extra trips and prolonged searches. A pad and pencil should be at each telephone, together with a directory.

DETAILS
Lamps

- Avoid installing any sconce that protrudes more than 4 in. into the space (between 27 and 80 in. a.f.f.)
- Floor lamps can be moved out of the way and easily positioned from a wheelchair for task lighting. Specify adjustable-height floor lamps with touch controls.
- Plan lamps at each task location. The lamps should have heavily weighted bases for stability.
- Squeeze switches on cords are easy for many people to operate. A touch converter eliminates the switch. Touching the metal surface of the lamp turns it on and off.
- Plastic shades and fixtures are prone to volatile outgassing when exposed to high lamp temperatures. These gases may cause problems for people with allergies.[10]

Figure 12-3 Room service with china and linens. *Courtesy of Chambers Lorenz Design Associates.*

Figure 12-4 Inlaid floors and polished granite finishes. *Courtesy of Chambers Lorenz Design Associates.*

Satin pajamas and satin sheets are more than a luxury; some guests maintain that this is the only way they can sleep, as the satin allows them to turn over more easily with less pain. But others slip when getting into or out of bed.

A comfortable sleeping system with storage within reach is a necessity (see Details below). A custom footboard provides patient support and a custom headboard connects two storage cabinets. A reading light is installed on the bridge between the two cabinets (see Figure 12-5).

DETAILS
Patient Beds

- Specify a twin bed; its edges are easier to grip for turning than a wider bed.
- A fitted bedspread will not catch in a wheelchair or gurney.
- If the bed is too low for transfer from a wheelchair, consider adding locking casters to raise it to 17 to 19 in. a.f.f.[11]
- Consider the installation of ceiling eyebolts above the bed for trapezes, tracks, frames, or lifts to aid in transfer or a change of position in bed. As an alternative, attach a trapeze to the headboard.
- Side rails, if used on the bed, should be removable for ease of entry and exit. Latches for the side rails should be within reach, not at the foot of the bed. They should be below mattress level to prevent injury in transfer.
- Specify a bed with adjustable head and foot levels. Many patients struggle to find a comfortable angle for sleeping. Patients who are not susceptible to pressure sores can elevate their knees to relieve lumbar pressure. Elevated beds can also be helpful to clients with respiratory ailments or nausea. Some designs are more hospitable in appearance than others.
- When using an adjustable bed, choose a mattress that does not bunch and become lumpy at the bends.
- Specify footboards (at handrail height of 34 to 38 in.)[12] to provide stability when walking around the bed. This higher footboard can also be used to hold the blanket or bedspread to relieve pressure on the feet.
- As beds are used for support, install nonskids if necessary.
- Make sure the bed is of substantial weight for stability.
- A headboard with an upper edge approximately 10 in. above the mattress level may be used for support to rise to a standing position.
- A headboard (or head wall) with built-in compartments or shelves can hold television controls, clocks, telephones, communication devices, bed controls, and alarm systems.
- A mattress should provide good heat retention, offer sufficient absorption to allow ventilation, and be flame retardant. It should be firm with little side play.
- Systems that allow a person to lie motionless while the mattress adapts to simulate position changes are also available.
- All mattress systems should be evaluated for ease of transfer to and from a wheelchair and for dressing in bed. Specify a mattress with a firm edge to help in transferring.
- The mattress cover should be changeable and washable. People with allergies often require cotton box spring covers and mattresses with cotton batting and ticking.
- People with limited circulation may prefer to sleep on sheepskin because the fleece serves as a soft support, conforming to the body and improving ventilation and absorption. The sheepskin should be washable.
- Keep the mattress and nightstand at equal heights so that the patient can slide a hand across the mattress to the nightstand to locate objects (see Details on page 267).

Figure 12-5 Patient room. *Courtesy of Chambers Lorenz Design Associates.*

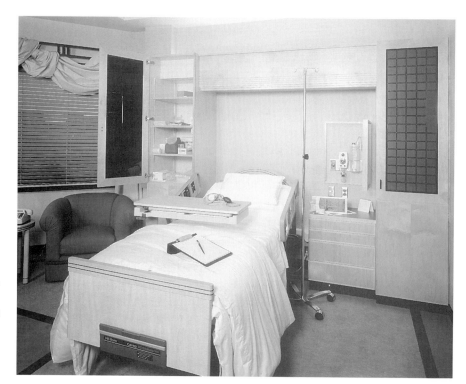

Figure 12-6 Art swings
away to reveal medical
gases. *Courtesy of
Chambers Lorenz
Design Associates.*

A choice of art may be offered to each guest. Permanent art can also be placed to conceal medical gases (see Figure 12-6). Hang some permanent artwork at the eye level of a person using a wheelchair or gurney. Also include mirrors usuable from a wheelchair in the bedroom and by the front door. Elevate glass at least 10 in. from the floor to avoid damage from wheelchair footrests.

Most suites have large bathrooms, some with two bathtubs (see Details below). The bathroom may also feature a laundry (see Details on the next page). Bathroom lighting should be designed to enhance the patient's

---

DETAILS
Bathtubs

- A soak in the bathtub relieves pain for many people, but standard bathtub design can make it difficult to get in and out. It can be especially difficult to transfer from a wheelchair into a poorly sized tub or a tub with a track. For a tub and shower combination, specify a trackless installation.

- For seated users, the height of the tub should match the height of the chair seat. The height that serves most adults and children is 17 in. a.f.f., but the needs may vary from 11 in. for children to 19 in. for an adult (see Details on page 191).

- A seat installed on the end of bathtub is helpful when transferring from a mobility assistance device. The extra length of the tub and seat may extend the floor space in the bathroom to allow a 5 ft. turnaround space for wheelchair users.

- Bevel the edge of the seat so that it can be used as a headrest and slant the end of the tub to make it easy to slide slowly into the tub from the seat, using the adjacent grab bars. For additional comfort, the slant may be contoured for extra back support.

- Install a handheld shower to use from the seat. This is useful to people who do not have the strength to lower themselves into the tub.

- Generally, a bathtub should have a flat (not round) bottom for stability.

- The floor of the tub must be slip resistant.

- Look for tubs with narrow rims or handles that can be grasped when getting in and out.

- Soft tubs provide a nonslip surface that may prevent falls and will certainly cushion the blow if a fall does occur.

- Use a contrasting stripe to identify the bathtub rim and base perimeter. Vertical stripes in the tub help to identify the amount of water through refraction or bending of the stripes at the level of the water.

- Choose a lever-type faucet and drain control for easy operation. Controls must be installed toward the approach side.

- To eliminate controls, specify an automatic fill system that programs use and presets the temperature and water level. This is especially helpful if sensitivity to temperature is a factor.

DETAILS
VIP Patient Bathroom Amenities

- A truly hospitable patient bathroom includes a combination washer-dryer. Most people cannot reach the bottom of a top-loading washer from a wheelchair. Front-loading machines also make it easier to lift wet and heavy clothes. Side-hinged doors allow closer wheelchair access than do bottom-hinged doors.

- Install an ironing board that drops down from the wall. Portable ironing boards are awkward to set up from a wheelchair and are bulky to store.

- Install a retractable clothesline or wall-mounted hanger over the bathtub. Add a second line at 48 in. a.f.f. for seated users.

- Storage areas in the patient bathroom are often insufficient and require extra planning. With higher cabinets, interior shelves should be of reinforced glass or clear plastic to make the contents more visible to children, shorter people, and wheelchair users.

- A cabinet mounted to the side of the sink is more convenient for access from a wheelchair than a cabinet mounted above the sink. When reaching over a counter from a wheelchair, anything over 44 in. a.f.f. is out of reach.

- Drawers beside the sink area, perhaps in a cabinet on wheels, can fill most remaining bathroom storage needs. On all drawers, C-grip handles should be horizontal and centered.

- Recess a soap holder so that it does not interfere with wheelchair use and transfer; plan multilevel soap dispensers. A liquid soap dispenser may require less coordination than retreiving bar soap from a holder.

- A spa can be made accessible to many people through the addition of a series of steps, the highest of which should be at the height of a wheelchair seat (17 to 19 in. a.f.f.). The user can slide from one step to the next, employing natural buoyancy to help with transfer.

- A fold-down utility tray in the bathtub or spa is another convenience.

appearance, not for use in diagnosis. A warm white or slightly pink luminaire should be selected to improve the appearance of patients with jaundice, cyanosis, or the sallow complexion that may result from a hospital stay. Patients may also experience weight loss, skin texture changes, and stress while in the hospital. Flattering lighting improves self-image and confidence. Use indirect sources, preferably behind the user, to avoid grazing the face with down light, which emphasizes textural changes and shadows.

All of this luxury can be offered in a VIP suite for as little as $31 per day more than a semiprivate room in a hospital.[13] For this cost, the med-

RESEARCH ABSTRACT
Experiential Research in Detailing Patient Rooms

Jain Malkin, Inc., a San Diego based interior architecture firm, has planned over 500 health-care facilities around the world. Jain Malkin provides the following patient-centered design details:

1. Add a user's guide to the patient room similar to that found in hotel rooms. The guide should provide written instructions for controlling room lights, using the telephone, and reaching auxiliary services like complementary therapies, newspaper delivery, and meal options. The guide should include a hospital map and an explanation of hospital policies together with the nursing philosophy.

2. Three types of lighting should be planned in the patient room: indirect ambient lighting supplemented by natural light, examination lighting in a color temperature of 3500 Kelvin, and task lighting for the patient, including a good reading light. Lighting, the nurse call system, and the window treatments should be easily controlled by the patient from bed.

3. The patient room should be private, with the bed placed to maximize a view of the outdoors. The windowsill should be no higher than 30 in. a.f.f.

4. The television should be built into a cabinet at the foot of the bed. The cabinet could also feature a reachable shelf for flowers.

5. The room should contain a message board, a comfortable place for a family member to sleep, and an interesting ceiling, preferably of gypsum board instead of acoustic tile.

ical hotel can maintain a nursing staff ratio of one to four, just as in an acute-care hospital. For the right patient, the medical hotel provides a high quality of care at a reasonable cost in a comfortable, often luxurious environment (see Research Abstract above).

REFERENCES

1. Norman Cousins, "Anatomy of an Illness," *New England Journal of Medicine* 295 (1976): 1458.
2. Anthony J. Grieco et al., *Family Partnership in Hospital Care* (New York: Springer Publishing, 1994), 215.
3. John Morrissey, "Cooperative Care Acutely Less Costly," *Modern Healthcare* (Sept. 19, 1994): 181.
4. Grieco, 212.
5. Bruce Komiske, "Innovations of Note: Cooperative Care—The Ultimate in Patient-Centered Care at a Lower Cost," *Journal of Healthcare Design* 7 (1995): 181.
6. Walter B. Kleeman, *The Challenge of Interior Design* (Boston: CBI Publishing, 1981), 121.

7. *Americans with Disabilities Act Accessibility Guidelines for Buildings and Facilities; Building Elements Designed for Children's Use*, 4.32.5(2).

8. North Carolina State Building Code Council, *North Carolina State Building Code*, vol. 1-C (Raleigh: NCSBCC, 1989), 7.2(d).

9. Kleeman, *Challenge of Interior Design*, 118.

10. Robert J. Kobet, "The Tight House Syndrome: Causes and Cures" (paper presented at the American Society of Interior Designers National Conference, Washington, D.C., August 1988).

11. *Americans with Disabilities Act Accessibility Standards*, 1991, 4.35.4.

12. *ADA Standards*, 4.8.5 (5).

13. E. Aldridge, L. D. Smith, and L. A. Sperling, "VIP Suites: A New Trend," *Journal of Healthcare Design* 3 (1991): 94.

13 GENERAL HOSPITALS

General hospitals have fallen on hard times. Health care is moving away from general hospital delivery systems to ambulatory specialized facilities, away from urgent care to primary care. As previously stated, close to 1000 hospitals have closed since 1987. Many remaining hospitals have found a niche, a service delivery style that differentiates them from their competition. Some provide state-of-the-art research from a central location, disseminating the research to satellite hospitals. Others offer an unusual form of health care or a distinctive facility planned to attract patients.

In tertiary care hospitals, patients are categorized into the very sick, the early sick, and the worried well. These hospitals have shifted from hierarchical to functional management styles with fewer corporate dictates and more patient participation in decision making. Hospitals have finally acknowledged that patients don't always fit into a particular department or hospital hierarchy; they require a system that is flexible enough to meet individual needs. In this model, patients and families are expected to take a more active role in treatment, collaborating with providers rather than submitting to them. These models provide more choices to consumers, increased access to information, and patient-centered services. The patient may be offered the option of bypassing crowded waiting rooms, for example, and going directly to the patient room. Admitting takes place in the patient room with staff using a computer that also charts blood pressure, temperature, and other data.

Health-care provision is changing. In the past, research and teaching hospitals charged heavy fees for routine procedures to cover the cost of medical research and the education of physicians. As it became increasingly difficult to do so, research and teaching hospitals were forced into staff reductions. Registered nurses were replaced by aides and physician specialists by generalists. Primary care physicians became more powerful as they increasingly served as gatekeepers to the specialists.

Patients are discharged quicker and sicker. With fierce competition for patients and budget reimbursement reductions by managed care, the number of research and teaching hospitals continues to decline. The remaining facilities provide specialized care in a high-tech hub serving a growing network of satellite clinics. Physicians and patients are flown to and from these clinics as needed, and the use of telemedicine is increasing. This seems to be the emerging model.

INNOVATIONS IN SERVICE PROVISION

The high-tech hub of the network may provide laser surgery with fiber optics inside the patient before, during, and after surgery. Genetic engineering may lead to cures for cancer, AIDS, arthritis, Alzheimer's disease, chronic mental illnesses, and the common cold. Digital diagnostic imaging continues to improve. Telemedicine and teleradiology are fast becoming the standard in health research centers.

Kaiser Permenente is testing an interactive telemedicine unit about the size of a microwave oven. The unit has a two-way color video monitor, blood pressure cuff, and telephonic stethoscope. A nurse at the hospital can monitor pulse and blood pressure and listen to the lungs without requiring the patient to leave home. Patients may receive services in both rural and urban areas. Patient and staff education is enhanced.

At some sites, telesurgery is guided electronically. In the future, remote control robotics will be coupled with this technology. For now, design requirements are simple: user-friendly equipment and high-quality audio and video monitors. The downside to telemedicine is a possible loss of privacy as medical records are transferred via the Internet. Encryption, password protection, and electronic data interchange standards are all methods being used to reduce the risks.

A large number of smaller general hospitals survive by providing unique services or innovative facilities that set them apart from the competition. Many have embraced complementary medicine, offering perks like massage therapy in the patient room, a storyteller to break the monotony, pet therapy (see Figure 13-1) and a healing garden that serves as a waiting room (see Details on page 234). Aromatherapy may be provided for relaxation inside a frightening MRI. Acupuncture may supplement traditional medicine for pain control, and art therapy may provide a flight of imagination from the anxiety of illness. In some hospitals, patients participate in the design, and their priorities may differ from those of the staff. They may want dimmers on the room lights to allow staff to check-in without disturbing their sleep. They may want coin-return lockers or a coat room in the lobby. They may enjoy sources of laughter and joy, like clowns for children.

Some hospitals practice anthroposophic medicine, using color to aid in the healing. Practitioners maintain that color should progress from clear primary colors to soft, muted tones as patients move from outside to inside, with pastels used in the most intimate and vulnerable spaces, like patient rooms. Warm colors are used to build up from a cold illness like arthritis and cool blue or violet tones are used to dissolve or break down inflammation[4] (see Details on page 82). Illness is viewed as an opportunity for spiritual development, a chance to renew strength and gain insight into one's purpose.

CASE STUDIES

Our discussion has already included most of the design details required in a general hospital. In previous chapters, arrival, parking, reception, corridors, waiting areas, and specialized treatment spaces have all been considered from a family-centered perspective. The design of patient bedrooms and baths has been addressed. Now we take a look at examples of design detail in action.

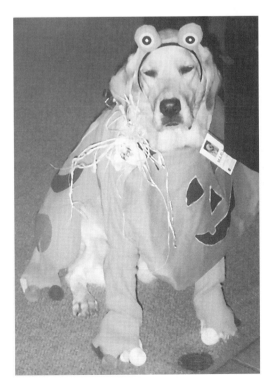

Figure 13-1 Pet therapy. *Courtesy of Desert Samaritan Medical Center, Phoenix.*

DETAILS
Planning a Healing Garden

Jacob Lieberman has linked sunlight exposure to well-being[1] and Williamson has shown a correlation between the soothing sounds of moving water and relaxation,[2] but a healing garden can do more: It may actually produce the medications for a cure.

Each plant in a healing garden is labeled with an explanation of the medication it produces. As patients learn the derivations of their medications, they also learn that nature is responsible for many of their cures. Madagascar periwinkle yields the drug vinblastine, which is used to treat Hodgkin's disease, and the drug vincristine sulfate, for the treatment of leukemia. Yew is the basis for Taxol, which is given to patients with ovarian and breast cancer, and mayapple is used to produce Etoposid, which fights testicular cancer. Garlic and lavender are traditional homeopathic remedies. Herbs are used in aromatherapy. Patients may even be inspired to grow herbs at home or pick a bouquet for their hospital room.

James Burnett, an innovative Houston landscape architect, would like to do more. He would like to plan a bed-accessible garden. "I [want] the option to be rolled outside into a garden instead of staying inside with *Jeopardy* on the TV all day and the smell of Lysol everywhere," says Burnett. "We lost our connection to nature because we thought we could solve everything with technology." In his design, the garden becomes a part-time patient room. Beds would be equipped with weatherproof medical gases and call system (see Details on page 225).

Bed in the garden. *Courtesy of the Office of James Burnett.*

Clare Cooper Marcus at the University of California at Berkeley has studied the correlation between hospital gardens and change of mood. From a survey of 24 hospitals, she determined that 95 percent of patients, employees, and families derived a therapeutic benefit from hospital gardens.[3] Gardens can be used for structured physical therapy, horticultural therapy, and recreation therapy. The garden is a place where patients and family can be distracted from their pain and anxiety. Windows to

Family garden. *Courtesy of The Office of James Burnett.*

the garden reveal patterns of sunlight filtering through plants of various colors, a sensory environment that contrasts sharply with the sterility of the hospital. Terminally ill patients have a spiritual need for a meditative garden. As time in the hospital increases, the patient's sense of time and location can decrease. A garden can put everything back in order.

A well-maintained garden inspires confidence in the care provided at the hospital. It provides sensory stimulation, especially when plants are varied in size, blooming cycle, texture, color, and fragrance. The garden should be safely planned for use by children (see Details on page 204); avoid hazardous and thorny plants. Specify nontoxic plants to protect children, pets, and people with allergies. Some garden seating should be movable so families can sit together. Some should be stable with supportive backs, extended arms and clear floor space for transferring from a wheelchair. Elevated gardens can be planned for patient use. For those in wheelchairs, pots and planters should be at least 2 ft. in height and accessible from both sides if they exceed a 2 ft. depth. They can be mounted on stands, walls, or racks. A vertical garden offers easy access to both ambulatory and seated patients.

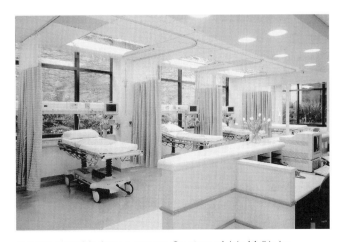

Garden viewable from a gurney. *Courtesy of Jain Malkin Inc. Photography: Steve McClelland.*

Lessons from Planetree

A growing number of small hospitals have joined the Planetree family, health-care providers with a mission to support the physical, emotional, and spiritual needs of patients. "I found it ironic that we spend so much time and effort to create splendid airport terminals so we're comfortable during a two-hour layover, but there's virtually no attention to the environments where we may spend the most significant hours of our lives," says Angelica Thieriot, the founder of Planetree.[5]

The Planetree difference begins with classical music in the parking lot (see Details on page 128). Inside, the performance softly continues on a grand player piano in the lobby. The receptionist invites you to wait in the patient library until your appointment. From the size of the book collection, you realize that Planetree is committed to empowering patients with research, demystifying the medical system in the process. Books and research articles are organized by subject for self-directed research. On-line research is also available. An adjacent health bookstore provides paperbacks and audiotapes to go.

When you are called for your appointment, you walk by a fountain through clutter-free carpeted corridors. You may notice one of the live performances taking place off of the corridor (see Figure 13-2). Art and gardens also invite inspection along the way (see Research Abstract on next page).

After treatment, you decide to visit a friend in the hospital. There is no need to worry about visiting hours; the patient rooms are always accessible—to ambulatory visitors as well as wheelchair users (see Details on page 238). Corridor signage is clear and accessible (see Details on page 240 and Research Abstract on page 242), with no messy work areas or frightening equipment in sight. Staff and equipment are in a separate corridor, and 80 percent of the diagnosis and treatment is done at the patient's bedside.[6]

Figure 13-2 Musical performance in the corridor. *Courtesy of The S/L/A/M Collaborative, Architects and Engineers.*

RESEARCH ABSTRACT
Experiential Research in Healing Art

Joan Baron designs original custom tile work in her Scottsdale, Arizona, studio. She focuses on the contribution of art to healing environments, and offers the following thoughts:

- Art can stimulate the viewer's consciousness. It can help to develop a heightened sense of self. It can make people capable of feeling another's pain and bliss. Art can elevate the soul to clarity about our true connection to one another. Shells represent cross-cultural connections; people worldwide collect shells to remind them of their adventure.

- Art can inspire the viewer to shout out the grand experience of life and to never lose hope. Joan believes art has the power to affect people in a deep and spiritual way.

- Art can empower the viewer to participate. Some participate by sponsoring a wisdom circle on a column designed to represent the true essence of the person they honor. Joan works collaboratively with the donor to elevate the memory of a loved one. The placement is low enough for children and people in wheelchairs to touch and read (see Details on page 188). The low walls in the garden are used as seats to encourage patients to touch the water, even patients in wheelchairs.

- Art reflects the importance of staying in balance. The strength of 12-in. columns is balanced by the fluid and organic mosaic tile. Balance leads to health and harmony.

- Art can free the imagination. To be burdened with shame, anger, and hopelessness is a block to creativity. The process of creating art can free the body of negative emotions by creating a pathway to new expression.

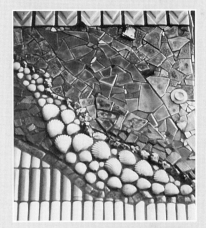

Shells: a cross-cultural connection. *Courtesy of Joan Baron, artist/educator. Project: Good Samaritan Hospital, Phoenix.*

Accessible water feature. *Courtesy of Joan Baron, artist/educator.Project: Good Samaritan Hospital, Phoenix.*

Solid columns balanced by fluid tile. *Courtesy of Joan Baron, artist/educator. Project: Good Samaritan Hospital, Phoenix.*

DETAILS
ADA Requirements in Health-Care Facilities

In addition to general ADA requirements, the following standards apply to medical treatment facilities where people may need assistance in responding to an emergency and where the period of stay may exceed 24 hours.[7]

- Where emergency warning systems (alarms) are provided, their design may be modified to suit standard health-care alarm design practice.

- At least one accessible entrance complying with ADA must be protected from the weather by a canopy or roof overhang. Such entrances must incorporate an accessible passenger loading zone. Even though operating force requirements on exterior doors have been placed on reserve, the doors must still be accessible — generally defined as operable with no more than 8.5 lbf.

- An accessible patient room provides a 36 in. accessible route to each side of the bed. There must be an unobstructed turning space within each room. This space can be either a 60 in. diameter circle or a T-shaped space. In rooms with two beds, it is preferable that this space be located between the beds.

- An accessible toilet room must also include a turning space and the accessibility requirements of the ADA Standards 4.22 and 4.23 (see Chapter 8). Common mistakes include the location of the flush control (it must be located on the approach side), lack of insulation on the hot water supply and drain lines, clothing hooks above 48 in. a.f.f. (or without a clear floor space), and toilet tissue dispensers with a controlled flow.

- In general-purpose hospitals, psychiatric facilities, and detoxification facilities, at least 10 percent of patient bedrooms and toilets, and all public and common use areas, are required to be accessible.

- In hospitals and rehabilitation facilities that specialize in treating conditions that affect mobility, all patient bedrooms and toilets, and all public and common use areas, are required to be accessible.

- In long-term care facilities, at least 50 percent of patient bedrooms and toilets are required to be accessible.

- Although 44 in. wide patient room entry doors are exempted from latch side maneuvering clearances, it is still necessary to provide them. Doors 44 in. and wider functionally require at least 24 in. of maneuvering clearance on the latch side of the door.

In addition to general ADA requirements, the following standards apply to all health care facilities (unless specifically noted):

- Common protruding hazards in health-care facilities include fire extinguishers and door closers protruding more than 4 in. (between 27 and 80 in. a.f.f.).[8]

- Patient rooms are considered primary function areas. If alterations take place in a patient room, up to 20 percent of the cost must be spent to bring an inaccessible path of travel into compliance (including restrooms, telephones, and drinking fountains along the path).[9]

- The following equipment must be available for installation in patient rooms if required: text telephones, closed-caption TV decoders, visual smoke detectors, visual door knock alerting devices, and any other devices necessary for effective communication with people with hearing differences. Other examples include handset amplifiers and assistive listening devices. Qualified sign language interpreters must be provided upon request.

- Controls in the patient room must be operable with one hand without tight grasping, pinching, or twisting.[10] For example, use a wand on draperies instead of a cord and C-grips on cabinets instead of knobs.

- Provide adjustable-height rods in the closet. Lockers and storage (when provided) must also be available at a reachable height.[11]

- Electrical outlets over sinks may be required to be as low as 44 in. a.f.f. An electrical outlet must be provided within 48 in. of the telephone outlet for use with a portable text telephone.[12]

- If a health-care facility must provide a plan to evacuate patients in the event of a fire, it must also provide a plan to evacuate people with disabilities.

- Ten percent of the total number of parking spaces at outpatient facilities must be accessible.[13]

- Twenty percent of the total number of parking spaces provided at facilities that specialize in treatment or services for persons with mobility impairments must be accessible.[14]

- If valet parking is offered, provide a compliant passenger loading zone located on an accessible route to the entrance of the facility.[15]

- The elevator exemption cannot be used in the office of a health-care provider. If these buildings have more than one floor, elevators must be provided.[16]

- If public pay telephones are located in or adjacent to a hospital emergency room, recovery room, or waiting room, one public text telephone must be provided at each such location.[17]

- Where dressing and fitting rooms are provided for use by patients, customers, or employees, 5 percent but at least one of the dressing rooms for each type of use in each cluster of dressing rooms must be accessible.[18]

- An accessible dressing room with a swinging or sliding door must feature a turnaround space; the door must not swing into any part of the space.[19]

- Every accessible dressing room must have a 24 by 48 in. bench fixed to the wall along the larger dimension. The bench must be mounted 17 to 19 in. above the finish floor. Clear floor space must be provided alongside the bench to allow a person using a wheelchair to make a parallel transfer onto the bench.[20]

- Where mirrors are provided in dressing rooms of the same use, then, in an accessible dressing room, a full-length mirror measuring at least 18 in. wide by 54 in. high must be mounted in a position affording a view to a person on the bench as well as to a person in a standing position.[21]

DETAILS
Accessible Signage

- Identify accessible facilities and parking with the international symbol for accessibility. Under the symbol, additional signage may be required. For example, parking for vans requires a sign stating "van accessible." "Area of refuge" signs are also required.

- Text telephones must be marked with the international symbol for a TTY.

- Volume control telephones and assistive listening systems must be identified by the international symbol of access for hearing loss. The symbol also may be used to notify persons of the availability of other auxiliary aides and services such as real-time captioning, captioned note taking, sign language interpreters, and oral interpreters.

- Inaccessible elements like entrances, exit stairways, toilet rooms, drinking fountains, and elevators must have signage providing directions to accessible features.

- Directional signage mounted over 80 in. a.f.f. must employ 3-in. characters, at a minimum.

- Contrast, proportion, and redundant cuing are important signage features. Light yellow or white letters on a black background are the most readable for partially sighted users.[22] The *ADA Accessibility Standards* recommend a contrast level of 70 percent. Contrast in percent must be determined by the following formula: contrast = $[(B1 - B2)/B1] \times 100$, where B1 is the light reflectance value (LRV) of the lighter area and B2 is the light reflectance value (LRV) of the darker area.[23]

- People who are color-blind have difficulty with signs relying on contrast between red and green.

- People using different languages and learning skills may understand colored pictograms more easily than words.

- Signs that provide tactile and audible cues as well as visual cues are important to people with differences in vision, reading, and learning abilities.

- Tactile signs must include letters or symbols raised a minimum of ½₂ in. and must be accompanied with Grade 2 braille. It should be angled for ease of use. Raised Arabic numerals and standard block uppercase letters without serif are required. Raised characters must be ⅝ in. high but no higher than 2 in.[24]

- In the event of an emergency, exit signs should be backed up with a middle-frequency audible signal to aid in location of an exit.[25]

- Tactile maps lead users from larger to smaller details about a space. The metal ball on a tactile map indicates the location of the sign.

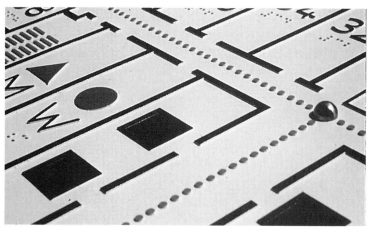

Tactile map.
Courtesy of Roger Whitehouse.

- Required tactile signs must be mounted at a height of 60 in. a.f.f. (48 in. for children) on the latch side of the door. A person must be able to approach within 3 in. of signage without encountering protruding objects or standing within the swing of a door.[26]

- Audible signs may have touch controls or, with a controlled audience, include infrared or low-frequency radio signals. Receivers can be distributed in stadiums, auditoriums, hotels, convention centers, museums, schools, etc. The receiver scans the area for audible messages.

- Some facilities offer an interactive audiovisual tour on a handheld unit with large touch buttons and a visual printout. This unit is helpful to people with hearing, coordination, and visual differences.

- All signs should be placed to avoid glare from windows and light sources, and glare-free materials should be selected.

- Illumination levels on the sign surface should be in the 100 to 300 lux range (10 to 30 fc) and uniform over the sign surface. Signs should be located such that the illumination level on the surface of the sign is not significantly exceeded by the ambient light or visible bright lighting source behind or in front of the sign.[27]

- Proportion can also improve visibility. Letters and numbers must have a width-to-height ratio between 1:1 and 3:5. The letter X, for example, could be 3 by 5 in. The ratio of the stroke width to the height must be between 1:5 and 1:10. If each line used to make the X is 1 in. wide, then the line itself could be between 5 and 10 in. long.[28]

- Spacing between lines of text should be 25 to 30 percent of the point size.[29]

- Many people with disabilities have limitations in movement of their heads and reduced peripheral vision. Thus, signage positioned perpendicular to the path of travel is easiest for them to notice. People can generally distinguish signage within an angle of 30 degrees to either side of the centerline of their faces without moving their heads.[30]

- Raised borders around signs containing raised characters may make them confusing to read by touch.

RESEARCH ABSTRACT
Signage Summary

So often, commonsense details are overlooked on signage. Research has confirmed a need for the basics. Signage must be as succinct as possible, readable for all users (composed at a sixth-grade reading level), stated in positive terms, understandable, and in need of no further clarification.[31] Simple terms like *walkway* and *general hospital,* for example, are more easily understood than *overhead link* or *medical pavilion.*[32] Multilingual signage may be necessary in some hospitals, although this does add information. Probably the most common error is made by putting too much information on the sign.

Move from general information at the start of wayfinding to specific signage at the destination. Place directional signage at corridor intersections; use room numbers and arrows to help wayfinders decide which way to turn. Do not use arrows on nondirectional signs. Reinforce the message beyond the intersection, if necessary, perhaps every 150 to 250 ft.[33] Additional signage may be necessary when an architectural feature, like a change in finishes, indicates a different part of the building. Coordinate electrical and mechanical fixture placement so that prime signage locations are not taken. Don't forget to sign the destination.

Reinforce the wayfinding plan with a "you are here" map. On a map, forward is up. Include icons of memorable architectural elements, like sculpture and gardens. Deemphasize staff areas on the map and highlight public corridors. Provide an inset showing the relationship between the mapped area and the rest of the building. Maps with a perspective view are preferred over maps with a plan view.[34]

Draw the "you are here" arrow pointing in the direction the viewer is facing while looking at the map. Color code explanations with map colors and use language corresponding to the signs on the walls. Place the map near an unusual building feature, like a donor's column in the lobby, so users can remember the location of the map. Don't limit map placement to the entry or parking area; place maps at key destinations (with reverse signage) showing the way back to the parking lot.

Be consistent in signage. Use the same terminology on each sign; don't put "Psychology" on one sign and "Behavioral Science" on another. Be consistent in placement to maintain expectations. For example, place signage at all intersections, not just some. All rooms beginning with the number 5 should be on the fifth floor. Keep odd numbers on one side and even numbers on the other. Coordinate patient room numbers with phone numbers.

Floor numbers should logically relate to the entry and to the other floors. Avoid linking floor 3 of one building with floor 5 of another. Do not mix letters and numbers to identify spaces (e.g., room A101). *I* can be confused with *1* and *0* can be confused with "O" and "Q." One exception: Sub 1 and Sub 2 are the preferred floor titles for basement locations.[35] Larger numbers may indicate patient destinations and smaller may be used on staff rooms, or use names on patient rooms and numbers on staff rooms. Sliding message panels add flexibility so that room numbering systems can accommodate future renovation, but select a system that is not *too* easy to change. Align words on the left margin of the sign.

When you arrive at the private room, you find your friend's name framed in a beautiful ceramic nameplate outside. A small sign invites you to knock on the door. It is opened by the patient's care partner, who stays with the patient in the room. The partner invites you to wait in one of the adjacent lounges while the patient gets dressed. You can choose between a quiet lounge or the entertainment lounge with music, television, and games (see Details on page 137). The fragrance of baking cookies drifts through the lounge from the family kitchen (see Details on pages 94, 95, 96, and 97 and Research Abstract on page 59). A cooking class in progress. This is really quite a hospital!

A hospital can be a cold, impersonal, lonely place, more akin to a body shop than a healing environment. Patients are expected to adjust to these surroundings while facing financial problems, lack of information, fear of pain and medication, threat of severe illness or death, and other stresses resulting from lack of control. In addition, the hospital requires them to separate from family and friends and to obey providers. The nursing station traditionally looks like a prison, often elevated and surrounded by glass like a guard tower protecting the nurses from the patients.

Planetree has decentralized the nursing station into a series of pods serving three to four patients (see Figure 13-3). Each pod is equipped with a computer, phone, office supplies, medications (other than controlled substances), and dressings. This is more convenient for both nurses and patients. Patients have access to their records and the right to insert comments. This has eliminated much of the confusion between patients and providers; many patients actually serve as a liaison between specialists. As an added benefit, patients who are well informed about medications are more compliant about taking them.

Figure 13-3 Decentralized nursing station. *Courtesy of The S/L/A/M Collaborative, Architects and Engineers.*

Planetree philosophy and design detail produce measurable results. A study conducted by the University of Washington showed that only 8.2 percent of Planetree inpatients needed to use the emergency department during their stay versus 14.9 percent of patients from other units. Complaints at the Bergen Mercy Trauma Center dropped from 37 in 1994 (before Planetree took over) to only two in 1995. The average length of stay declined from 7.0 to 4.3 days in the diabetes unit, from 3.2 to 2.5 days in ICU, and from 2.7 to 2.1 days in surgery.[36] Patient-centered design detail makes a measurable difference (see Research Abstract on the next page).

A Study in Context

The Alaskan Native Medical Center is a fascinating study in wayfinding and orientation within a cultural context. This hospital serves patients from small native villages. Many have never even been in an elevator. Most cannot read. To add to the challenge, seven distinct native groups (which may not always get along) are served. These Alaska natives are from cultures centered on the outdoors; they value their relationship to nature. They resist entering a building, let alone a hospital. Yet this hospital became one of the major native gathering places in the state of Alaska.

To identify their cultural values, Richard Dallam, the NBBJ architect, spent 18 months researching these societies; he actually lived with native families in each village for several weeks. He was looking for common links, shared traditions, and beliefs that could be reflected in the design of the hospital. He did a survey of the native architecture and identified a common concept: each village consisted of a number of small buildings constructed around the perimeter of a central meeting place or lodge. In this common area, natives sat on the floor around the perimeter, basking in sun, if possible.

Most of the buildings were very small. Many incorporated unique solutions to the problem of living in a severe climate. Arctic entries reduced the admission of cold air. Structures were heavy and nonlinear. Buildings were planned to admit daylight and reduce snow drifting. Natural materials, including bones, animal skins, and spruce, were used for protection from the elements.

The architect noticed how the natives put things together. The Athabascan traditionally decorated sparingly, with only seams and joints embellished with intricate, ornamental design. Clothing seams are often the boundary between life and death in this harsh climate. Seasonal clothing is so important that it has become an art form.

Dallan learned about the interdependence of the villagers. They give more to the village than they take. He learned that they honor death as much as birth, that the hospital morgue would be as important to them as the birthing rooms. He found a basic lifestyle, dependent on land and

RESEARCH ABSTRACT
Experiential Research in Detailing Hospitals for Patient-Centered Care

Karrie Frasca-Beautieu, ASID, heads the interior design team at the S/L/A/M Collaborative in Glastonbury, Connecticut, one the nation's leading health-care architecture firms. She provides the following recommendations:

- Reduce stress with wayfinding. Strong architectural elements like a spiral staircase create unmistakable reference points for navigation. Striking furniture arrangements, like a console table with flowers, or a special effect with lighting can also be used as landmarks.

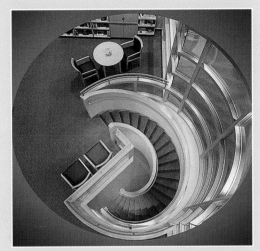

Strong architectural element. *Courtesy of The S/L/A/M Collaborative, Architects and Engineers.*

- The healing power of nature has been documented by clinical research. Muscle tension and blood pressure have been significantly reduced after viewing natural scenes. SLAM projects reflect the importance of courtyards, gardens, and terraces. The deleterious effects of disturbing repetitive sound and unvarying light are exacerbated in rooms without windows. Glass-block windows and walls allow natural light to penetrate patient rooms without compromising privacy.

- Sound can be used as a positive distraction. When patients focus on music, they tend to tune out disturbing sounds. The sound of bubbling water in a fish tank can also block out unpleasant noises (see Details on pages 265 and 266).

- Patients need to enhance their sense of control over personal space. Provide a secure area with wardrobe space to store personal items (see Details on page 24).

- Encourage family visits with a comfortable lounge featuring hospitable furnishings specified in a variety of sizes to accommodate different ages and body types.

- Create a comfortable and friendly hospital atmosphere by replacing plastic handrails with wood, colored corner guards with acrylic, and vinyl furniture with natural choices. Introduce color through carpeting, draperies, artwork, and upholstery. For an inviting atmosphere, vary the lighting and add decorative accessories, plants, bedspreads, flowers, and lamps (see Details on page 223).

- Hospital food is a primary source of complaints. To broaden the patient's choices, plan a family kitchen and encourage patients and families to cook their own meals. With the help of a nutritionist, they can learn new habits that lead to a healthier lifestyle.

- Custom cabinets reduce clutter in patient rooms by providing functional storage for monitors, supplies, medical gases, televisions, VCRs, small refrigerators, and hampers.

Figure 13-4 Entrance canopy. *Courtesy of NBBJ. Photography: Assassi Productions.*

Figure 13-5
Gathering place.
*Courtesy of NBBJ.
Photography:
Assassi Productions.*

water. He learned that the native people rely on their visual acuity to survive, to find their way through the endless white snow and diffused sky. They orient themselves with natural landmarks and navigate on the basis of color value, the degree that the landscape pales in the distance.

He took these lessons to heart. The Alaska Native Medical Center is a series of small-scale one-story pavilions in a village-like setting. The dark colors on the base of the structures lighten in ascent, reflecting the relationship between color value and viewing distance. The building seams appear to be stitched together with brickwork. The entrance canopy looks like a combination of whalebone and seal gut (see Figure 13-4). The landscaping includes a nature walk through mature trees.

The building steps back to the north, allowing the never-ending summer daylight to flood the interior. The Arctic stone entryway reduces the flow of cold air and catches some of the grit. The interior is filled with gathering places where people can meet and socialize with family and friends while they bask in the sun. The center of each gathering place is empty, a place to display familiar land and sea forms crafted of terrazzo and aluminum (see Figure 13-5). Low seating around the perimeter meets the needs of these shorter people. Other gathering areas provide a place for families to be on the floor but out of the way of staff, or a place for prayer and meditation. Even the pediatric natural sand area is designed as a gathering place. Children in wheelchairs can approach on a ramp with a very gradual slope (1:20) (see Details below).

DETAILS
Ramps

- To prevent segregation by design, ramps should be designed universally and appear to be an integral part of the architecture.

- A universal ramp does not exceed a grade of 1:20. Over two thirds of wheelchair users cannot use an ADA-compliant ramp with a 1:12 slope and a 30-ft. length.[37]

- The slope of the landings and the cross slope of the ramp should not exceed 1:50.[38]

- Wood ramps are easy to build (and to dismantle). Use fire-retardant wood that has been pressure-treated (or is decay resistant, like redwood). Hot-dip galvanized bolts and screws (with washers) should be used to resist corrosion.

- Commercial nonskid surfaces are appropriate for wood ramps. Do not specify carpet for ramps, especially indoor-outdoor carpeting, which may become slippery when wet. Sheet vinyl and painted surfaces are also slippery when wet or dusty.

- Permanent concrete ramps should be surfaced with a sand-float or broom finish brushed across the slope, not with it, to prevent slipping.

- Cover exterior ramps in climates with ice and snow. Built-in electric heating coils can also be considered.

Continued

DETAILS
Ramps *(continued)*

- Curbs with a minimum height of 2 in. must be installed on both sides of the ramp to serve as guardrails for wheels and crutch tips.[39] Use these low curbs instead of side walls to prevent scrapes and bumps.
- Shorter ramps without handrails should have flared sides to prevent tripping accidents.
- The flat landings at the beginning and end of ramps and at any turnaround point should be at least 5 ft. in length.[40]
- The ramp should be directed toward the handle side of the door if the door opens onto the ramp. If the door opens into the building, orient the ramp to the hinge side of the door.
- The width should be a minimum of 36 in. for one-way traffic, including wheelchairs, 48 in. for two-way ambulatory traffic, and 60 in. for two wheelchairs to pass.[41]

Ramp oriented to door swing. *American National Standards Institute. A117.1, 1986.*

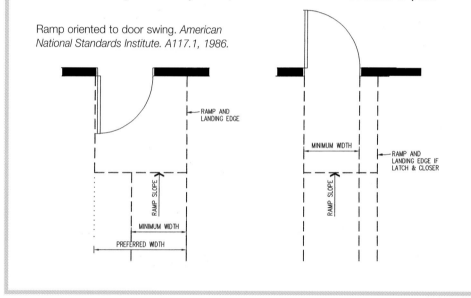

The finishes relate to a people who spend most of their time outdoors. Solid wood beams reflect the log construction of native Alaskan buildings (see Figure 13-6). Wainscoting tiles are the color of Alaska jade. Custom-blown glass sconces resemble ice formations (see Figure 13-7). Door frames are contrasted like the piping on the native clothing.

The hospital's interior is a blend of traditional culture and modern health-care design. The patient rooms are simple in design, mirroring the basic lifestyle of the patients. A large window is the focal point of each patient room, affirming the importance of nature. Hospital research has shown that patients assigned to rooms with window views of a natural setting showed significant improvement over those with windows facing brick walls. The patients with a view had shorter postoperative stays,

Figure 13-6 Solid wood beams. *Courtesy of NBBJ. Photography: Assassi Productions.*

Figure 13-7 Light and ice sconces. *Courtesy of NBBJ. Photography: Assassi Productions.*

fewer negative evaluations by nurses, and required less medication (potent analgesics).[42]

A 59-room hostel provides a place for families and community health aides who travel to the hospital to learn skills they can take back to the villages. The training emphasizes treatment of orthopedic injuries and burns. A satellite link is provided between the villages and the hospital.

Wayfinding was particularly challenging, as many patients cannot read. Spectacular native art and crafts are used as wayfinding cues at critical intersections, acknowledging the visual acuity of the native people (see Figure 13-8). Patients are told to turn right at the halibut bone carving (see Details on the next page). The nonlinear, asymmetrical shape of the building and the small scale contribute to orientation (see Details on page 252).

Figure 13-8 Crafts as wayfinding cures. *Courtesy of NBBJ. Photography: Assassi Productions.*

DETAILS
Environmental Wayfinding Cues

How do I get there from here? To find the way through a building, cues must be read from signage and from the environment. Yet in most hospitals there is little spatial differentiation; walls are all the same color (for ease of maintenance), and all floors are finished with the same material.

- The form of the building provides the strongest wayfinding cue. Reduce the number of corridors and limit the building symmetry. Logically place the points where directional choices must be made.

- Secure displays of personal collections provide important wayfinding and orientation cues.

- A unique patient room entrance can help locate a specific room from down the corridor. The floor tiles in front of each patient room doorway can be differentiated. Gateways and footprints can be added to the carpet. A private mailbox can be installed next to each patient room so the patient can look forward to receiving mail each day.

- Color and pattern can be planned for wayfinding. Corridors can be color coded for easy directions.

- Lighting is also used in wayfinding. Include a night-light so patients can find their way to the toilets.

- Visual connection of spaces also improves wayfinding. In some hospitals, patients can view corridors from the common area. Other spaces provide patients a chance to observe activities prior to entering. Views to the outside also help.

- Convert corridors into atriums and galleries to improve wayfinding.

- Use consistent lighting details at all major decision-making points. Repeat a hospital icon or logo at these points. Use only one symbol per sign.

- To guide patients into the hospital, the vehicular approach needs to be clear and visually differentiated from the ambulance entrance.

- A lowered ceiling subtly delivers the message that the space is changing from public to private.

- Ensure direct visual access to the reception desk from the entrance. The information desk should be easily distinguished from other counters and windows. Olsen and Pershing (as reported by Carpman et al.) found that 74 percent of all of patients stopped at this desk to receive wayfinding information.[43]

- Floor stripes are best used in small facilities, where only a few colors are necessary.

DETAILS
Environmental Orientation Cues

Where am I now? Stress caused by disorientation can raise blood pressure, increase fatigue, cause headaches, and produce feelings of helplessness.[44]

- Small, clearly differentiated spaces aid in orientation. Plan unique layouts for each entry and courtyard. Interior entrances can be recessed for additional spacial differentiation.

- Redundant cuing that appeals to all five senses can improve orientation and reduce loss of memory. Patients rely on tactile cues, like objects and air currents, for orientation. Fragrances and visual shapes are also important orientation cues.

- A view of the sky and ground helps to maintain circadian rhythms and to prevent hallucinations and disorientation. Patients often experience disorientation between day and night, especially in spaces without windows. Exterior views can also help with awareness of seasonal changes.

- A clock in the patient room can help with time orientation. Also, write the date and day of the week on a whiteboard using nontoxic markers. Don't mark off days on the calendar, which can reinforce a sense of loss of another day.

- Disorientation may also be caused by too many repetitive elements in the design. For example, doors repeated the full length of double-loaded corridors (corridors with rooms off both sides) are confusing. Long corridors themselves can be disorienting.

- Side lights and other accent lighting (instead of flat fluorescent light) can help people to maintain orientation within a room.

- Plan chairs in a variety of sizes to accommodate both small and large visitors as well as children of all ages. Styles can also be varied to serve as cues for orientation.

- To help with orientation and to accommodate people with hearing impairments, avoid tall arrangements of flowers and accessories on furniture that block visual cues.

- Side lights and vision panels in doors help with orientation, allowing patients to look inside to see if this is where they really belong. At the entrance to each waiting room, glass block serves as a nice transition, allowing patients to see through from the corridor for orientation.

- An outdoor play area or garden can serve as a strong reference point to help with orientation to the building. A wind chime provides a sense of direction to all users.

- Visually confusing mirrors produce distracting patterns that can make concentration and orientation difficult. These problems are exacerbated in hospitals by constant interruption, drug intervention, and other medical treatments.

- Because patients are prone much of the time, it is more important to differentiate between the ceiling and walls than between walls and the floor.

- Overhead paging can reduce orientation. It seems to come from all directions at once and makes the area seem uniform.

DETAILS
Stairs

- People with reduced balance may be able to manage steps more easily than ramps.
- People with mobility differences have difficulty negotiating spiral and curved staircases, which require balance and dependence on the handrails.
- Straight staircases must provide a safe stopping place midway between floor levels to help those who are prone to dizziness or who need to conserve energy. A seat on the landing is helpful to many. Landings at frequent intervals minimize the distance a user can fall.
- Landings at exterior stairway entrances may become slippery when wet, so they must be slightly sloped (not exceeding 1:50) for drainage.
- Do not design steps with abrupt or square nosings that project more than 1½ in.[45] It's easy to catch a toe on this overlap. Use wedge-shaped fillers on existing square nosings.
- Open risers are nearly impossible for people with canes or other mobility aides to use. For a similar appearance, consider a clear filler for an open riser.
- Keep every riser a constant height (7 in. maximum preferred) and every tread a constant depth (11 in. minimum).[46]
- Tread width must also be consistent within each flight, as varied widths can create optical illusions that affect the balance of users.[47] Avoid confusing patterns on stairway floor coverings for the same reason.
- To prevent people from walking into hanging stairways or other elevated protruding objects, install wing walls or curbs under them. Guardrails or planters can also be used.
- Color-contrast the edges of treads and risers so they can be spotted more easily. This is especially important on the first and last steps. With self-illuminating strips, the edges can be seen in the dark.
- Single stairs can be difficult to see and are dangerous when they are not expected or lighted properly. Many building codes do not allow their use, but when it is allowed, changing the texture or color on a single stair helps.
- Texture should be used to mark stairway landings and other areas that are hazardous to people with differences in vision.

Strong architectural shapes provide additional cues. The stairway opens all the way to fifth floor (see Details above and on page 254). The integrated display of native jewelry cases makes climbing the stairs an event and encourages use of the stairs by those unfamiliar with elevators. Multiple windows acknowledge that native Alaskans orient themselves with natural landmarks. The interior courtyard provides another opportunity to spend time outdoors; it uses reflected light to melt the snow in the winter. Patients are encouraged to dine outside, and the restaurant serves reindeer stew.

DETAILS
Handrails

- A handrail diameter of 1¼ in. allows the strongest and most comfortable grip.
- The handrail should have rounded ends or return to the wall, floor, or post to minimize the chance that it will snag clothing and cause a fall. It should not extend into the pedestrian pathway by more than 4 in.[48]
- A handrail should also clear the adjacent wall by 1½ in.[49] This gap is enough to allow a panic grab during a fall, but not wide enough to be dangerous. Many people place their entire lower arm on the handrail to push up; the arm can become wedged between the wall and the rail if a larger clearance is allowed.
- To prevent scraped knuckles, the wall surface behind the handrail must not be abrasive.[50] Texture can be used on the handrail itself for improved grip and orientation. Notches or grooves can be cut in the rail to identify location. Braille and audible cues may also be added.
- Handrails should not rotate within their fittings.
- Contrast the handrails from the wall so that they can be seen quickly in an emergency.
- Handrails should be continuous on the inner rail at switchbacks and doglegs, and the gripping surface must be uninterrupted. Mount handrails for accessible ramps and stairs at a height of 34 to 38 in. above the stair nosing or ramp surface.[51]
- Handrails should always be installed on both sides of a stair or ramp to accommodate people who are stronger on one side than the other.
- Handrails are required on ramps if the rise is greater than 6 in. or its horizontal projection greater than 72 in.[52]
- A handrail can be recessed to a maximum of 3 in. if the recess extends at least 18 in. above the top of the rail.[53]
- The handrail should extend 12 in. beyond the top and 12 in. plus the width of one riser beyond the bottom of stairs and ramps. At the bottom, the handrail should continue to slope for a distance of the width of one tread. The remaining 12 in. should be horizontal.
- At least 3 ft. of clearance must be provided between the handrails on stairs (4 ft. on stairs adjacent to an area of refuge).

REFERENCES

1. Michael Leccese, "Nature Meets Nurture," *Landscape Architecture* 85, no. 1: 68.
2. J. Williamson, "The Effects of Ocean Sounds on Sleep After Coronary Artery Bypass Graft Surgery," *American Journal of Critical Care* 1 (1992): 91–97.
3. Susan Edge-Gumbel, "Flower Power: The Proper Garden Can Cultivate a Wealth of Hospital Benefits," *Health Facilities Management* 9, no. 6 (June 1996).
4. Gary Coates and Susanne Siepl-Coates, "Vidarkliniken," *The Healthcare Forum Journal* (September/October 1992): 27–29.
5. Steve Schwade, "Hospitals with the Human Touch," *Prevention* (December 1994): 6–7.
6. Ellen Weisman, "Built-In Care," *Health Facilities Management* (November 1994): 25.
7. *Americans with Disabilities Act Accessibility Standards,* 1991, 6.1.
8. Ibid., 4.4.1.
9. Ibid., 4.1.6 (2).
10. Ibid., 4.27.4.
11. Ibid., 4.25.3.
12. Ibid., 4.2.5.
13. Ibid., 4.1.2 (5)(d)(i).
14. Ibid., 4.1.2 (5)(d)(ii).
15. Ibid., 4.1.2 (5)(e).
16. Ibid., 4.1.3 (5), Exception 1.
17. Ibid., 4.1.3 (17)(c)(iii).
18. Ibid., 4.1.3 (21).
19. Ibid., 4.35.2.
20. Ibid., 4.35.4.
21. Ibid., 4.35.5.
22. John Salmen, ed. "Low Vision Print Legibility," *Universal Design Newsletter.* (January 1994): 8.
23. *ADA Standards,* A4.30.5.
24. Ibid., 4.30.4.
25. Janet Reizenstein Carpman, Myron A. Grant, and Deborah A. Simmons, *Design That Cares,* (Chicago: American Hospital Publishing, 1986), 52.
26. *ADA Standards,* 4.30.6.
27. Ibid., A4.30.8.
28. Ibid., 4.30.2.
29. Salmen, "Low Vision Print Legibility," 8.
30. *ADA Standards,* A4.30.1.
31. Carpman et al., *Design That Cares,* 26.
32. Ibid., 27.
33. R. Downs, "Mazes, Minds, and Maps," in *Sign Systems for Libraries,* eds. D. Pollet and P. Haskell (New York: R. R. Bowker, 1979).
34. Carpman et al., *Design That Cares,* 79.
35. Janet Reizenstein Carpman, Myron A. Grant, and Deborah A. Simmons, "Wayfinding in the Hospital Environment: The Impact of Various Floor Numbering Alternatives," *Journal of Environmental Systems* 13, no. 4 (May 1984): 353–364.
36. Mark Harris, "Designing for Patient-Centered Care: Making It Happen in Today's Marketplace," *The Quality Letter* 9, no. 6 (June 1997): 11.
37. D. J. M. Van der Voordt, "Accessibility by Means of Ramps," *Proceedings of the Built Environment and the Handicapped: Toward a Normal Life for the Disabled and Elderly* (Gotheberg, Sweden: Swedish Council for Building Research, 1981), 38–40.

38. *ADA Standards,* 4.3.7.
39. Ibid., 4.8.7.
40. Ibid., 4.8.4.
41. Ibid., A4.2.1 (3).
42. Roger S. Ulrich, "View Through a Window May Influence Recovery from Surgery," *Science* 224 (1984): 420–421.
43. Carpman et al., *Design That Cares,* 43.
44. S. Schumaker and J. E. Reizenstein, "Environmental Factors Affecting Inpatient Stress in Acute Care Hospitals," in *Environmental Stress,* ed. G. W. Evans (New York: Cambridge University Press, 1982).
45. Ibid., 4.9.3.
46. Ibid., 4.9.2.
47. Ibid., 4.9.2.
48. Ibid., 4.4.1.
49. Ibid., 4.8.5 (3).
50. Ibid., 4.26.4.
51. Ibid., 4.8.5 (5).
52. Ibid., 4.8.5.
53. Ibid., 4.26.2.

14 CRITICAL CARE

EMERGENCY DEPARTMENTS

Dr. Frederick Scott had a vision: an inviting center for emergency care that looks nothing like a stereotypical emergency department (ED). He envisioned original art on the walls and a real piano playing softly in the background. He saw children frolicking on a sunny patio next to a healing garden (see Details on page 234), Mom reading on a comfortable sofa, and Dad studying the exotic fish in the aquarium (see Figure 14-1). Instead of medicinal odors, the fragrance of baking bread was drifting through the space.

Dr. Scott maintained this vision until it became the Samaritan West Valley Health Center outside of Phoenix, Arizona. Although the center looks nothing like a typical ED, many patients with life-threatening emergencies receive critical care there. Some arrive by ambulance, are stabilized, and are then transferred, by helicopter if necessary, to a hospital for further care. However, this standalone emergency care center provides more than health care. It houses a community room for group meetings, a gallery of children's art, and a learning center with up-to-date health information. Families access the Internet on a computer tucked away in a beautiful armoire (see Details on page 139).

Figure 14-1 Aquarium. *Courtesy of the Orcutt/Winslow Partnership.*

On arrival, the patient is not put through even a minimal registration process. Each patient and family is taken immediately to an emergency suite for a medical assessment by a triage nurse. Registration information is taken after the examination in the suite. Most often the patient is treated immediately, but if a wait is required, the patient knows that someone has taken his or her injury seriously enough to do an assessment. During the wait, patients and their family can watch television in the exam room or use a private phone. In addition to these amenities, the rooms are inconspicuously equipped for the best health-care provision, including negative pressure systems for infection control.

This 36,000 sq. ft. center devotes 4,500 sq. ft. to medical imaging, providing CT scans, ultrasound, tomography, and X-ray. Most laboratory studies are completed in-house. The center also offers a large array of outpatient services and houses the offices of many physicians and other providers. A private space was planned for police and paramedics, encouraging them to choose this center. This space is equipped with supplies for restocking ambulances.

A private space was also planned for family members who have lost a loved one. This grieving area is separated from a body-viewing room by a stained-glass window. An outside exit means distraught family members need not pass through the waiting room.

Indirect lighting creates a welcoming ambience in the waiting and reception area (see Details on page 83). The context of the setting is maintained by the desert colors—warm sand tones with cactus green—offset by natural wood finishes and slate floors. An original art collection is displayed in the space, including paintings, sculpture, and a handmade quilt (see Figure 14-2).

Large windows fill the center with natural light. Three courtyards provide access to the outdoors, and a fountain soothes with the sounds of moving water. It's hard to believe this is an emergency care center (see Research Abstract on page 260).

Most patients arrive at an ED with unexpected injuries and sudden illnesses. They are often under stress and sometimes make poor decisions. Wayfinding is critical. The vehicular approach needs to be very

Figure 14-2 Comforting quilt in emergency department. *Courtesy of the Orcutt/Winslow Partnership.*

Figure 14-3 Clear vehicular approach. *Courtesy of Mackey Mitchell Associates.*

RESEARCH ABSTRACT
Experiential Research in Critical Care Design

Nancy Pattyn with Phoenix-based Orcutt/Winslow led a team of interior designers to produce a spectacular critical care center, the Samaritan West Valley Health Center. She considers the following elements critical to producing a healing environment:

- Considering the extended waiting times in emergency rooms, plan space and furnishings to support a variety of activities. Include some outdoor space and keep interior spaces intimate and relaxing. Include tables with comfortable chairs for writing or doing puzzles. Include lounge chairs for reading, sofas for resting or consoling, and movable lightweight seating for family groups.

- Provide interior views to outdoor spaces, bringing natural elements inside. Use natural materials with a low sheen, like stone and wood, to reduce glare from patios and gardens.

- Reinforce wayfinding cues with redundancy. Signage can be reinforced by a change in lighting or in room finish at decision points. Art can serve as landmarks to help patients and their families locate a destination and return from it.

- Develop a full-spectrum color scheme by using complementary colors. Use both natural and artificial lighting sources, including both indirect and task lighting. This creates balance in the space and a calmer, more harmonious environment.

- In an effort to create comfort, appeal to all of the senses. Eliminate clinical odors and introduce soothing scents, such as vanilla. Comfort visually with textural furnishings, sculpture, and artwork like quilts. Comfort acoustically with music, which establishes a mood while masking unwanted sounds.

clear (see Figure 14-3) and visually differentiated from the ambulance entrance. One entrance should be planned for ambulance patients and another for walk-in patients providings privacy and dignity (see Details on pages 63 and 149). For patient and family security, staff must have visual access to both entrances.

Arrival, entry, triage (evaluation to help prioritize treatment), and registration are seamlessly facilitated at Samaritan. The patients are moved through the space with the help of signage (see Details on page 240 and Research Abstract on page 242), logical space planning, and other wayfinding techniques (see Details on pages 251 and 252). To track patients during the process, Smartcard technology is used. The card speeds registration and access to medical records.

In an ED, furniture and finishes in the waiting area must be extremely serviceable, yet comfortable for extended waits. Lighting should be indirect and flattering to minimize the stress of illness and injury. Patient and visitor waiting areas should feature individual reading lamps (see Details on page 223) and some reclining seats for sleep (see Details on page 119). Public telephones should be located outside of the waiting rooms to provide privacy. A television should be located where it will not disturb others, and a children's play area should be strategically placed (see Chapter 6). Patients and their families should be offered a choice of music in the waiting area as well as in the treatment areas. In one excellent study, patients who listened to music while undergoing laceration repair in an ED experienced significantly less pain.[1]

The challenge of designing an ED treatment area is to create an environment that limits patient-to-patient contact yet maintains staff-to-patient and staff-to-staff contact, either physically or electronically. Many hospitals have moved the essential nursing functions to treatment modules, creating small nursing stations called *podiums*.[2] Each module can be modified in size from two to six beds, depending on patient acuity levels. Patients are separated from one another but retain visual and aural contact with the nurses, who can monitor up to six patients at once.

In this model, each treatment area is differentiated from others by changes in color, floor plan, ceiling height, and finishes. Neutral corridors are established around the perimeter of the treatment modules for use by other patients, families, and visitors. These corridors should not be used to store visible hospital equipment, which can appear threatening (see Figure 14-4). Typically, the corridors have high ceilings and low-intensity lighting to reduce stress. To improve wayfinding, ceilings are lowered as space changes from public to private. Public corridors, reception areas, and registration and triage areas are differentiated from staff areas and patient treatment modules. Postobservational rooms are positioned away from the major trauma rooms, closer to the waiting areas for better access.

Figure 14-4 Concealed storage and corridor seating. *Courtesy of Shepley, Bulfinch, Richardson, and Abbott.*

INTENSIVE CARE UNITS

In the past, the intensive care unit (ICU) was a large, rectangular room with a nursing station in the center and beds around the perimeter. Patients and their families were continually annoyed by noise from other patients, staff interruptions, and beeping medical equipment. The overhead illumination was unrelenting and windows were seldom provided. Patients could not differentiate between day and night, so they were prone to "ICU psychosis"—extreme disorientation exacerbated by constant interruption, drug intervention, and other medical treatments.

In a well-meaning but misguided attempt to soften the blow, some ICUs were decorated to look like home. Incongruous ruffles and lace, wallpaper with confusing patterns, and abstract art only added to patient and family disorientation (see Details on page 214). Patients and their families began to wonder whether the medical treatment was as makeshift as the decoration.

Today, the best ICUs feature professionally designed private rooms with visual access to the outdoors as well as to the nursing station (see Figure 14-5). In one study, window access improved memory, orientation, and sleep. Patients experienced fewer hallucinations and visual disturbances.[3] A view of the sky and ground helps to maintain circadian rhythm and prevent hallucinations and disorientation. A clock within sight also helps, but not on the wall at the foot of the bed, where patients would have to stare at it all day.

In addition, spacial differentiation techniques can be used to prevent disorientation. Because patients are prone most of the time, it is more important to differentiate between the ceiling and walls than between the walls and the floor of the ICU. Use indirect lighting without glare, not a fluorescent fixture, over patient beds. Movable lighting can be used to increase lighting levels when required.

Visual access to the nursing station is necessary for both the nurse and the patient. Some patients may be too weak to operate a call system. They depend on visual and aural contact. For those who can use the call system, ensure that all controls are lighted for nighttime use, usable by either hand, and operable without tight grasping, pinching, or twisting. They should be intuitively operable and visible, with large, high-contrast lettering.

Visual access from outside the room must be controlled by the patient for privacy in bathing and toileting. Window treatments can be provided to offer privacy and to prevent glare from corridor lights as well as from

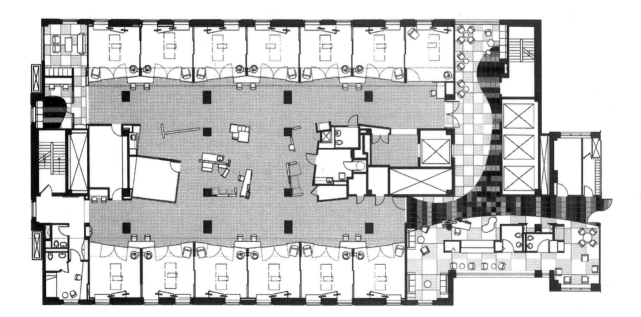

Figure 14-5 ICU floor plan. *Courtesy of Spector Group with Guenther Petrarca.*

Figure 14-6 Cubicle curtains in the ICU. *Mt. Sinai Neurosurgical Intensive Care Unit. Peter Maus, Esto, Photographer. Courtesy of Guenther Petrarca, formerly Architecture + Furniture.*

the outdoors (see Details on page 80). The ICU is a good place for motorized window treatments and cubicle curtains (see Figure 14-6).

Acoustical privacy is also a priority. Private rooms give the family an opportunity to have confidential conversations with the patient and protect from ambient noise. ICU noise levels may be hazardous to health. In one interesting study, 105 healthy women were exposed to noise levels characteristic of critical care units and experienced poorer sleep.[4] Noise has been shown to contribute to fewer visits by family and more staff turnover.[5] Design detail can make a significant contribution to acoustical control (see Details on pages 265 and 266).

ICU patients and their families should also be offered options in lighting and HVAC control. Individual HVAC systems should be planned in the private rooms. Some patients may prefer ambient temperature levels of 75° or more and humidity levels as high as 50 percent.[6] Controls for lighting and HVAC could be combined with the call system described above (lighted for nighttime use, usable by either hand, easily operable and visible). Night-lights allow nurses to check on patients without disturbing their rest; supplemental lighting can be used for examinations.

To allow accurate examination of the patient's color, yellow and blue should not be used on the headwall.[7] Examination equipment should be stored out of sight when not in use. When equipment is in use, it should be placed out of the direct sightline of the patient and family whenever possible.

DETAILS
Ambient Noise

Noise in hospitals contributes to sleep deprivation, confusion, and disorientation, whereas the relaxing sounds of running water and music can stimulate production of endorphins, lower heart rates, and reduce the need for anesthesia. Even under general anesthesia, patients exhibit a significant decrease in anxiety when listening to music.[8] Ocean sounds (produced by a sound simulator) have been shown to improve sleep in postoperative patients.[9] High noise levels increase pain perception levels and may even increase the need for medication.

- Studies show that carpeting can reduce ambient noise by up to 70 percent.[10] It also prevents generation of surface noise and reduces impact noise transmitted from floor to floor. Even noise from mechanical equipment can be significantly reduced by carpeting when used with floor insulation and padding. Cut pile absorbs more sound than loop pile.[11]

- A wall of drapery can absorb nearly half the ambient noise in the space.[12]

- In relaxation areas, use textured sound-absorbing wall coverings. Specify products with a high noise reduction coefficient (NRC) rating.

- Work areas should be planned to reduce ambient noise generation. Add padding under printers and telephones. Attach a felt strip to the edge of file drawers. Avoid noisy metal chart holders and racks. Doors should be equipped with silent closers.

- Spring-mount transformers and isolate vibration from mechanical equipment.

- Low, highly reflective ceilings amplify sound, increasing ambient noise. The reflected sound can be reduced using ceiling tiles with a high NRC.

- Long, rectangular rooms increase sound reflection and resulting noise levels. Low-frequency noise generated within the space can be absorbed by sound panels. Place the panels on at least two adjacent (not opposite) walls at the critical height for sound absorption (between 2 ft. 6 in. and 6 ft. 8 in. a.f.f.).[13]

- Hard surfaces facing one another produce reverberation. Irregularly shaped recessed areas along walls and ceilings defuse sound waves, improving acoustics as much as 10 percent.[14]

- Ceiling light fixtures that reflect sound should be replaced with suspended or wall-mounted fixtures.

- Sound baffles used across a corridor can be effective in absorbing ambient noise while visually reducing the length of the space.

DETAILS
Transmitted Noise

- It is especially important to control sound transmission between the social and private spaces of the interior. Locate noisy public spaces away from patient rooms. Window and door openings should be oriented away from sources of noise.

- In shared patient rooms, noises from the bathroom should be contained, not transmitted. To quiet water flow, specify pipes with as large a cross section as possible and install low-pressure cisterns instead of high-pressure heads. Back-to-back outlets and medicine chests in bathrooms are also sources of transmitted noise that can be avoided.

- Transmitted noise from mechanical rooms can often be controlled with wall insulation.

- Reduce background noise and vibrations by isolating forced-air heating units in a separate room. Insulate heating and ventilation ducts to control fan noise. Replace or line metal ductwork with 1 in. insulated duct board. Silencers may also be installed near fans. Regulate airflow velocities to control turbulence-induced noise and select registers with low sound-production ratings.

- Avoid the noise of forced-air heating systems by installing electric baseboard heating, radiant ceiling heat, or a hot water radiator.

- Stagger interior doors so they do not face each other in corridors.

- Be sure there are no acoustical leaks between the ceiling and the wall.

- Make sure all door and wall assemblies eliminate acoustical leaks. Inspect gaskets and use laminated or double-glazed glass in doors and windows.

- Staggered stud construction is a simple idea that can be easily applied to reduce sound transmission. This construction technique opens an air space in the wall that can be filled with insulation.

- Products with a high sound transmission class (STC) rating prevent transmitted noise that adds to the ambient noise levels.

- Many window treatments that insulate the space from temperature changes also insulate the interior from exterior noise. Consider heavy draperies with a separate liner or heavy roman shades that seal around the perimeter of the window. Tambour window treatment can be used to control street noise.

- Unwanted noise is known to produce stress. It is most annoying when its source is not evident and when it is not predictable. Overhead paging systems are responsible for much of the unpredictable noise in hospitals. Overhead paging can even reduce orientation, as it seems to come from all directions and makes the area appear more uniform.[15] Replace or supplement this system with pocket pagers.

- Corridor maintenance should be timed to prevent transmitted noise from disturbing patients' rest.

- Even if transmitted noise cannot be eliminated, the resulting stress can be reduced by providing a means to control the stressor.[16] White noise is a mixture of frequencies used to cover distracting sounds; it has been proven to reduce stress as long as patients control it themselves. Patients and their families should be able to choose their own soothing music or tapes of running water, surf, rain, and other calming sounds.

DETAILS
Nightstands and Overbed Tables

- A cantilever table projects over the bed to keep things within reach. Ensure that the base fits under an adjustable bed or a bed with box springs.
- Some tables attach to the headboard. Another choice is a table that sits on the bed.
- Specify a table that adjusts for reading, writing, and working. It should also adjust for use as a writing surface when the patient is seated in a chair.
- A lazy Susan on a large overbed table can provide easier reach than a standard table.
- An adjustable mirror can be added to the table. A two-sided mirror allows the table to be used from either side of the bed.
- Keep the mattress and nightstand at equal heights. This makes it easier for people who depend on the sense of touch more than vision or for any patient reaching for a drink of water in the night.
- Specify a nightstand large enough to privately store assistive devices.
- The nightstand top should be large enough to accommodate a telephone or call system.
- A gallery rail or edge around the top prevents items from being accidentally pushed to the floor.
- A console or wall-mounted countertop can be used as a nightstand with clearance for wheelchair footrests, making it easier to approach the bed or answer the phone from a wheelchair.
- Brightly colored furniture that contrasts with the background improves visual acuity.
- Plan sufficient storage to prevent clutter, which reduces visual acuity.

Storage must address security and display. Most ICU patients are not alert enough to notice a theft, and lockable storage should be planned, perhaps in the nightstand (see Details above). A movable wardrobe can be used to bring clothing close to the bed (see Details on page 269). A display case for personal possessions is a thoughtful addition. Consider storage for the television (if provided). The TV should be placed for easy viewing and the controls integrated into the call system. The telephone should be placed within reach. For ease of use in bed, specify large push buttons in the handset, not in the base unit.

A clear path must be maintained between nurse and patient; this path should not be obstructed by family seating. Clear space should also be planned around the patient bed for equipment, so guest seating is generally limited. At least one guest chair in each private ICU room should recline for sleeping (see Figure 14-7).

Figure 14-7 Reclining chair for sleeping. *Courtesy of Spector Group with Guenther Petrarca. Photography: Colin McRae Photography.*

UNIVERSAL PATIENT ROOMS

In the traditional general hospital, the ICU was located close to ED and surgery suites. Patient were triaged in ED, transferred to surgery if necessary, stabilized in the ICU after surgery, and moved to a patient room. But are all of these moves necessary? Can critical care (including ED and ICU functions), intermediate care, acute care (including some surgery), and ambulatory care be provided in the same patient room?

The universal patient care room is planned to reduce the number and frequency of patient transfers and to accommodate the rising acuity level of hospital patients. With the growing number of ambulatory care facilities, hospitals are left with the most acutely ill patients. General hospitals have become large critical care units that treat patients with life-threatening diseases. ICU rooms are increasingly demanded and patient rooms are more often empty.

DETAILS
Wardrobes and Dressers

- A wardrobe on wheels can be used to move clothing and shoes to the dressing area. This is particularly helpful for people who dress on the bed.

- Specify lockable carpet casters on the wardrobe.

- Hooks, shelves, and hanger bars in wardrobes should be adjustable for access by children, shorter people, and wheelchair users. Many can reach 4 ft. a.f.f., although a maximum of 3 ft. is optimal.

- Keep upper shelves transparent or wire for visual access by children, shorter people, and those in wheelchairs.

- Utilize space at a reachable level with racks and shelves attached to the backs of swinging wardrobe doors. Sliding wardrobe doors or bifold doors swing out of the way of the wheelchair but cannot be used for storage.

- A locking drawer and a shoe shelf at 9 in. a.f.f. are handy features.

- Drawers are a good indication of quality. As a test for ease of use, grasp one corner to see if the drawer opens easily.

- Patients often use dressers for support when walking or transferring to a wheelchair, so structural integrity is important.

- To allow one-handed use, look for drawers narrow enough to open with one central C-grip.

- Look for hardware that can be operated with a closed fist or slightly opened hand.

- Drawers or bins under the bed may be handy for people who dress while seated or lying on the bed. Check the floor clearance to make sure that nothing interfers with the base of the overbed table.

- Interiors of wardrobes and dressers should be light-colored to increase visibility.

- Look for rounded corners on case goods. The General Services Administration (GSA) Federal Supply Service has required all furniture corners and edges to be rounded to a minimum ⅛ in.[17] Rounded corners are especially good for clients with vision problems and those who bruise easily.

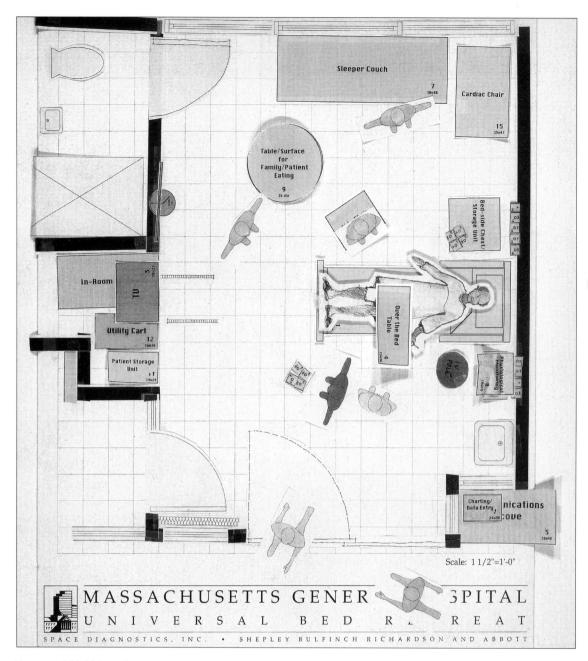

Figure 14-8(a) Universal room. *New England Deaconess Hospital, Clinical Facility Corridor, Boston, MA. Courtesy of Shepley Bulfinch Richardson and Abbott.*

Universal rooms are planned with acuity adaptable design, which means the room flexes to the needs of various acuity levels (see Figure 14-8 a and b). The universal room is an inclusive concept that involves patients, family, and friends in care patterns. Four functions take place in a patient room: (1) activities of daily living, (2) interactions with the environment, (3) therapies and diagnostic services, and (4) communication among staff, visitors, families, patients, and students.[18] Of the four, the communication needs are most frequently overlooked.

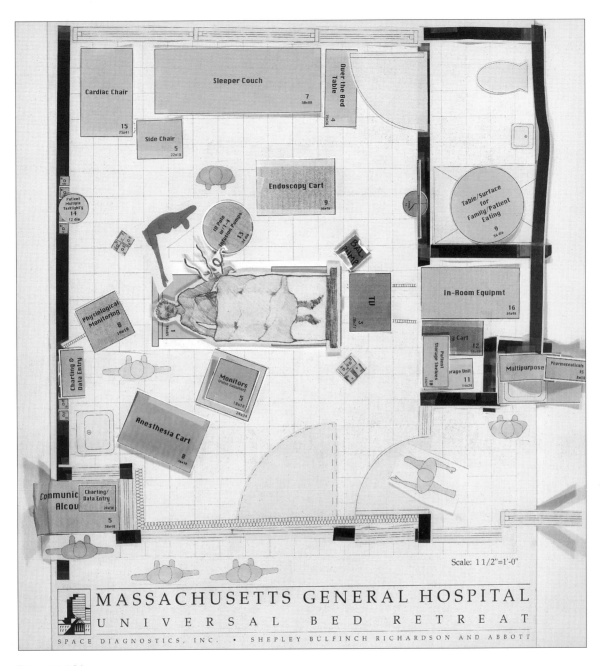

The labels visible in the figure include:

Cardiac Chair 15 / Sleeper Couch 7 / Over the Bed Table 4 / Side Chair 5 / Patient Multiple Tasklight'g 14 / Endoscopy Cart 9 / IV Pole w/ 4 Infusion Pumps 13 / Table/Surface for Family/Patient Eating 9 / Bar Pump / TV 3 / In-Room Equipmt 16 / Physiological Monitoring 8 / Cart 12 / Patient Storage Shelves / Storage Unit 11 / Multipurpose / Pharmaceuticals 15 / Charting & Data Entry / Monitors (Pulse Oximeter) 5 / Anesthesia Cart 8 / Communic Alcov / Charting/Data Entry 5

Scale: 1 1/2"=1'-0"

MASSACHUSETTS GENERAL HOSPITAL

UNIVERSAL BED RETREAT

SPACE DIAGNOSTICS, INC. • SHEPLEY BULFINCH RICHARDSON AND ABBOTT

Figure 14-8(b)

Communication must be planned for privacy as well as audibility. Accommodations may be necessary for people with hearing impairments. A flashing light can be added to the telephone to indicate that the phone is ringing. A strobe light reinforces the smoke alarm and a pillow or bed shaker replaces an alarm clock. A decoder for closed-captioned television and a text telephone may also be required. For the latter, an electrical outlet must be provided within 4 ft. of the telephone connection. All electrical and communication outlets for patient and family use should be within reach,

271

not under furniture (see Details on page 99). Many older people have difficulty hearing certain frequencies, and increased volume may not help. Amplified phones that boost high frequencies and improve clarity are available. A cordless headset allows the television to be used without increasing the ambient noise level in a shared room or adjacent spaces.

Communication systems must address the need for education by both the patient and the family. Time in the hospital is filled with teachable moments—periods in which the motivation to learn about health care is high. Internet access should be provided on a laptop computer and a VCR should be available for use in the patient room. Staff should be prepared to answer questions. One focus group of patients were quite adamant about the need for personal communication with a "real person." They didn't want to just watch videotapes.[19]

SPECIALIZED INTENSIVE CARE UNITS

Cardiac Intensive Care Units

The newest cardiac ICUs (CICUs) are taking a universal approach. In one impressive project, 56 universal rooms were added to the Methodist Hospital in Indianapolis, Indiana, to address the needs of cardiology patients and their families. In the past, these patients were moved as many as ten times from ICU to step-down care units. These moves were difficult for patients as well as family members, who had trouble even finding the patient. With the new rooms, the patient remains in place throughout the entire stay.

To develop the design program, a focus group of patients was used and a mockup room was constructed. It was determined that the room must be oversized and planned with three zones to accommodate patient, family, and staff. The patient zone features a hospitality decor with cabinets on the head wall to conceal the medical gases. The staff zone, between the patient bed and the nursing station, is divided by glass that electronically frosts to provide privacy. The family zone incorporates a chair that makes into a bed for rooming-in (see Figure 14-9).

Neonatal Intensive Care Units

Babies of very low birthweight may now be saved by medical science, and these infants require increasing lengths of stay in neonatal ICUs (NICUs), where they are exposed to high levels of noise and light. In an excellent summary of the problems, Jain Malkin cites a study that documents a NICU as noisy as the hospital's boiler room.[20] The infants' circadian rhythms may be interrupted for months at a time as they remain

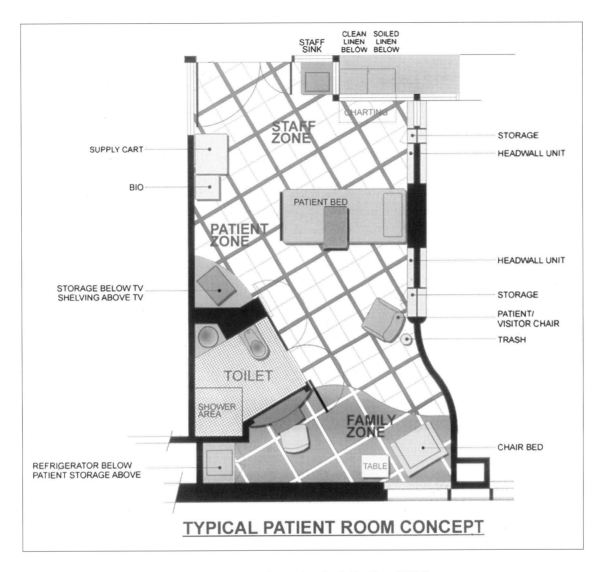

TYPICAL PATIENT ROOM CONCEPT

Figure 14-9 Universal CICU. *Project name: Cardiac Comprehensive Critical Care (CCCC). Typical Patient Room Plan—Clarian Health. Courtesy of BSA Design, Indianapolis.*

under fixed lighting, and their vision may be distorted as they look through an oxyhood.

One strong study documented longer sleeping, less time feeding, and increased weight gain when the intensity of light and noise was reduced between 7 P.M. and 7 A.M.[21] Another study of cycled lighting confirmed the weight gain, also reporting that the infants were able to be fed orally sooner, spent fewer days on the ventilator and on phototherapy, and displayed enhanced motor coordination.[22] But studies differ on a causal relationship between intense lighting and retinal damage. One study found no difference in the incidence and severity of retinopathy of prematurity among groups of infants exposed to intensities between 15 and 55 fc.[23] Another found higher incidence in infants with birthweights below 1000g.[24]

Ambient lighting levels should be adjustable between 1 and 60 fc, measured at the mattress level of the incubator.[25] Higher levels of light can cause infants to lose their eye blinking reflex. Separate procedure lighting (between 150 and 200 fc) should be available without increasing the lighting level for other babies in the same room. Full-spectrum lighting and warm reflecting color are important choices when monitoring jaundiced or cyanotic babies. Yellow and blue tones should not be used (or should be limited to a high border) (see Details on page 82). Windows providing exposure to natural light may help to establish circadian rhythms while improving staff morale.

Although infants do require sensory stimulation, the quality of tactile, visual, and aural stimulation must be controlled. One strong study documented reduced stress levels in infants in an NICU when exposed to music. The infants also improved their feeding, retained weight, and reduced their length of stay in the hospital.[26]

In general, however, ambient noise levels must be reduced. Control both ambient and transmitted noise through acoustical design. Keep peak noise levels below 90 decibels.[27] In the NICU, specify incubators with reduced motor noise levels. Other noisy equipment that should be replaced includes monitors, respirators, and oxyhoods. Soft surfaces, like carpeting, absorb the ambient noise generated within the room.

In the NICU, maintain an ambient temperature of 72–78°F and a relative humidity of 30–60 percent without condensation on wall and window surfaces.[28] In one study, severe apneic spells were reduced with higher humidity levels.[29] A minimum of six air changes per hour is required, with two of those changes being outside air. The air should be filtered to 90 percent efficiency. Fresh air intake must be located at least 25 ft. from exhaust outlets of ventilating systems, combustion equipment stacks, medical-surgical vacuum systems, plumbing vents, and areas that collect noxious fumes.[30] Research suggests increased outbreaks of infection result when an open window is located near exhaust ducting from an isolation room.[31]

In addition to the needs of the infant, the NICU must be planned to support the family. Family members may stay by the side of the infant for hours, so stools should be available for observation of the infant at the height of the isolette porthole. Choose stools with an adjustable seat height, seat angle, armrest, backrest, and footrest, if provided. Hardware for adjustment should be easy to reach and operate.

A rocking chair can be provided to soothe and feed the infant. A high-backed rocker provides head support. Make sure the chair cannot tip and that the arms are positioned for comfort and support. Armrests should seldom be higher than 8½ in. above the seat for maximum support and reduction of fatigue (see Details on page 117).

FAMILY WAITING ROOMS

The design program should accommodate intensive care for families as well as patients, providing emotional support, realistic expectations, understanding of medical procedures, and an opportunity to participate in care.[32] From individual reading chairs to reclining seats, design detail can be carefully planned to support these objectives. Adjacent to the seats, plan storage for pillows and blankets.

Space planning should be flexible to support private groupings of furnishings that allow families to sit together. The lounge should be equipped with a desk and telephone where a hospital volunteer can provide families with information about the patient. Telephones for visitor use should be located outside the waiting room for privacy.[33]

Adjacent to the lounge, a small kitchen is often provided (see Details on pages 94, 95, 96, and 97 and the Research Abstract on page 59). It is best to locate the bathroom outside of the waiting room so that its use is not advertised (see Details on pages 166, 167, and 168). Plan a private adjoining consultation room with a movable sign on the door to indicate that the room is being used. This room can also be used for crying and grieving. A nearby chapel is a thoughtful addition.

> The fruit of silence is prayer.
> The fruit of prayer is faith.
> The fruit of faith is love.
> The fruit of love is service.
> The fruit of service is peace.
>
> MOTHER TERESA

REFERENCES

1. J.J. Menegazzi, P. Paris, and C. Kersteen, "A Randomized Controlled Trial of the Use of Music During Laceration Repair," *Annals of Emergency Medicine* 20 (1991): 348–350.
2. Jim Lennon, "New Design Skills Toolbox: A Workshop for Designing the ER of the Future," *Journal of Healthcare Design* 8 (1996): 145.
3. P.J. Keep, J. James, and M. Inman, "Windows in the Intensive Therapy Unit," *Anesthesia* 35, no. 3 (March 1980): 257–262.
4. M. Topf, "Effects of Personal Control over Hospital Noise on Sleep," *The Mount Sinai Journal of Medicine* 60, no. 6 (1993): 522–527.
5. Lorraine G. Hiatt, "Long-Term Care Facilities," *Journal of Health Care Interior Design* 2 (1990): 201.
6. F.D. Hickler, "Symposium on Design and Function of the Operating Room Suite and Special Areas," *Journal of Anesthesiology* 31, no. 2 (August 1969): 103–106.
7. Jain Malkin, *Hospital Interior Architecture* (New York: John Wiley and Sons, 1992), 223.
8. V.A. Moss, "Music and the surgical patient. The effect of music on anxiety," *AORN Journal* 48, no. 1 (1988): 64–69
9. J. Williamson, "The Effects of Ocean Sounds on Sleep after Coronary Artery Bypass Graft Surgery," *American Journal of Critical Care* 1 (1992): 91–97.

10. Walter B. Kleeman, *The Challenge of Interior Design* (Boston: CBI Publishing, 1981), 243.

11. Virginia Beamer Weinhold, *Interior Finish Materials for Health Care Facilities* (Springfield, Ill.: Charles C. Thomas, 1988), 25.

12. Robert Marshall, "Carpet as an Acoustical Material," *Canadian Interiors* 1 (1970): 36–39.

13. Margaret Milner, *Breaking Through the Deafness Barrier: Environmental Accommodations for Hearing-Impaired People.* (Washington, D.C.: Physical Plant Department, Galludet College, 1979, 9.

14. Millicent Gappell, "Hospice Facilities," *Journal of Health Care Interior Design* 2 (1990): 79.

15. Janet Reizenstein Carpman, Myron A. Grant, and Deborah A. Simmons, *Design That Cares* (Chicago: American Hospital Publishing, 1986), 228.

16. G. W. Evans and S. Cohen, "Environmental Stress," in *Handbook of Environmental Psychology*, ed. D. Stokols and I. Altman (New York: John Wiley and Sons, 1987), 571–610.

17. Walter B. Kleeman, *The Challenge of Interior Design* (Boston: CBI Publishing, 1981), 40–41.

18. Meredith Spear, "Current Issues: Designing the Universal Patient Care Room," *Journal of Healthcare Design* 9 (1997): 82.

19. Ibid., 83.

20. Malkin, *Hospital Interior Architecture,* 259–261.

21. N.P. Mann, R. Haddow, and L. Stokes, "Effect of Night and Day on Pre-Term Infants in a Newborn Nursery: Randomized Trial," *British Medical Journal* 293 (1986): 1265–1267.

22. C.I. Miller, R. White, D.L. Hagar, and T.R. Denison, "The Effects of Cycled versus Non-cycled Lighting on Growth and Development in Pre-term Infants," *Infant Behavior and Development* 18 (1995): 87–95.

23. Sherwonit Ackerman and J. Williams, "Reduced Incidental Light Exposure Effect on the Development of Retinopathy of Prematurity in Low Birth Weight Infants," *Pediatrics* 83 (1989): 958–962.

24. P. Glass, G.B. Avery, and K.N. Subramanian, "Effect of Bright Light in the Hospital Nursery on Incidence of Retinopathy of Prematurity," *New England Journal of Medicine* 313 (1985): 401–404.

25. Judith A. Smith, *The Family Birthplace: Planning and Designing Today's Obstetric Facilities* (Chicago: American Hospital Publishing, 1995), 101.

26. J. Caine, "The Effects of Music on the Selected Stress Behaviors, Weight, Caloric and Formula Intake, and Length of Hospital Stay of Premature and Low Birth Weight Neonates in a Newborn Intensive Care Unit," *Journal of Music Therapy* 28, no. 4 (1991): 180–182.

27. American National Standards Institute, *Acoustical Terminology* (S1.1) (New York: ANSI, 1992).

28. "Energy conservation in New Building Design, Standard 90A-80," *ASHRAE Applications Handbook* (Atlanta: American Society of Heating, Refrigerating, and Air Conditioning Engineers, 1991).

29. T.K. Belgaumaker and K.E. Scott, "Effects of Low Humidity on Small Premature Infants in Servocontrol Incubators," *Biology of the Neonate* 26 (1975): 348–352.

30. American Institute of Architects *Guidelines for Construction and Equipment of Hospital and Medical Facilities* (Washington, D.C.: AIA Press, 1993).

31. S. Cotterill, R. Evans, and A.P. Fraise, "An Unusual Source for an Outbreak of Methicillin-Resistant Staphylococcus Aureus in an Intensive Therapy Unit," *Journal of Hospital Infection* 32 (1996): 207–216.

32. Hoover, M.J. "Intensive Care for Relatives." *Hospitals* 53, no. 14 (16 July 1979): 219–222.

33. Carpman, Janet. "Design Research: Emerging Trends." *Journal of Healthcare Design* 5 (1992): 109.

DIRECTORY OF DESIGNERS AND CONSULTANTS

Aktivitetcentret Sophielund
Sophielund 25–27
270 Hørshol
Denmark

Alterra Health Corporation
450 North Sunnyslope Road #300
Brookfield, WI 53005

Anshen + Allen, Architects
901 Market Street #600
San Francisco, CA 94103

Joan Baron
8325 E. Monte Vista Road
Scottsdale, AZ 85257

Barrier Free Environments Architecture, P.A.
410 Oberlin Road, #400
Raleigh, NC 27605

Elizabeth Brawley
Design Concepts
30 Princess Court
Sausalito, CA 94965

BSA Design
9365 Counselors Row, Suite 300
Indianapolis, IN 46240

Bumgardner
101 Stewart, Suite 200
Seattle, WA 98101-1048

The Office of James Burnett
1973 W. Gray, Suite 5
Houston, TX 77019

Celebration Health
Florida Hospital
400 Celebration Place
Celebration, FL 34747

Chambers Lorenz Design
6770 N. West Avenue, Suite 105
Fresno, CA 93711

Cini & Associates, LLC
919 Old Henderson Road
Columbus, OH 43220

Russell Coile
Chi Systems, Inc.
5229 Willowross Way
Plano, TX 75093

Delawie Wilkes Rodriques Barker & Bretton
2827 Presidio Drive
San Diego, CA 92110

Engelbrect and Griffin Architects, P.C.
12 Auburn Street
Newburyport, MA 01950

Ellerbe Becket
800 Lasalle Avenue
Minneapolis, MN 55402

Ellerbe Becket
1875 Connecticut NW #600
Washington, DC 20009

ETV arkitektkontor AB Evan Terry
Associates P.C.
One Perimeter Park South #200S
Birmingham, AL 35243

Evan Terry Associates
One Perimeter Park
South #200S
Birmingham, AL 35243

Ewing Cole Cherry Brott
100 N. 6th Street
Philadelphia, PA 19106

Louis Feinstein Alzheimer's Center
25 Brayton Avenue
Cranston, RI 02920

Gruppbostäder i Sverige AB
Tunhemsvägen 58
461 43 Trollhättan
Sweden

Guenther Petrarca LLP
Formally Architecture + Furniture
157 Chambers Street
New York, NY 10007

Guynes Design
1555 E. Jackson Street
Phoenix, AZ 85034

Hailey Designs
11140 Petal Street, Suite 200
Dallas, TX 75238-2441

Healthcare Environment Design
2625 Elm Street #212
Dallas, TX 75226

H & L Architecture LTD
1621 18th Street #110
Denver, CO 80202

Huelat Parimucha
635 S. Fairfax Street
Alexandria, VA 22314

Cynthia Leibrock
Easy Access
1331 Green Mountain Drive
Livermore, CO 80536

Lifease, Inc.
2451 15th Street NW, Suite D
New Brighton, MN 55112

Mackey Mitchell Associates
800 St. Louis Station
St. Louis, MO 63103

Eva Maddox Associates, Inc.
300 West Hubbard, Suite 201
Chicago, IL 60610

Jain Malkin, Inc.
7855 Fay Avenue
San Diego, CA 92037

Moore Iacofano Gottsman
809 Hearst Avenue
Berkeley, CA 94710

NBBJ
111 S. Jackson Street
Seattle, WA 98104

OWP&P Architects
111 W. Washington Street, Suite 2100
Chicago, IL 60602

Ohlson Lavoie Corporation
1860 Blake Street #300
Denver, CO 80202

The Orcutt/Winslow Partnership
1130 N. 2nd Street
Phoenix, AZ 95004

Anita Rui Olds
P.O. Box 312
Woodacre, CA 94973

Presbyterian Senior Care
1215 Hulton Road
Oakmont, PA 15139

Reese, Lower, Patrick & Scott, Ltd.
1910 Harrington Drive
Lancaster, PA 17601-3992

Rhode Island School of Design
Two College Street
Providence, RI 02903-2784

Robinson Design
405 Douglas Pike
Smithfield, RI 02917

Robinson Green Beretta Corporation
50 Holden Street
Providence, RI 02908

Samaritan Health
1441 N. 12th Street
Phoenix, AZ 85006

The Schunkewitz Partnership, LLP
Healthcare Systems Architects
99 Madison Avenue
New York, NY 10016

Seccomb Design Associates, Inc.
77 DeBoom Street
San Francisco, CA 94107

Sekisui House, Ltd.
Tower East, Umeda
Sky Building
1-88 Oyodonaka
1-Chome, Kita-Ku
Osaka 531, Japan

Shepley Bullfinch Richardson and Abbott
40 Broad Street
Boston, MA 02109

SHG Architects, Inc.
500 Griswold Street
Suite 200
Detroit, MI 48226

Smith Hagar Bajo
6265 Riverside Drive
Suite 150
Dublin, OH 43017

Stichting Humanitas Rotterdam
Keizersgracht 321
1016 EE Amsterdam
Holland

The S/L/A/M Collaborative, Architects & Engineers
Somerset Square
80 Glastonbury Boulevard, 2nd Floor
Glastonbury, CT 06033-4415

The Stratford
601 Laurel Avenue
San Mateo, CA 94401

Summer Hill Company, Inc.
RR1 Box 3184
Sherburne, NY 13480

TBG Development
226 South Meramec, Suite 200
Clayton, MO 63105

Thompson Design Associates
751 Marsh Avenue
Reno, NV 89509

TRO/The Ritchie Organization
80 Bridge Street
Newton, MA 02458

Watkins Hamilton Ross Architects, Inc.
6575 W. Loop South, Suite 300
Bellaire, TX 77401

Kai-Yee Woo & Associates
2 Henry Adams Street #322
San Francisco, CA 94103

Mino Yokoyama
Concertino
3-11-14 Create Bldg. #2F
Ginza, Chuo-ku, Tokyo 104-0061
Japan

Directory of Manufacturers

Access Industries
4001 East 138 Street
Grandview, MO 64030
816-763-3100

ADD Specialized Seating
Technology
6500 South Avalon Boulevard
Los Angeles, CA 90003-1934
213-752-0101

Accessible Designs
94 North Columbus Road
Athens, OH 45701
614-593-5240

Aiphone Corporation
1700 130th Avenue NE
Bellevue, WA 98009
425-455-0510

Alva Access Group, Inc.
5801 Christie Avenue, Suite 475
Emeryville, CA 94608
510-923-6280

American Olean Tile Company
1000 Cannon Avenue
Lansdale, PA 19446-0271
215-393-2705

American Standard
One Centennial Avenue
Piscataway, NJ 08855
908-980-3000

Ameriphone Inc.
12082 Western Avenue
Garden Grove, CA 92841
800-874-3005

Amerock Corporation
4000 Auburn Street
Rocktord, IL 61101
800-435-6959

American Telecare
7640 Golden Triangle Drive
Eden Prairie, MN 55344
612-941-5862

Andersen Windows, Inc.
100 Fourth Avenue North
Bayport, MN 55003-1096
612-430-5928

Aqua Glass Corporation
PO Box 412, Industrial Park
Adamsville, TN 38310 901-632-091 1

Armstrong World Industries, Inc.
P.O. Box 3001
Lancaster, PA 17604
888-361-1696

Asko, Inc.
1161 Executive Drive West
Richardson, TX 75081
800-367-2444

A-Solution, Inc.
1332 Lobo Place NE
Albuquerque, NM 87106
505-256-0115

Audex Assistive Listening System
710 Standard Street
Longview, TX 75604
800-237-0716

AVSI
17059 El Cajon Avenue
Yorba Linda, CA 92886
714-524-4488

Baker Furniture
1661 Monroe Avenue NW
Grand Rapids, Ml 49505
616-361-7321

Banner Scapes
7106 Mapleridge
Houston, TX 77081
800-344-3524

Barclay Products Limited
4000 Porett Drive
Gurnee, IL 60031
847-244-1234

Benicia Foundry
2995 Bayshore Road
Benicia, CA 94510
800-346-4645

Bernhardt Furniture Company
PO Box 740
Lenoir, NC 28645
704-758-9811

Better Living Products
International, Inc.
150 Norfinch Drive Toronto,
Ontario, Canada M3N 1 X9
519-685-1501

Bobrick Washroom
Equipment, Inc.
11611 HartStreet
North Hollywood, CA 91605
818-764-1000

Boltaflex
175 Gent Road
Fairlawn, OH 44333
330-869-4571

Bonar Floors
647 Bunker Hill Road
Salem, NY 12865
800-852-8292

Bonar Floors, Inc.
961 Busse Road
Elk Grove Village, IL 60007
800-852-8292

Brown Jordan
9860 Gidley Street
El Monte, CA 91734
626-443-8971

C/S Group
3 Werner Way
Lebanon, NJ 08833
800-233-8493

Capstone Products, Inc.
203 Flagship Drive
Lutz, FL 33549
813-948-0107

Carolina Mirror Company
201 Elkin Highway
North Wilkesboro, NC 28659
910-838-2151

Center for Rehabilitation
Technology Georgia Institute
of Technology
Atlanta, GA 30332-0130
404-894-2000

Century Products, Inc.
9600 Valley View Road
Macedonia, OH 44056
216-468-2000

The Chamberlain Group, Inc.
845 Larch Avenue
Elmhurst, IL 60126
630-279-3600

The Charles Stewart Company
PO Box 5400
Hickory, NC 28603
704-322-9464

Chicago Botanic Garden
1000 Lake Cook Road
Glencoe, IL 60022
847-835-5440

Closet Maid
650 SW 27th Avenue
Ocala, FL 34471
352-401-6000

Cluster Seating Systems
1000 Philips Knob
Burnsville, NC 28714
704-682-3985

Coco Raynes Associates, Inc.
569 Boylston Street
Boston, MA 02116
617-536-1499

Collins & Aikman
Floorcovering, Inc.
311 Smith Industrial Boulevard
Dalton, GA 30720
706-259-2042

Color Guild International
P.O. Box 390569
Cambridge, MA 02139-0007
800-225-1141

Constantine
2050 Eastchester Road
Bronx, NY 10461
718-792-1600

Construction Specialties
P.O. Box 380, Route 405
Muney, PA 17756
800-233-8493

Custom Laminations, Inc.
932 Market St.
Paterson, NJ 07509-2066
973-279-9332

Dacor
950 South Raymond
Pasadena, CA 91109
800-793-0093

The Dorma Group
Dorma Drive
Reamstown, PA 17567-0411
717-336-3881

Dor-O-Matic
7350 West Wilson Avenue
Harwood Heights, IL 60656
502-339-8891

Du Seung Trading Co.
3190 Northeast Expressway
Suite 240
Atlanta, GA
800-274-7267

DuPont Corian®
Barley Mill Plaza
Price Mill Building
PO Box 80012
Wilmington, DE 19880-0012
800-426-7426

DuPont Flooring Systems
One Town Park Commons
Suite 400
125 Town Park Drive
Kennesaw, GA 30144
770-420-7700

Dwyer Products Corp.
418 North Calumet Avenue
Michigan City, IN 46360
219-874-5236

Egan Visual International
300 Hanlan Road
Woodbridge, Ontario, Canada
L4L 3P6
905-851-2826

Eljer Plumbingware, Inc
14801 Quorum Drive
Dallas, TX 75240-7584
800-423-5537

Elkay Manufacturing Company
2222 Camden Court
Oak Brook, IL 60523
630-574-8484

Elsafe, Inc.
4303 Vineland Road
Suite F15
Orlando, FL 32811
407-423-7233

Eurotex
165 West Ontario Street
Philadelphia, PA 19140
800-523-0731
215-739-8844

EVAC+CHAIR Corporation
17 East 67th Street
New York, NY 10021
212-734-6222

Fantagraph
P.O. Box 371805
Cincinnati, OH 45237
800-888-4000

Fieldstone Cabinetry
600 East 48th Street N
Sioux Falls, SD 57104
605-335-8600

Fleetwood
PO Box 1259
Holland, MI 49422-1259
616-396-5346

Fritz Industries
500 Sam Houston Road
Mesquite, TX 75149-2789
800-955-1323

Fyrnetics, Inc.
1055 Stevenson Court
Suite 102W
Roselle, IL 60172
800-654-7665

Gaggenau USA Corp.
425 University Avenue
Norwood, MA 02062
781-255-1766

Garcia Imports
P.O. Box 5066
Redwood City, CA 94063
650-367-9600

GE Appliances
Appliance Park
Louisville, KY 40225
502-452-3071

Gemini Bath and Kitchen
Products
PO Box 43398
Tucson, AZ 85733
520-770-0667

Genon Wallcoverings
Three University Plaza
Suite 200
Hackensack, NJ 07601
201-489-0100

Goelst Corporation
915 Bridge Street
Winston-Salem, NC 27104
910-917-0001

Hafele America Co.
3901 Cheyenne Drive,
Archdale, NC 27263
336-889-2322

Harris Communications, Inc.
15159 Technology Drive
Eden Prairie, MN 55344-2277
612-906-9144

Hausmann Industries, Inc.
130 Union Street
Northvale, NJ 07647
800-526-0289

Haworth, Inc.
One Haworth Center
Holland, Ml 49423
800-344-2600

Haws Drinking Faucet
Company
PO Box 1999
Berkeley, CA 94710-1499
510-525-5801

Herman Miller, Inc.
Zeeland, Ml 49464
616-654-8909

Hewi, Inc.
2851 Old Tree Drive
Lancaster, PA 17603
717-293-1313

Holtkötter International, Inc.
155 Hardman Avenue S
St. Paul, MN 55075
612-552-8776

The Hon Company
200 Oak Street
Muscatine, IA 52761
319-264-7080

Honeywell, Inc.
1985 Douglas Drive
Golden Valley, MN 55422
612-954-4574

Horton Automatics
4242 Baldwin Boulevard
Corpus Christi, TX 78405-3399
800-531-3111

Howe Furniture Corp.
12 Cambridge Drive
Trumbull, CT 06611-0386
800-888-4693

Hunter Douglas Window Fashions
2 Park Way
Upper Saddle River, NJ 07458
800-444-8844

Intogrip, Inc.
1141 East Main Street
Ventura, CA 93001
805-652-0770

In-Sink-Erator
Division of Emerson Electric Co.
4700 21st Street
Racine, WI 53406-5093
414-554-5432

International Cushioned Products, Inc.
8360 Bridgeport Road #202
Richmond, British Columbia,
Canada V6X 3C7
604-244-7638

The Ironmonger, Inc.
122 West Illinois Street
Chicago, IL 60610-4506
312-527-4800

J. Piercey Studios, Inc.
1714 Acme Street
Orlando, FL 32805
407-841-7594

J.C. Penney Co., Inc.
PO Box 10001
Dallas, TX 75301
972-431-1000

Jack Cartwright, Inc.
PO Box 2798
High Point, NC 27261
910-889-9400

JBliss Imaging Systems
650 Saratoga Avenue
San Jose, CA 95129
408-246-5783

JCDecaux USA
212-604-9160

Jenn-Air
403 West 4th Street N
Newton, IA 50208
800-JENN-AIR

Joerns Healthcare, Inc.
5001 Joerns Drive
Stevens Point, WI 54481
800-826-0270

Johnsonite
16910 Munn Road
Chagrin Falls, OH 44023
800-899-8916

Julius Blum, Inc.
Stanley, NC 28164
800-438-6788

Kimball Office Group
1155 West 12th Avenue
Jasper, IN 47549
800-482-1616

Kindred Industries
1000 Kindred Road
Midland, Ontario, Canada
800-456-5586

King Products, Inc.
195 The West Mall
Suite 915
Etobicoke, Ontario, Canada
M9C SKI
416-620-1230

KitchenAid
2000 M-63 North MD #4302
Benton Harbor, MI 49022
616-923-5000

Knickerbocker Partition Corp.
193 Hanse Avenue
Freeport, NY 11520
516-546-0550

Kohler Co.
444 Highland Drive
Kohler, WI 53044
920-457-4441

KraftMaid Cabinetry, Inc.
PO Box 1055
Middlefield, OH 44062
800-571-1990   (consumer);
440-632-5333   (trade)

Krueger International
1330 Bellevue Street
Green Bay, WI 54308-8100
920-468-8100

Lee Rowan
900 South Highway Drive
Fenton, MO 63026
800-325-6150

Lernout & Hauspie
20 Mall Road
Burlington, MA 01803
617-238-0960

Leviton Manufacturing Co.
59-25   Little Neck Parkway
Little Neck, NY 11362-2591
800-323-8920

Lifespec Cabinet Systems, Inc.
100 Lifespec Drive
Oxford, MS 38655
601-234-0330

The Lighthouse, Inc.
111 East 59th Street
New York, NY 10022-1202
212-821-9556

Ligne Roset USA
200 Lexirgton Avenue
Suite 601
New York, NY 10016
212-685-2238

Loewenstein
1801 North Andrews Extension
Pompano Beach, FL 33061-6369
954-960-1100

Lumex
100 Spence Street
Bay Shore, NY 11706-2290
800-645-5272

Lutron Electronics Co., Inc.
7200 Suter Road
Coopersburg, PA 18036-1299
610-282-3800

Lux Steel Contract
P.O. Box 1085
Elkart, IN 46515-1085219-
295-0229

Lyons Industries, Inc.
30000 M-62 West
Dowagiac, Ml 49047
616-782-3404

Maddak, Inc.
6 Industrial Road
Pequannock, NJ 07440-1992
973-628-7600

The Maiman Company
3839 East Mustard Way
Springfield, MO 65803
800-641-4320
417-862-0681

Mat Factory, Inc.
760 West 16th Street
Building E
Costa Mesa, CA 92627
800-628-7626

Maxi Aids, Inc.
PO Box 3209
Farmingdale, NY 11735
516-752-0521

Maytag
403 West 4th Street
Newton, IA 50208
888-4MAYTAG

McGuire
1201 Bryant Street
San Francisco, CA 94103
415-626-1414

Metropolitan Furniture Corp.
1635 Rollins Road
Burlingame, CA 94010-2301
650-697-7900

The MoMA Design Store
44 West 53rd Street
New York, NY 10019
800-793-3167

Nichols Design Associates, Inc.
2016 Mt. Vernon Avenue
Suite 200
Alexandria, VA 22301
703-519-2198 tty

Nutone, Inc.
Madison and Red Bank Roads
Cincinnati, OH 45227
800-543-8687

Olsonite Corp.
25 Dart Road
Newnan, GA 30265
770-253-3930

Otto Bock Rehab
3000 Xenium Lane North
Minneapolis, MN 55441
800-328-4058

OXO International
230 Fifth Ave #1100
NewYork, NY 10001
212-213-0707

Palazzetti, Inc.
10-4045th Avenue
Long Island City, NY 11101
718-937-1199

Pella Corp.
102 Main Street
Pella, IA 50219-2147
515-628-1000

Phillips Consumer Communications
5 Wood Hollow Road 3H10
Parsippany, NJ 07054
888-582-3688

Pinecrest
2118 Blaisdell Avenue
Minneapolis, MN 55404
800-443-5357

Research Products Corp.
1015 East Washington Avenue
Madison, WI 53701-1467
608-257-8801
800-334-6011

Rev-A-Shelf, Inc.
2409 Plantside Drive
Louisville, KY 40299-
502-499-5835

Robern, Inc.
7 Wood Avenue
Bristol, PA 19007
215-826-9800

Roppe Corporation
1602 N. Union Street
Fostoria, OH 44830-1158
800-537-9527

Rubbermaid, Inc.
1147 Akron Road
Wooster, OH 44691-6000
800-643-3490

Rutt Custom Cabinetry
1564 Main Street
Box 129
Goodville, PA 17528
800-240-7888

Senior Technologies
1620 North 20th
Lincoln, NE 68503
402-475-4002

Shaw Industries, Inc.
1000 South Harris Street
Dalton, GA 30722
706-275-1755

SICO North America, Inc.
7525 Cahill Road
Minneapolis, MN 55439
800-328-6138

SIS human factor technologies, inc.
SSC Harvey Road
Londonderry, NH 03053
603-432-4495

Sloan Valve Company
10500 Seymour Avenue
Franklin Park, IL 60131
847-671-4300

Smart Design, Inc.
137 Varick Street
8th Floor
New York, NY 10013
212-807-8150

Sub-Zero Freezer Co., Inc.
4717 Hammersley Road
Madison, WI 53711
800-222-7820

Summitville Tiles, Inc.
PO Box 73
Summitville, OH 43962
330-223-1511

Sunrise Medical
7477 East Dry Creek Parkway
Longmont, CO 80503
888-333-2572

Superior Millwork Ltd.
2502 Thayer Avenue
Saskatoon, Saskatchewan,
Canada 57L 5Y2
306-373-8588

Symmons Industries, Inc.
31 Brooks Drive
Braintree, MA 02184
800-SYMMONS

T.L. Shield & Associates, Inc.
PO Box 6845
Thousand Oaks, CA 91359-6845
818-509-8228

Talking Signs, Inc.
812 North Boulevard
Baton Rouge, LA 70802
504-344-2812

Tempo Industries, Inc.
2002A South Grand Avenue
Santa Ana, CA 92705
714-662-4860

Thomasville Furniture Industries
PO Box 339
Thomasville, NC 27360
910-472-4000

Thonet Industries, Inc.
403 Meacham Road
Statesville, NC 28677
704-878-2222

Tielsa
IZ-NO-Sud, Strasse 3,
Obj. 41, A-2355
Wiener Neudorf, Austria
02236161525

TOTO USA
1155 Southern Road
Morrow, GA 30260
770-282-8686

Truth Hardware
700 West Bridge Street
Owatonna, MN 55060
800-866-7884

Tub-Master, LC
413 Virginia Drive
Orlando, FL 32803
407-898-2881

Ultratec
450 Science Drive
Madison, WI 53711
800-482-2424

United Chair Company
114 Churchill Avenue
Leeds, AL 35094
205-699-5181

Universal Furniture
2226 Uwharrie Road
High Point, NC 27263
910-861-7200

Visible Interactive
1000 Sansome Street
Suite 375
San Francisco, CA 94111
415-433-7781

Walker Equipment
4009 Cloud Springs Road
Ringgold, GA 30736
800-HANDSET (426-3738)

Whirlpool Corp.
2000 M-63
Benton Harbor, MI 49022
800-446-0724

White Home Products
PO Box 2656
Union, NJ 07803
800-200-9272

Whitehouse & Co.
18 E. 16th Street
New York, NY 10003
212-206-1080

Wilsonart
P.O. Box 6110
Temple, TX 76503-6110
254-207-7000

Winona Manufacturing, Inc.
24 Laird Street
Winona, MN 55987
507-454-3511

Wm. Ohs Showrooms, Inc.
115 Madison Street
Denver, CO 80206
303-321-3232

Workstations, Inc.
11 Silver Street
South Hadley, MA 01075
413-535-3340

York Wailcoverings Inc.
750 Linden Avenue
York, PA 17404
717-846-4456

Zygo Industries
PO Box 1008
Portland, OR 97207-1008
503-684-6006

INDEX